Build Your Own Home Security System

Build Your Own Home Security System

Delton T. Horn

TAB Books
Division of McGraw-Hill, Inc.
Blue Ridge Summit, PA 17294-0850

Notices

GE™	General Electric Co.
Radio Shack™	The Tandy Corp.

FIRST EDITION
FIRST PRINTING

©1993 by **TAB Books**.
TAB Books is a division of McGraw-Hill, Inc.

Library of Congress Cataloging-in-Publication Data

Horn, Delton T.
   Build your own home security system / by Delton T. Horn
     p.   cm.
   Includes index.
   ISBN 0-8306-3870-9   ISBN 0-8306-3871-7 (pbk.)
   1. Dwellings—Security measures—Amateurs' manuals. 2. Electronic security systems—Design and construction—Amateurs' manuals.
   I. Title.
   TH9745.D85H67 1993
   643'.16—dc20   92-41602
                                      CIP

Acquisitions Editor: Roland S. Phelps
Editorial team: B.J. Peterson, Editor
          Susan Wahlman, Supervising Editor
          Joanne Slike, Executive Editor
          Joann Woy, Indexer
Production team: Katherine G. Brown, Director
          Jan Fisher, Typesetting
          Ollie Harmon, Typesetting
          Lisa Mellott, Typesetting
          Brenda Plasterer, Typesetting
          Wanda S. Ditch, Layout
          Lorie L. White, Proofreading
Design team: Jaclyn J. Boone, Designer
          Brian Allison, Associate Designer
Cover design: Graphics Plus, Hanover, Pa.   EL2

Contents

Projects

Introduction

ANYONE WHO HAS SO MUCH GLANCED AT A NEWSPAPER OR TURNED on the television in the last few years knows that security is a growing concern. Burglaries occur with disgusting frequency. Then there are disasters such as fires and floods.

How can you protect yourself? A good security system can certainly help. Such a system can alert you when a worrisome condition occurs.

A very simple security system is a stack of empty tin cans near the door. If an intruder comes in, he or she will knock over the cans, and the clattering noise will alert you to the intruder's presence. But modern electronics permits you to come up with security systems that are far superior and more reliable than this rather crude example. The purpose of this book is to demonstrate some of the many ways you can use electronics to protect your security and peace of mind.

The main focus in this book is burglar alarms and related devices, because this area of electronic security is the one most people seem interested in today. But I also cover fire alarms and other devices designed to offer increased security against various environmental conditions. A good security system does more than simply keep out potential intruders.

Certain features are common to most security systems. These basic elements are introduced in chapter 1; two of the most important of these elements (sensors and alarm-sounding devices) are examined in somewhat more detail in the next two chapters.

Chapter 4 features a number of projects designed for protecting your electrical and electronic equipment from theft, unauthorized use, and dangerous power conditions. Electronic combination lock circuits are covered in chapter 5.

Chapters 6 through 8 cover home and office burglar alarm or intrusion-detector systems. Basic instrusion-detector circuits are featured in chapter 6. Time-delay functions are added in the projects of chapter 7. Chapter 8 offers some important tips on the proper installation of an intrusion-detection system.

Several practical antitheft systems and other security projects for your automobile are presented in chapter 9. Chapter 10 discusses some sophisticated, special-purpose security devices that are now available. This discussion emphasizes determining just when it is or isn't necessary to invest in a deluxe security system.

Fire alarms and temperature sensors (both too hot and too cold) are covered in chapter 11, and chapter 12 wraps things up with a variety of security devices for monitoring a number of environmental conditions including light, flooding, impending electrical storms, and even microwave radiation.

I believe almost any electronics hobbyist reading this book should be able to find at least a few projects that will help him or her relax and sleep a little better. After all, who can't use a little added security?

Basics of electronic security systems

IT'S A SAD FACT THAT THIEVES ABOUND IN THE WORLD. THEY might steal material possessions, or they might steal access to information. Either way, their theft hurts.

So what are you going to do about it? Will you just shrug and hope it won't happen to you (or maybe, that it won't happen to you again)? Or will you attempt to do something about it?

Presumedly, if you are reading this book, you intend to do something about it. This book gives you as much solid information about protecting yourself and your property with electronics as the author can.

Although the main emphasis in this book is burglar alarms, it also considers alarms and devices to help warn and protect you from fire and other potentially hazardous conditions. In some of the general discussion in this chapter, *intruder*, can mean a fire or other environmental problem as well as a human intruder. The same electronic principles apply to burglar alarms and most other types of alarms.

The three parts of an alarm system

Most practical burglar (and other) alarm circuits consist of three basic sections, as shown in Fig. 1-1. Some sort of sensor detects the intruder, activating the control circuitry and sounding the alarm or other indication device. In some cases, the output indication is visual only and doesn't actually sound at all. In most alarm systems, however, an audible output alarm of some sort is the norm.

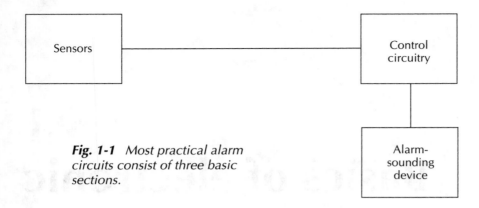

Fig. 1-1 *Most practical alarm circuits consist of three basic sections.*

Each of these sections might be very simple or very complex, but it is hard to imagine any practical alarm system without these three sections in one form or another.

Alarm circuit sensors of various types are discussed in detail in chapter 2. For now, consider just the most generalized sensors. Similarly, sounding and indication devices for alarms are covered in detail in chapter 3. For now, you don't need to pay any real attention to just what happens when the alarm is set off. In this general discussion, the text simply states "the alarm sounds."

The control circuitry for alarm systems is usually the most complex section. The actual projects presented throughout the later chapters of this book deal extensively with actual control circuitry of a wide variety of designs, ranging from the very simple to the sophisticated.

The sensor section of an alarm system

Most, though not all, sensor devices used in alarm circuits are essentially specialized switches. Like an ordinary switch, the sensor is either open or closed, with no in-between values. In this respect, it is like a binary, digital circuit, the output of which always must be either HIGH or LOW, with no other possibilities.

Usually alarm sensors function much like momentary-action switches. An ordinary slide switch is a nonmomentary device. Once you've set it to one position or the other (either open or closed), it stays there. It doesn't change its state again until you physically move the slider again. Some switches, especially push-button switches, are momentary-action devices. They are spring-loaded, so that they automatically return to one particular setting unless they are being physically held in the opposite position. A momentary-action switch can be either normally open (NO) or normally closed (NC), depending on which position it automatically returns to when it is released.

The standard schematic symbol for a normally-open switch is shown in Fig. 1-2. Notice that the switch contacts are shown with an open circuit. The normal (unactivated) switch position is always shown in the schematic. If you leave this normally open switch alone, it remains open indefinitely. There is no electrical connection between its contacts, and no current can flow between them. When the switch is physically activated, the contacts are mechanically forced to touch one another, completing the circuit. The switch is now closed, and current can flow from one switch contact to the other. But as soon as you release the switch, its internal spring mechanism forces the contacts apart again, and the switch returns to its normal, open position.

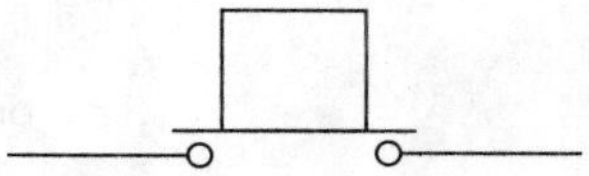

Fig. 1-2 *This is the standard schematic symbol for a normally open switch.*

Not surprisingly, a normally closed switch works in just the opposite way as a normally open switch. The standard schematic symbol for a normally closed switch is shown in Fig. 1-3. Notice that this time an electrical connection is shown between the switch contacts. The normal (unactivated) position of a switch is always shown in the schematic. If you leave this normally closed switch alone, it will remain closed indefinitely. There will be a continuous electrical connection between its contacts, and any applied current can flow between them. When the switch is physically activated, the contacts are forced to move away from one another, opening the circuit. The switch is now open, the circuit is broken, and no current can flow from one switch contact to the other. But as soon as you release the switch, its internal spring mechanism forces the contacts together again, and the switch returns to its normal, closed position.

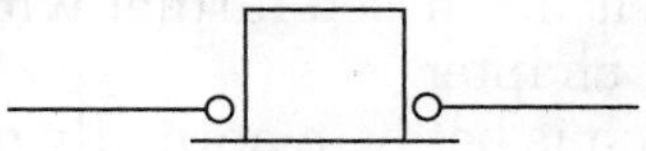

Fig. 1-3 *This is the standard schematic symbol for a normally closed switch.*

Thus far, you have been considering only SPST (single-pole, single-throw) switches. Momentary-action switches with more than one pole or more than one *throw* (position) are possible. For example, an SPDT (single-pole, double-throw) momentary-action switch is illustrated in Fig. 1-4. Notice that this switch has two sets of switch contacts. One set is normally open, and the other set is normally closed. It works just like a normally open switch and a separate normally closed switch, which are always operated in unison. The center contact is known as the *common*, and it is used by both the normally open and normally closed switch contacts when their circuits are completed. Sensors used in alarm circuits usually has SPST contacts, which helps simplify the circuitry.

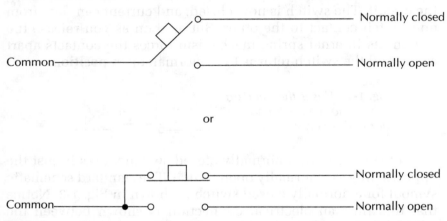

Fig. 1-4 *A momentary-action SPDT (single-pole, double-throw) switch has both normally open and normally closed contacts.*

The phrase *normally open* is often abbreviated as *N.O.* or *NO.* Similarly, *normally closed* is commonly abbreviated as *N.C.* or *NC.*

Most alarm sensors mimic the action of either a normally open switch or a normally closed switch, but that doesn't necessarily mean that the sensor is much like an ordinary mechanical switch in appearance or design. For example, an alarm sensor might not be spring loaded, but its contacts still function in either a normally open or a normally closed fashion. This concept is discussed further with actual alarm sensor devices in the next chapter.

Which is better, a normally open switch or a normally closed switch? Well, that depends on the specific application you have in mind. Usually either will work, but in some cases, a normally open switch might require more complex circuitry than a comparable normally closed switch, or vice versa.

In intrusion detection, normally closed switching will usually (though not always) provide greater security than normally open switching. To understand why, consider the simple alarm system illustrated in Fig. 1-5. The sensor in this alarm circuit is a normally open switch of some sort. When the intruder enters the protected area, he or she closes the switch, setting off the alarm. But what if the intruder knows the alarm system is there? The intruder could cut the wire between the normally open sensor and the control circuitry, as shown in Fig. 1-5. Now, if the sensor switch is closed, it will be ignored. As far as the alarm control circuit is concerned, the sensor switch is permanently open. The intruder has defeated the alarm system.

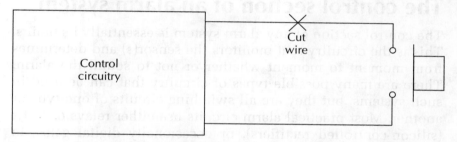

Fig. 1-5 *A normally open burglar alarm system can be easily defeated if the intruder cuts a connecting wire.*

Now, consider the same situation with a normally closed alarm system, as shown in Fig. 1-6. Everything is the same as before, except the intrusion sensor device is normally closed instead of normally open. When the intruder enters the protected area, the switch is opened and the alarm sounds. If the intruder cuts the wire from the switch to the control circuitry, the alarm circuit simply "thinks" that the sensor switch has been activated (opened), and the alarm sounds.

Of course, this is a very simple example. If the intruder doesn't have access to the connecting wires, it probably won't make much practical difference in the degree of protection offered if either normally open or normally closed switching is used. As discussed in chapter 2, some types of sensing naturally take a normally open form, and others just naturally work as normally closed devices. Often practical alarm systems incorporate

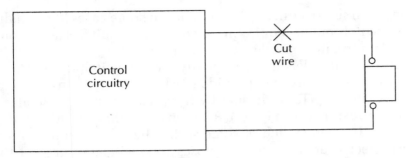

Fig. 1-6 *A normally closed burglar alarm system cannot be defeated by cutting a wire. In fact, cutting the wire will set off the alarm.*

both normally open and normally closed switching together for maximum protection and security.

The control section of an alarm system

The control section of any alarm system is essentially its brains. This is the circuitry that monitors the sensor(s) and determines from moment to moment whether or not to sound the alarm. There are many possible types of circuitry that can be used in such systems, but they are all switching circuits of one type or another. Most practical alarm circuits use either relays or SCRs (silicon-controlled rectifiers), or occasionally digital gates, to perform the main switching functions.

Of course, a number of specific control circuits are shown in detail for the actual projects in this book. For now, however, spend a little time learning about (or reviewing) the basic principles of switching devices commonly used in such circuits.

Relays

A relay is much like an ordinary mechanical switch, except it is operated by electromagnetic means. A relay consists of two main parts—a coil and a set of mechanical switch contacts. The wiper of the switch contacts is a small, springy piece of metal. A magnetic field can bend the wiper from one position to the other. When the magnetic field is removed, the springiness of the wiper returns it to its normal, denergized position.

Whenever current flows through a conductor, that conductor is surrounded by a small magnetic field. The magnetic field is stronger for a coil, because each loop of coiled wire adds to the overall effect. When a voltage is fed across a relay coil, a magnetic field is created, moving the wiper. The relay is said to be *activated*, or energized. When there is no voltage applied to the coil, there is no magnetic field, so the wiper stays in (or returns to) its normal, deactivated, or de-energized position.

One nice feature of relays, which can be very important in certain applications, is that there can be complete electrical isolation between a relay control circuit (connected to the coil) and its load circuit (connected to the switch contacts). This can add a touch of extra safety to some circuits, although this isn't usually too critical for most practical alarm systems, which generally use only very small voltages. More relevant is that the control circuit and the load circuit (the actual alarm output device) can use different supply voltages, as needed by each. For example, a low-power control circuit can operate a high-power alarm horn.

A relay can have any standard switch configuration. The four most common and standard switch configurations are SPST (single-pole, single-throw), SPDT (single-pole, double-throw), DPST (double-pole, single-throw) and DPDT (double-pole, double-throw). Other more exotic and complex switch configurations are possible, but these four are certainly the most widely used.

You might occasionally run across a SPST relay, but they aren't very common. DPST relays are very, very rare. Most readily available relays are either SPDT or DPDT. This availability is not a practical limitation in constructing electronic projects. The single-throw switches (SPST or DPST) can be simulated directly by their double-throw counterparts—simply leave the unneeded switch contact(s) open and unused. If you don't connect anything to it, it effectively doesn't exist in the circuit. In fact, a DPDT relay (or switch) can easily be used in place of any of the four basic switching configurations.

A relay switch contacts function like a momentary-action switch, like a push button. The switch contacts can be either normally open or normally closed. A normally open SPST relay closes its switch contacts only when it is energized. When this relay is de-energized (no voltage across its coil), the switch contacts are open. A normally closed SPST relay works in exactly the opposite manner. Its switch contacts are opened only when it is energized. When this relay is de-energized (no voltage across its coil), the switch contacts are closed.

An SPDT relay has three switch contacts, as shown in Fig. 1-7. The movable wiper is always shown in the middle. This is the part that physically moves in response to the magnetic field

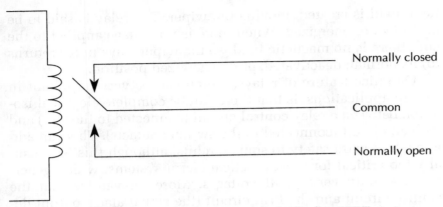

Normally closed

Common

Normally open

Fig. 1-7 *One of the most common types of relay has SPDT contacts.*

surrounding the coil when a suitable voltage is applied across it. The wiper connection is often labeled "common." Do not confuse this connection with a common-ground connection.

One of the remaining two fixed switch contacts is the normally closed contact, usually labeled "N.C." or "NC". The vast majority of schematics show the normally closed contact at the top, or to the left, but there are exceptions. The wiper (common) will always be shown in its normal (de-energized) position in the schematic, so you can easily tell which is the normally closed contact—it will be shown as a closed switch, in contact with the wiper, or common. The relay switch contacts are also labeled in many (but not all) schematic diagrams.

The remaining switch contact, of course, is the normally open connection. It is shown as an open switch, and is often labeled "N.O." or "NO".

If you are using an SPDT relay as an SPST relay, you will use only the wiper (common) and just one of the end contacts (either normally open or normally closed), leaving the other switch contact disconnected from the circuit. This contact will usually be shown in the schematic diagram anyway, but it won't be connected to anything. It might be labeled "N.C." for *no connection*. Unfortunately, this can lead to some confusion because N.C. can also stand for normally closed. Remember, the switch contacts will always be shown in their normal (de-energized) position, so don't be thrown if you see an unused normally open contact labeled N.C. for no connection. Most good technicians will do their best to avoid such ambiguity when drawing schematic diagrams, but such potentially confusing markings appear on some published schematics.

The schematic symbol for the DPDT relay usually shows two sets of SPDT switch contacts either side by side, or one over the other, as illustrated in Fig. 1-8. The switch contacts will almost always be shown as close as possible to the relay coil to indicate this is a single component, and not a separate coil and pair of mechanical switches.

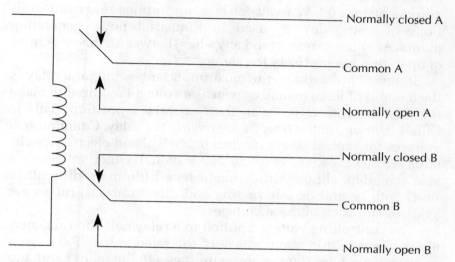

— Normally closed A

— Common A

— Normally open A

— Normally closed B

— Common B

— Normally open B

Fig. 1-8 *A DPDT (double-pole, double-throw) relay is like two SPDT relays in parallel, operated in unison.*

A DPDT relay operates just like two electrically separate, but mechanically linked, SPDT relays that always operate in perfect unison with one another. One complete set of contacts can be left completely unused, and the DPDT relay used as a simple SPST relay or SPDT relay. This might seem wasteful, but often DPDT relays are easier to find and even less expensive than SPDT or SPST units with similar specifications. The unused switch contacts won't hurt anything, and will not affect the operation of the circuit in any way. At worst, the relay used might be slightly larger than it really needs to be for the requirements of the applications. (Actually, there is usually little or no difference in the mechanical size of an SPST relay and a DPDT relay for the same basic ratings. They generally use the same plastic housings.)

Relays vary greatly in size, depending primarily on the amount of power they can safely carry. Some relays fit comfortably on the tip of your little finger, and there are industrial relays that an adult would have difficulty lifting. In hobbyist electronic circuits, relays are seldom more than a few inches in dimension and weigh no more than a few ounces.

Usually separate power ratings are given for a relay coil and its switch contacts, because they are generally used in separate circuits (or subcircuits), and often (though no always) have independent power supplies. Practical relays range from tiny units intended for use in transistorized equipment, where power requirements are 0.5 W (watt) or less, up to huge megawatt (millions of watts) devices used in industrial power-generating plants. At either extreme (and anywhere between), the principles of operation are precisely the same.

In most applications, the most important rating for a relay is the amount of force (usually given as a voltage) required to make the switch contacts move to their energized position. This is called *tripping, activating,* or *energizing* the relay. Common trip voltages for typical relays used in hobbyist level electronics circuits are 6, 12, 24, 48, 117, and 240 V (volts). Other voltages are also available, although they might be a little more difficult to find. Both ac and dc (alternating and direct current) relays are available for each of these voltages.

The controlling voltage applied to a relay coil should generally be kept within about ±25% of the rated value. Too large a voltage could burn out the coil windings. On the other hand, too small a control voltage could result in erratic or no operation of the relay.

In some applications, it might be necessary to drive a relatively high-power circuit with a fairly low-power control signal. This is accomplished using separate power supplies for the control (coil) circuit and the load (switch contact) circuit, as illustrated in Fig. 1-9. High-voltage supply b is in operation only when the relay is energized. This has the added advantage of minimizing power consumption.

Occassionally, the available control signal might not be sufficient to drive a large enough relay for the load circuit to be controlled. In a situation like this, the solution might be to add a cascaded medium-power relay to act as an intermediate stage as shown in Fig. 1-10.

To drive moderately high-power relays from low-power control signals, an amplifier circuit of some sort is often used. This usually is a simple transistor amplifier, like the one illustrated in Fig. 1-11.

The fairly delicate coil winding of a relay could self destruct if the current flowing through it is changed very suddenly. One

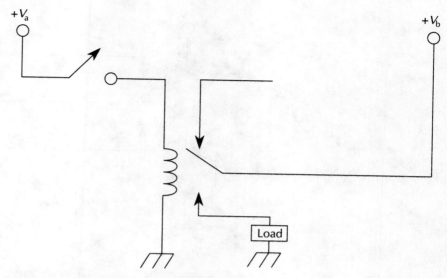

Fig. 1-9 A relay control circuit and its load can use independent power supplies.

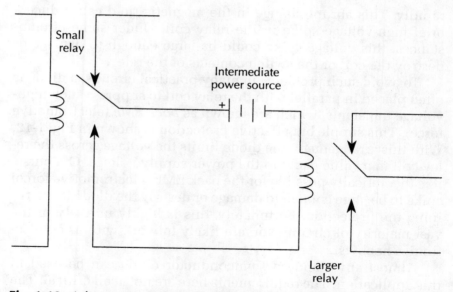

Fig. 1-10 A low-power relay can drive a second, larger relay to control a heavy load.

way this could happen is if a series switch (like the one shown in Fig. 1-9) is opened. The voltage across the relay coil abruptly drops from V+ down to 0 V in a tiny fraction of a second. This causes the magnetic field surrounding the coil to collapse very

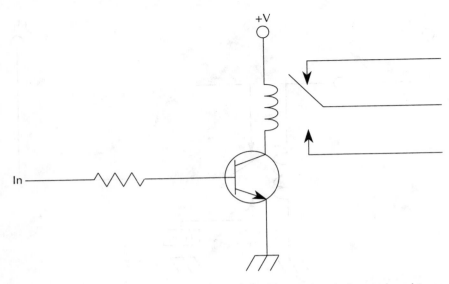

+V

In

Fig. 1-11 *A simple transistor amplifier can be used to help a relay drive a large load.*

rapidly. This abrupt change in the magnetic field can induce a brief high-voltage spike in the relay coil. Under some circumstances, this voltage spike could be large enough to damage or destroy the coil or the switch contacts of the relay.

To avoid such problems in many practical circuits, a diode is often placed in parallel with the relay coil to suppress such high-voltage transients, which are known as *back EMF* (electromotive force). This simple but effective protection is shown in Fig. 1-12. With this arrangement, the diode limits the voltage across the relay coil to a value equal to the power supply voltage. Of course, it is theoretically possible for the back EMF (electromotive force) spike to be large enough to damage or destroy the diode itself, ruining the protection. Fortunately, this is highly unlikely in the vast majority of circuits you are likely to work with as an electronics hobbyist.

Almost any standard semiconductor diode can be used in this application. The requirements here are not at all critical. The only specification you must be concerned with is the PIV (peak inverse voltage) rating of the diode. The diode PIV rating should always be high enough to cover any anticipated voltage that will be applied across the device. When in doubt, use a diode with a higher PIV rating. For the alarm projects, which generally use very low voltages only, a standard 1N4001 diode will almost always be sufficient for this purpose.

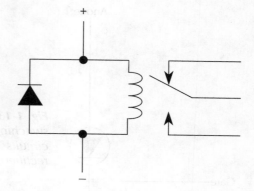

Fig. 1-12 *A diode in parallel with the relay coil can help protect against damage from back EMF (electromotive force).*

A protective diode might not be strictly necessary in all practical relay circuits, but it never hurts, and it won't add significantly to the cost of the project. It could save a lot of grief and frustration in the long run. Use such cheap insurance routinely, whether it appears to be "necessary" or not.

Most common relays are momentary-action types. They are energized only for as long as sufficient voltage is applied to the coil. When the current flowing through the coil drops, the relay switch contacts are released to their de-energized positions.

Some specialized relays are of a latching type. Not surprisingly, a device of this sort is called a *latching relay*. One control pulse activates the switch contacts, which will remain activated, even if the control signal is removed. A separate control pulse deactivates the latching relay switch contacts. Each time a latching relay is triggered, its switch contacts latch into the appropriate position until the next trigger signal is received.

Unfortunately, latching relays are usually fairly difficult to find and are rather expensive when you can find them. Some of the projects in this book use some clever circuitry to make an ordinary momentary-action relay act like a latching relay.

SCRs (silicon-controlled rectifiers)

Another popular type of switching device often used in alarm circuits is the SCR, or silicon-controlled rectifier. The schematic symbol for this special semiconductor device is shown in Fig. 1-13.

The SCR is often misunderstood, and many electronics hobbyists are almost afraid of it. Actually, the SCR is fairly easy to understand in general principle if you just look at each individual word in its name. *Silicon*, of course, is simply the semiconductor material the SCR is primarily made of. Like a regular diode, the two end terminals are known as the anode and the

Anode

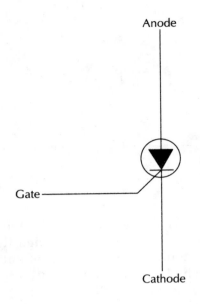

Fig. 1-13 *Another popular type of switching device often used in alarm circuits is the SCR (silicon-controlled rectifier).*

Gate

Cathode

cathode. The third word, *rectifier*, is also quite straightforward. It indicates that the SCR is a diodelike device, capable of rectification. The important term here is the one in the middle, *controlled*. The rectification of an SCR, unlike an ordinary diode, is externally controlled via an added third terminal, which is called the *gate*. You could consider an SCR to be an electrically switchable diode.

If a voltage is applied between the anode and the cathode of a SCR, as shown in Fig. 1-14, nothing at all will happen if there is no signal on the gate lead. In Fig. 1-14, the gate lead is shown grounded to emphasize that there is no signal at all on this terminal. In this circuit, the SCR acts like an open circuit. This is not at all a practical circuit, of course. It is completely nonfunctional. It won't do anything at all. This circuit is included here solely to demonstrate the operating concepts of the SCR.

But what happens if you apply an external voltage signal to the gate of the SCR, as shown in Fig. 1-15? If the gate voltage is very low, there is no change. The SCR will continue to block current flow from its cathode to its anode.

Now, assume that the gate voltage is being gradually increased. At some point, it will exceed a specific level (determined by the internal construction of the specific SCR used). At this point, the SCR will be *triggered* and the rectifier activated. Current can now flow from cathode to anode against only a small internal resistance, just as if it were an ordinary semiconductor

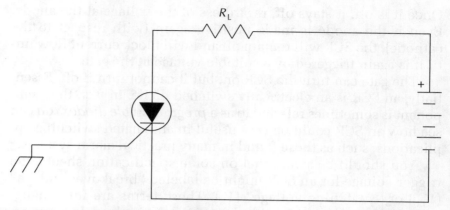

Fig. 1-14 *If a voltage is applied between the anode and the cathode of an SCR, nothing at all will happen if there is no signal on the gate lead.*

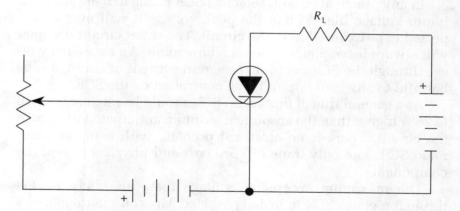

Fig. 1-15 *An SCR is turned on by applying a suitable voltage to its gate lead.*

diode. This current will continue to flow through the device, even if the external voltage on the gate terminal is removed. Once the SCR is switched on, it stays on regardless of the gate signal. The specific gate voltage level required to turn on an SCR is known as the *trigger voltage*.

The only way to stop the current flow through the SCR, once it has been turned on, is to decrease the positive voltage (with respect to the cathode) on the anode, or remove it altogether. When the anode voltage of an SCR drops below a specific level (once again, this value is determined by the internal construction of the particular SCR being used), current flow will be blocked. In other words, the SCR turns itself off when it is reverse biased.

Once it is off, it stays off, regardless of the voltage at the anode. Even if the anode is made positive again (with respect to the cathode), the SCR will remain off and will block current flow until it is again triggered by a suitable voltage at the gate.

The gate can turn the SCR on, but it cannot turn if off. Essentially, an SCR is an electrically switched diode. In fact, this component is sometimes referred to as a *programmable diode*. You can see how an SCR could be very useful in automated switching applications, such as those found in many practical alarm systems.

You should be aware that on some specification sheets, the trigger voltage for an SCR might be labeled "breakover voltage" (V_{bo}) or "switching voltage" (V_s). These terms are interchangable. Don't be thrown by the change in terminology. In some areas of electronics, unfortunately, there isn't much standardization.

In any practical circuit, select an SCR rating to handle a maximum voltage higher than the peak voltage it will ever be expected to be exposed to in the circuit. The smart circuit designer will always leave plenty of extra elbow room. An excessive voltage through the SCR could damage or destroy it. It could also be harmful to any load circuit being controlled by the SCR.

As a general rule of thumb, an SCR should be rated at least 10 to 25% higher than the absolute maximum anticipated voltage in the circuit. There is no electrical problem with using an overrated SCR. The only trade offs are cost and physical size of the component.

The maximum acceptable voltage that can safely be fed through a given SCR is usually labeled V_{drm} on manufacturer's specification sheets. This rating is more or less equivalent to the peak inverse voltage (PIV) rating for a standard rectifier diode. The V_{drm} rating will usually be at least 100 V greater than the trigger voltage.

SCRs are also given a current rating. This is the maximum current that the load can safely draw through the device. Obviously, in any practical project, the SCR must be selected to suit the intended load. When in doubt, always overrate an SCR. If you are not sure if the load will draw 2 or 3 A (amperes) use an SCR rated for 4 A or higher.

In most cases, substituting SCRs is fairly simple if you can't find the exact type number given in the project parts list. Generally speaking, if the SCR can handle the voltage and current in the circuit, it will probably work. But there are some exceptions, so be careful. Whenever you make any substitution in any electronic project, it is always a good idea to breadboard the circuit first, just to make sure it will work the way you think it will.

Digital gates

Some alarm circuits use digital gates in their control circuitry. A digital gate is, by definition, an electrically controlled switching device. An SPST switch can have either of two possible positions—open (off) or closed (on). Similarly, any digital signal must have one of just two possible states—LOW (0) or HIGH (1). Digital signals make a logical choice for electronically simulating the action of a switch.

Digital gates combine single-bit digital signals into various combinations, according to specific patterns, which are often outlined in charts known as *truth tables*. A bit is simply a BInary digiT, or a single digital LOW or HIGH signal.

The simplest possible digital gates have one input and one output. There are two possible types of single input/single output digital gates—the buffer and the inverter.

The buffer, shown in Fig. 1-16, always produces an output that is the same as its input. If the input is LOW, the output is LOW. If the input is HIGH, the output is HIGH. This might not seem to be very useful, and in terms of logic gating, it isn't. But in complex digital circuits, it might be necessary to feed the same signal many different places at once. A digital gate output can drive just so many inputs. A buffer permits a single output to drive more inputs without the problem of loading the driving device. A buffer is essentially the digital equivalent of an analog unity-gain buffer amplifier stage.

An inverter, shown in Fig. 1-17, is a bit more interesting and useful. This is sometimes called a NOT gate. It reverses or inverts the logic state of the input signal at the output. That is, the out-

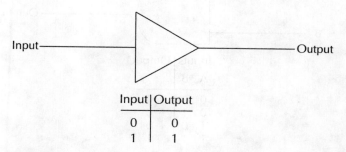

Input	Output
0	0
1	1

Fig. 1-16 *The buffer always produces an output that is the same as its input.*

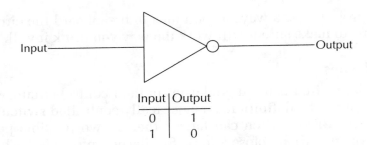

Input	Output
0	1
1	0

Fig. 1-17 *The output of an inverter is always the opposite state as its input.*

put signal is always at the opposite state as the input signal. If the input is LOW, the output is HIGH. If the input is HIGH, the output must be LOW. There are no other possibilities.

Single input/single output gates are clearly fairly limited. They can't do much useful work by themselves. Most digital gates have two or more inputs. Most simple gates still have a single output, although some have more.

With two inputs, each of which can take one of two possible states, there are four possible combinations of inputs:

$$0\ 0$$
$$0\ 1$$
$$1\ 0$$
$$1\ 1$$

A simple chart that shows the output state (or states) for all possible combinations of inputs is called the truth table of the gate.

A typical two input/single output digital gate is the AND gate, shown in Fig. 1-18. The output state is dependent on the interre-

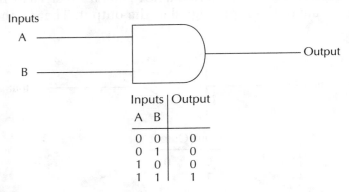

Inputs A B	Output
0 0	0
0 1	0
1 0	0
1 1	1

Fig. 1-18 *A typical two input/single output digital gate is the AND gate.*

lated states of two input signals. The output is HIGH if, and only if, both input A input B are HIGH. If either (or both) of the inputs is LOW, then the output will be LOW too. This relationship is shown in the truth table in Fig. 1-18.

The basic AND gate can be expanded to include three or more inputs. It still operates in the same way. All of the inputs must be HIGH to give a HIGH output. If any one or more of the inputs is LOW, then the output will be LOW. A three-input AND gate is shown in Fig. 1-19.

If you add an inverter to the output of an AND gate, as shown in Fig. 1-20, you reverse its operation entirely. Now, the output will

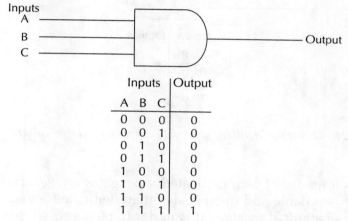

Inputs			Output
A	B	C	
0	0	0	0
0	0	1	0
0	1	0	0
0	1	1	0
1	0	0	0
1	0	1	0
1	1	0	0
1	1	1	1

Fig. 1-19 *An AND gate can have three or more inputs.*

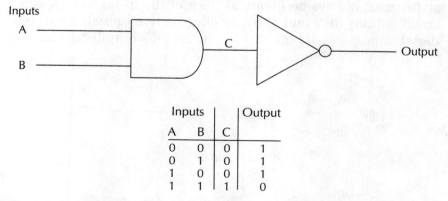

Inputs			Output
A	B	C	
0	0	0	1
0	1	0	1
1	0	0	1
1	1	1	0

Fig. 1-20 *Adding an inverter to the output of an AND gate produces a NAND gate.*

be LOW if, and only if both (or all) inputs are HIGH. If any one (or both) of the inputs is LOW, then the output will be LOW. This is no longer an AND gate. It is the opposite of an AND gate, made up of an AND gate and a NOT gate, so it makes sense to call this a *NOT AND* gate. This name is customarily shortened to *NAND* gate. This function is so useful that dedicated NAND gates are available. The schematic symbol for such a device is shown in Fig. 1-21. The small circle at the output of this gate symbol indicates inversion.

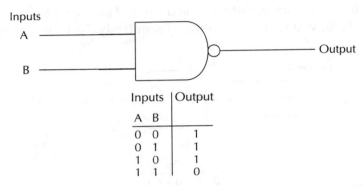

Inputs		Output
A	B	
0	0	1
0	1	1
1	0	1
1	1	0

Fig. 1-21 *This is the standard schematic symbol for a dedicated NAND gate.*

As a matter of fact, dedicated NAND gates are generally more readily available and inexpensive than dedicated AND gates. For various technical reasons, it is easier to etch a NAND gate circuit on an IC (integrated circuit).

What would happen if you shorted the two inputs of a NAND gate together, as shown in Fig. 1-22? Obviously, the two input states must always be identical. Two of the usual four possible combinations (0–1 and 1–0) are effectively eliminated and rendered impossible. If both inputs are LOW, the output is HIGH.

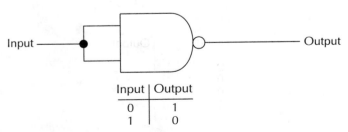

Input	Output
0	1
1	0

Fig. 1-22 *Shorting together the inputs of a NAND gate make it act like an inverter.*

If both inputs are HIGH, the output will be LOW. Because the two inputs cannot be different from one another in this case, there are no other possible input combinations. Shorting the inputs together turns a NAND gate into an inverter (or a NOT gate). This can be useful because there are typically four independent two-input NAND gates on a single IC. You can use a spare NAND gate as an inverter, without having to add another chip to the circuit. Figure 1-23 shows how two NAND gates can be combined to simulate an AND gate.

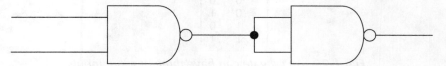

Fig. 1-23 *Two* NAND *gates can be combined to simulate an* AND *gate.*

Another very common type of digital gate is the OR gate, shown in Fig. 1-24. If either input A OR input B is HIGH, then the output will be HIGH. The output of an OR gate is LOW if, and only if, both inputs are LOW.

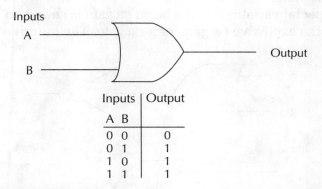

Inputs	Output
A B	
0 0	0
0 1	1
1 0	1
1 1	1

Fig. 1-24 *Another very common type of digital gate is the* OR *gate.*

Like the AND gate, the OR gate can be expanded for three or more inputs. The same principles of operation apply, but there are twice as many input combinations for each added input. A *three-input* OR gate is shown in Fig. 1-25. The output is LOW if, and only if all inputs are LOW. If any one or more of the inputs goes HIGH, the output will also be HIGH.

Again, you can reverse the logic function by adding an in-

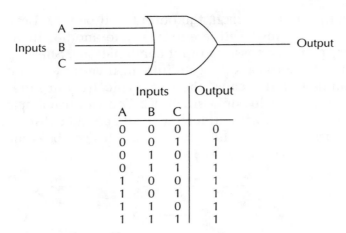

Inputs			Output
A	B	C	
0	0	0	0
0	0	1	1
0	1	0	1
0	1	1	1
1	0	0	1
1	0	1	1
1	1	0	1
1	1	1	1

Fig. 1-25 *An OR gate can have three or more inputs.*

verter to the output of an OR gate. This results in a *NOT OR* gate, or a *NOR* gate. A dedicated two-input NOR gate is shown in Fig. 1-26. NOR gate ICs are more widely available and less expensive than OR gate ICs, because of technical manufacturing processes.

Like the NAND gate, a NOR gate can be used as an inverter simply by shorting its two inputs together so they must always be at the same state.

A special variation on the basic OR gate is shown in Fig. 1-27. This is the exclusive-OR gate, or X-OR gate. The output of this gate

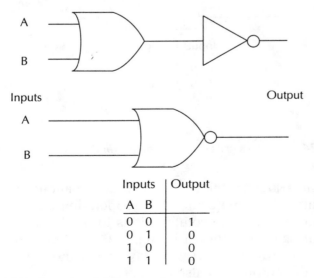

Inputs		Output
A	B	
0	0	1
0	1	0
1	0	0
1	1	0

Fig. 1-26 *Inverting the output of an OR gate produces a NOR gate.*

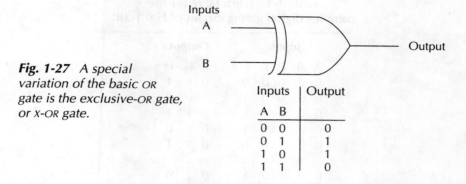

Fig. 1-27 *A special variation of the basic OR gate is the exclusive-OR gate, or X-OR gate.*

Inputs		Output
A	B	
0	0	0
0	1	1
1	0	1
1	1	0

is HIGH if either one of the inputs is HIGH, but not both. If both inputs are LOW, or if both inputs are HIGH, then the output of an X-OR gate will be LOW. You could consider the X-OR gate as a digital difference detector or as a one-bit digital comparator. X-OR gates with more than two inputs are extremely rare.

These basic simple gate types can be combined in countless ways to produce very complex digital switching networks. For example, Fig. 1-28 shows a complex digital gating circuit with five inputs and three outputs. The complete truth table for this circuit appears in Table 1-1.

A more sophisticated type of digital device is the flip-flop, or bistable multivibrator. Its output(s) reverses each time it is trig-

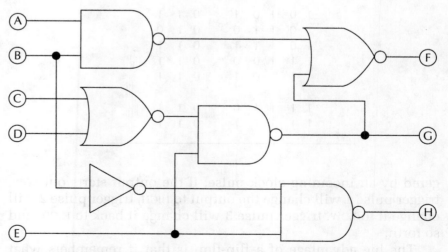

Fig. 1-28 *The basic simple gate types can be combined in countless ways to produce very complex digital switching networks.*

**Table 1-1 Truth table for the
complex digital gating circuit of Fig. 1-28.**

Inputs					Outputs		
A	B	C	D	E	F	G	H
0	0	0	0	0	0	1	1
0	0	0	0	1	1	0	0
0	0	0	1	0	0	1	1
0	0	0	1	1	0	1	0
0	0	1	0	0	0	1	1
0	0	1	0	1	0	1	0
0	0	1	1	0	0	1	1
0	0	1	1	1	0	1	0
0	1	0	0	0	0	1	1
0	1	0	0	1	1	0	1
0	1	0	1	0	0	1	1
0	1	0	1	1	0	1	1
0	1	1	0	0	0	1	1
0	1	1	0	1	0	1	1
0	1	1	1	1	0	1	1
1	0	0	0	0	0	1	1
1	0	0	0	1	1	0	1
1	0	0	1	0	0	1	0
1	0	0	1	1	0	1	1
1	0	1	0	0	0	1	0
1	0	1	0	1	0	1	1
1	0	1	1	0	0	1	0
1	0	1	1	1	0	1	1
1	1	1	0	0	0	1	1
1	1	1	0	1	0	1	1
1	1	1	1	0	0	1	1
1	1	1	1	1	0	1	1

gered by an incoming clock pulse. If the output starts out LOW, trigger pulse 1 will change the output to HIGH, trigger pulse 2 will change it to LOW, trigger pulse 3 will change it back to HIGH, and so forth.

The big advantage of a flip-flop is that it remembers what state it was set to. It can hold either a LOW output or a HIGH output indefinitely, until it receives suitable trigger pulse or until the power to the circuit is interrupted. Another way of looking at this is to say the flip-flop latches on to its last output state. For this reason, flip-flops are often called latches.

A number of the alarm projects in this book use digital gates or flip-flops, so it will be helpful for you to have at least some understanding of the principles of these devices. Refer to a basic digital electronics textbook for a detailed discussion of the principles of flip-flop operation.

Sensors

THE FUNCTION OF AN ALARM CIRCUIT IS TO ALERT YOU OF SOME condition in the real world (for example, to alert you that there is an intruder or a fire in the protected area). To know there is an intruder, or fire, the electronic circuitry must have some means of "looking at" the external world. Some sort of sensor is required.

Fortunately, modern electronics has progressed to a point where a great many different types of sensors are available. Almost any phenomenon in the real world can be monitored electronically.

Normally open and normally closed switches

Most (thought not all) practical alarm circuits use switching-type sensors. That is, the sensor unambiguously gives a simple yes/no indication of the monitored condition or event. Either there is an intruder or there isn't. Either the monitored temperature exceeds a specific preset level or it doesn't. Other types of sensors, such as a photoresistor, can offer a continuous range of values, which usually isn't needed in an alarm circuit. When such a continuous-range sensor is used in an alarm circuit, it is usually used with some sort of comparator circuit. The circuit converts the signal into a simple yes/no indication by comparing the continuous sensor signal with some specific reference value.

Because there are so many possible types of sensors, which may be useful in different practical applications, the schematic diagrams for the burglar alarm projects in this book will usually show just simple mechanical switches as the input devices. This is just for convenience and simplicity. The same alarm circuitry can be used with many different types of sensors, and it would be ridiculous to repeat the schematic diagram for each possible type of sensor. (Unless otherwise noted, the sensor switches shown in the schematics for the projects can be replaced with a comparable sensor suited to your specific intended application.)

Switches used as sensors in alarm circuits are almost always of the momentary-action type. Most inexpensive push-button switches are momentary-action type. (There are some exceptions.)

A standard slide switch is an example of a nonmomentary-action switch. When the slider is moved from one position to the other, it stays there, until you move it again. This type of switch can be left in either a closed position or an open position indefinitely.

A momentary-action switch always prefers one particular position and will go to the other position only when it is forced to. As soon as the switch is no longer being physically held in the nonpreferred position, it automatically reverts to its original state. You can see why this type of switch is called a *momentary-action device*.

Assuming an SPST (single-pole, single-throw) switch, there are two types of momentary-action switches; they work in exactly opposite ways.

A normally open switch, as shown in Fig. 2-1, will usually have no electrical connection between its contacts—it acts like an open circuit. Pressing the switch closes the contacts, completing the circuit connected across the device, but only as long as the switch is physically held down. As soon as the push button is released, the switch contacts automatically and immediately reopen. In a push-button switch, spring loading is used to mechanically return the slider to its nominally normal position.

The other type of momentary-action switch is the normally closed switch, which is illustrated in Fig. 2-2. It works in just the opposite manner as the normally open switch. For a normally closed switch, there usually is an electrical connection between the contacts—it acts like a closed or completed circuit. Pressing the switch opens up the contacts and breaks the circuit connected across the device, but the connection is broken only as long as the switch is

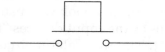

Fig. 2-1 *Some switching sensors have normally open contacts.*

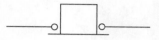

Fig. 2-2 *Some switching sensors have normally closed contacts.*

physically held down. As soon as the push button is released, the switch contacts automatically and immediately re-close.

The same principles apply to any other momentary-action switching sensor. A normally open sensor closes and completes the circuit only when it is tripped by the event of interest. A normally closed sensor opens and breaks the circuit only when it is tripped by the event of interest.

Most momentary-action switches (switching sensors) are the simple SPST type. More complex switching arrangements are possible. For example, a momentary-action SPDT (single-pole, double-throw) switch is shown in Fig. 2-3. The common slider is moved from one end contact to the other. One of these end contacts is the normally closed contact, and the other is the normally open contact.

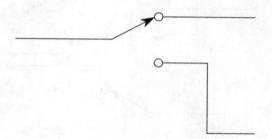

Fig. 2-3 *An SPDT switch has both normally open and normally closed contacts.*

Ordinarily, when the switch is not being activated, the common wiper makes electrical contact with the normally closed contact, but not with the normally open contact. When the switch is pressed, this condition reverses—the common wiper moves from the normally closed contact to the normally open contact. This condition will hold only as long as the switch is physically held down. As soon as the push button is released, the switch reverts back to its original condition—the common wiper is in contact with the normally closed contact and not with the normally open contact.

A DPST (double-pole, single-throw) switch, shown in Fig. 2-4, simply acts like a pair of SPST switches operating in unison. In almost all cases, both sets of switch contacts are of the same type—either both are normally open or normally closed. Dedicated DPST switches and switching devices are relatively rare. Usually a DPDT switch is used with some of its contacts left disconnected.

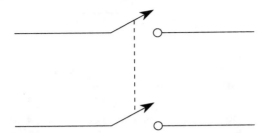

Fig. 2-4 *A DPST switch is like two linked SPST switches in parallel that are always operated in unison.*

A DPDT (double-pole, double-throw) switch, shown in Fig. 2-5, is like two simultaneously activated SPDT switches. A DPDT switch can be used in place of any of the three simpler switch types (SPST, SPDT, or DPST) simply by leaving some of the DPDT switch contacts disconnected, as if they didn't exist.

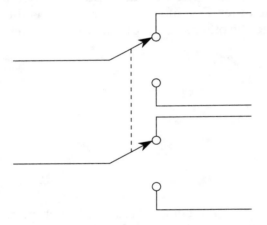

Fig. 2-5 *A DPDT switch is like two linked SPDT switches in parallel that are always operated in unison.*

Still more complex switching arrangements, with more than two poles and throws, are possible, but they are far less common. For example an SP8T (single-pole, 8 throw) switch has a single pole that can be moved to any of eight available positions. A 3P6T (3-pole, 6-throw) switch is like three six-position switches tied together with a single control. Most of the sensor switches used in alarm circuits are of the basic SPST type.

Now, why would anyone want to bother with the potential confusion between normally open and normally closed switches? Why not pick just one type and stick with it? Well, often a normally open switch is a better choice in one application, but a normally closed might be preferable in a different application. Certain types of sensors, as explained in this chapter, are most naturally of the normally open type, and others tend to be normally closed devices.

For an alarm system, a circuit using normally open switches will tend to be somewhat simpler than a comparable circuit using normally closed switching. But normally closed switches will often offer better security than normally open switches.

To see why, consider the simple alarm circuit shown in Fig. 2-6. A normally open switch is used as the sensor. What if an intruder manages to cut the wire connecting the sensor to the alarm circuit? Or what, if a fire burns through this wire in a fire alarm? The alarm circuit will think it sees a safe, open switch, even if the sensor is tripped. The sensor has been completely deactivated as far as the alarm circuit is concerned.

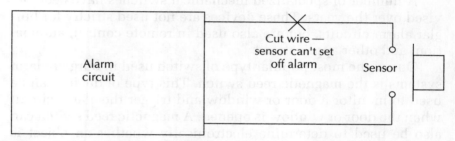

Fig. 2-6 *A normally open burglar alarm system can be easily defeated if the intruder cuts a connecting wire.*

On the other hand, in a normally closed switching system, as shown in Fig. 2-7, cutting, burning through, or breaking a connecting wire is interpreted by the alarm circuit as a tripped sensor. The alarm goes off as soon as the system is breached. In most practical circumstances, it is much more difficult to defeat an alarm system using normally closed sensors.

Specialized mechanical switches

You could post a note saying something like, "Dear Ms. or Mr. Intruder. Please press the button. Thank you." But it's highly doubtful that most intruders would be so cooperative as to set off your alarm system so directly. In a practical burglar alarm system, you need switches that the intruder activates whether or not he or she wants to do so (and almost certainly intruders do not want to). Ideally, the intruder should not be aware that a sensor switch has been tripped at all until it is too late, and the alarm has been set off.

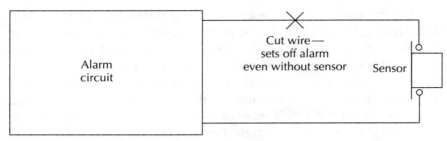

Fig. 2-7 *A normally closed burglar alarm system cannot be defeated by cutting a wire. In fact, cutting the wire will set off the alarm.*

A number of specialized mechanical switches have been devised over the years. These devices are not used strictly for burglar alarm circuits, but are also used in remote control, automation, and other applications.

One of the most popular type of switch used in burglar alarm systems is the magnetic reed switch. This type of device can be used to monitor a door or window and trigger the alarm circuit when the door or window is opened. A magnetic reed switch can also be used to determine electronically whether an object is moved away from some other object or from a specific position near a wall.

A magnetic reed switch consists of two physically separate parts. As Fig. 2-8 illustrates, these two sections of a magnetic reed switch don't really look like very much—just two plastic-enclosed rectangles with ear extensions for mounting screws. One of the pieces has contacts for two wires to be connected. The other piece is not electrically connected to anything.

The wireless half of the magnetic reed switch contains a small permanent magnet. The other section contains a light-weight reed switch. This switch is connected to the alarm circuit, just like an ordinary switch. Most magnetic reed switches are of the SPST type.

The slider of the magnetic reed switch is a magnetically operated reed. When there is a sufficient magnetic field in the vicinity of this reed, it will change its position, activating the switch. When the magnetic field is removed, the switch is deactivated, and the reed springs back to its normal position.

To monitor a door, the wireless magnet section is mounted on the door itself, and the reed switch section is mounted on the door frame, as shown in Fig. 2-9. These two sections should be mounted as physically close to each other as possible.

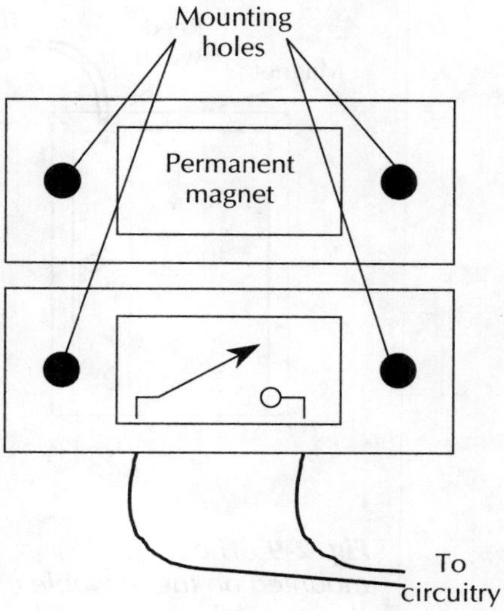

Fig. 2-8 *Magnetic reed switches are used to monitor doors and windows.*

Magnetic reed switches are available in either NO (normally open) or NC (normally closed) configurations. The choice depends on the particular requirements of the specific application.

Assume you have a normally open magnetic reed switch mounted on a door as shown back in Fig. 2-9. When the door is open, the magnetic field from the permanent magnet does not reach the reed within the switch section, so it is in its normal (deactivated) position—the switch contacts are open. When the door is closed, the magnet is brought close to the switch section, so the magnetic field activates the reed, and the switch closes.

Of course, a normally closed magnetic reed switch works in exactly the opposite way. In this case, when the door is open and the magnetic field from the permanent magnet cannot reach the reed within the switch section, so it is in its normal (deactivated) position—the switch contacts are closed. When the door is closed, the magnet is brought close to the switch section, so the magnetic field activates the reed, opening the switch contacts.

Summarizing the switch condition for the door position:

Door	NO	NC
Open	Open	Closed
Closed	Closed	Open

Now, it can be a little confusing using a magnetic reed switch with a burglar-alarm circuit. For the purposes of the alarm sys-

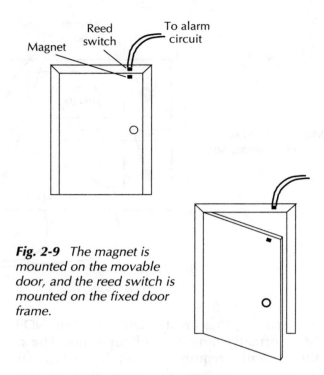

Fig. 2-9 *The magnet is mounted on the movable door, and the reed switch is mounted on the fixed door frame.*

tem, the normal position of the door is closed, not open. You want to trigger the alarm when the door is opened. Therefore, as weird as it sounds, if the schematic diagram for your alarm switch shows a normally open switch, you should use a normally closed magnetic reed switch, and if the schematic calls for a standard normally closed switch, use a normally open magnetic reed switch. The confusion comes from identifying which state is normal.

To add to the potential for severe confusion, many manufacturers of magnetic reed switches, knowing that their products are frequently used in alarm systems, designate the switch condition when the magnetic field is present as the normal state, even though this designation is not really technically correct. Read the manufacturer's description of any magnetic reed switch carefully. At worst, if you don't know which way a particular magnetic reed switch operates, you can easily check it out with an ohmmeter or a continuity checker. You should get low resistance (high continuity) when the switch is closed, and high (ideally infinite) resistance (or low to no continuity), when the switch is open. Which state do you get when the magnet is close enough to activate the reed switch, and what happens when the magnet is moved away?

Remember, what name you give the switch (normally open or normally closed) doesn't really matter. What matters is that it operates the way you want it to. If you make a mistake and use the wrong type of switch, the alarm will be set off when the door is closed, which probably isn't what you want the circuit to do so.

A magnetic reed switch also can be used to monitor a window, as shown in Fig. 2-10. Again, the magnet section (no wires) is mounted on the movable part of the window, and the actual reed switch is mounted on the window frame. If the window is opened past a specific point (depending on the positioning of the switch elements (you might have to experiment here), the alarm will be set off, just as when a protected door is opened.

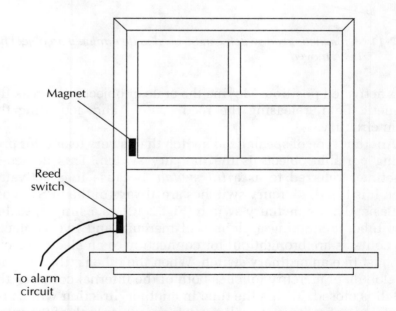

Fig. 2-10 *A magnetic reed switch can also be used to determine if a window is open or closed.*

Another use for a magnetic reed switch in a burglar alarm system is illustrated in Fig. 2-11. The magnet (no wires) section is mounted on a crate, or some other object you don't want moved, and the reed switch is mounted on the wall or some other immovable (preferably) object near where you want the protected object to stay. As long as the crate, or other protected object, is left undisturbed, the magnet will hold the reed switch

36 Sensors

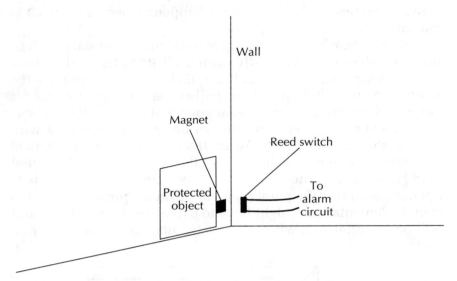

Fig. 2-11 *A magnetic reed switch can be used to determine if an object has been moved.*

in its activated position. Moving the crate or object will break the magnetic field, releasing the reed switch, and activating the alarm circuitry.

Another type of specialized switch that is very useful for protecting portable objects is the mercury switch. This device is sometimes referred to as a *tilt switch*, because it is activated when it is tilted. Mercury switches are always of the SPST type.

Basically, the mercury switch (Fig. 2-12), is a simple, sealed glass tube, containing a globule of mercury and two contacts. The contacts are brought out for connection to an electronic circuit, just like an ordinary switch. When the tube is tilted so that the globule of mercury touches both of the internal contacts, the switch is closed. Tilting the tube in another direction will cause the globule of mercury to roll away from one or both of the internal contacts, opening the switch. Mercury switches can be used to detect relatively small movement, although they generally require very careful and precise placement.

Closely related to the mercury switch is the vibration switch. This is a fairly sophisticated device, which just looks like a rather unimpressive little box, with a pair of wires coming out of it. Of course, these wires are used to connect the switch to the electronic circuitry. A vibration switch is almost always of the SPST, normally open type. When the vibration switch is just sit-

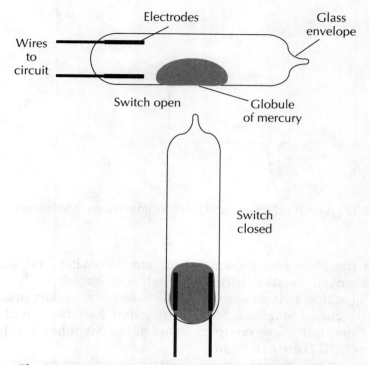

Fig. 2-12 *A mercury switch is sometimes called a* tilt switch.

ting there with no movement, the switch stays open and nothing happens. Any movement or disturbance sets off vibrations, which activate the switch, closing its contacts and setting off the alarm. Better vibration switches have some sort of adjustment control that permits you to determine just how much vibration will be required to activate the device. This feature is very useful for preventing irritating false alarms.

The chief disadvantage of vibration switches is that they tend to be rather bulky and expensive. You can probably buy half a dozen mercury switches for the price of one vibration switch, but a vibration switch is generally easier to use (it doesn't require such precise placement) and more reliable in most applications.

In some alarm applications, a snap-action switch might be useful in detecting relatively small motion. A typical snap-action switch is shown in Fig. 2-13. The switch is equipped with a small, relatively long but very lightweight lever, that touches the object you wish to sense or monitor. A very small, light pressure

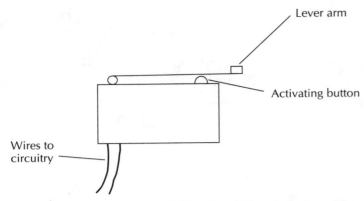

Fig. 2-13 *A snap action is useful for detecting relatively small motion.*

against the lever is sufficient to activate the switch. When the lever is moved, even slightly, the switch is activated.

Snap-action switches are available in either normally open or normally closed versions. Most snap-action switches are of the SPST type, but more complex snap-action switches (such as SPDT or DPDT) are available.

Snap-action switches can be obtained with many different lever arrangements, so the same basic principles can be adapted to a very wide variety of potential applications. Several separate snap-action switches can be used together to detect different possible positions of a single object.

Some burglar alarm systems use a pressure switch. It is a relatively large, flat package that is usually strategically placed under a rug or mat. When an intruder steps on the switch, it closes and activates the alarm.

Pressure switches are almost always of the SPST type, and usually have normally open contacts, although there are normally closed pressure switches.

To offer reasonable protection, a pressure switch must be very, very carefully placed to maximize the odds that the intruder will actually step on it. These devices also tend to be rather expensive, which further limits their use in most practical burglar-alarm systems. But they can be just what the doctor ordered in some specific applications.

Other, often more obscure, specialized switches are also available, and might be suitable under some circumstances. The switching devices covered here are generally the most appropriate for the vast majority of practical burglar-alarm systems.

Foil tape

A very useful item for burglar alarm systems is foil tape. Foil tape is a narrow strip of adhesive-backed tape, much like ordinary cellophane tape. Instead of cellophane, foil tape is made of a conductive metallic foil. Foil tape is used primarily to protect windows.

You read that a window can be protected with a magnetic reed switch, similar to the way doors are protected. But a reed-switch system works only if the intruder actually attempts to open the window. Often, intruders break or cut the glass and enter through the window without opening the frame. It doesn't even have to be a window that can be opened. If the window frame isn't physically moved, the magnetic reed switch won't notice the intrusion. Foil tape can take up the security slack here.

The tape is affixed around the perimeter of the window, something like the arrangement shown in Fig. 2-14. Notice that the tape is placed on the window in one continuous strip. If necessary, separate pieces of tape can be used, but they must be overlapped so that there is good electrical continuity between them. To the circuit, the separate pieces of tape "look" like a continuous strip. To minimize potential problems, it is very important to use as few separate pieces of tape as you possibly can.

A small contact block is placed at either end of the complete foil strip. It is just a little device that makes electrical contact

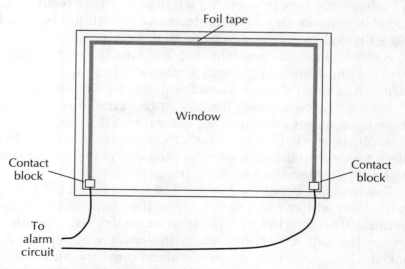

Fig. 2-14 *Foil tape applied around the perimeter of a window will act like an open switch if the window is broken.*

with the conductive foil of the tape and permits you to attach a wire to some sort of electronic circuit—presumably a burglar alarm circuit of some sort. Ordinarily, the foil tape provides a continuous current path from one contact block to the other. As far as the attached circuit is concerned, the foil is a closed switch or simply a continuous conductor or wire.

If an intruder breaks the glass, the odds are good that he or she will also break the foil tape at least partially. Careful placement of the tape can maximize the odds that the tape will be broken. Breaking the foil tape, of course, opens up the circuit between the contact blocks, which triggers the alarm circuit. Notice that the foil tape electrically acts just like a normally closed switch and can be used with any circuit calling for such a switch. (There is probably no way to create a foil tape normally open switch, but there is no particular reason you might want to.)

Foil tape can offer very good security, but it is not perfect. (What is?) It will almost always be visible to an intruder, which is good if it acts as a deterent. A careful burglar armed with a good glass cutter might be able to cut away enough of the glass to enter without breaking any of the foil tape, because the tape is visible. You can't very well cover up the entire window with foil tape—that would pretty much defeat the purpose of having the window in the first place.

Also, the foil tape will not be broken if the window is opened. An intruder could cut a small hole, enough to reach in and release the lock to open the window. For best security, any openable window should be protected with both foil tape and a magnetic reed switch, as described in this chapter.

Another potential problem with foil tape is that this tape is very thin and fragile. Very small breaks can cause annoying false alarms. At a retail store protected with foil tape, the alarm went off once or twice a week, usually in the middle of the night. These false alarms continued for several months, and each time an employer was called in to check the store and reset the alarm. There was never any sign of attempted entry nor any apparent reason for the alarm to have been triggered.

Eventually, a very thin, too small to see, crack in the foil tape on the front window was found. When the temperature changed significantly, the window expanded or contracted, opening or closing the gap. Of course, when the crack was separated, it looked like an open circuit to the alarm circuitry, so the alarm was set off to indicate the detected intrusion. If you run into periodic mysterious false alarms with your burglar alarm system, it would be a good idea to check any foil tape very carefully for possible hairline cracks.

Photosensors

Not all sensors used in alarm circuits are simply modified switches. Often, you will want an electronic circuit to respond to some specific phenomenon in the real world, such as light intensity. Light detection cannot be done with a mechanical switch, because an entirely different kind of energy is involved—photo (light) energy instead of mechanical energy. Obviously, you need a specialized photosensor component to do this. There are a number of such devices to choose from for different applications.

Figure 2-15 shows how photosensors are most commonly used in burglar alarm systems. A light source puts out a beam of light, which is focused on the photosensor, separated by some distance. If any nontransparent object (such as an intruder) passes between the light source and the photosensor, the light beam is broken. The photosensor detects this change in the light level, and the appropriate circuitry sets off an alarm. Either ordinary visible light or invisible infrared light can be used in such applications.

For best results, the light beam source and the photosensor should be shielded as much as possible from any stray, uncon-

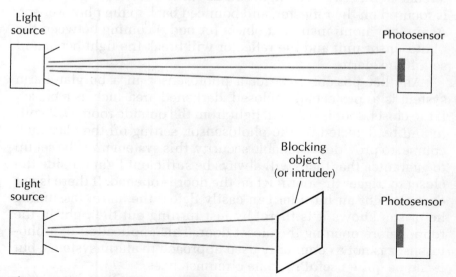

Fig. 2-15 A photosensor can trigger an alarm when the light beam is cut off.

trolled ambient light in the area. A pair of small cardboard tubes around the light source and the photosensor, as shown in Fig. 2-16, often provide sufficient focusing of the light beam. An infrared light beam and infrared photosensor will generally be less susceptible to interference from ordinary ambient light sources than a comparable system using visible light.

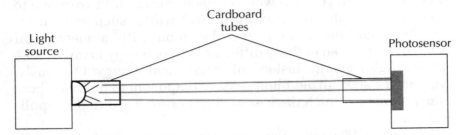

Fig. 2-16 *The light beam can be better focused by small cardboard tubes around the light source and the photosensor.*

In some cases, the light beam can be sent to the photosensor via one or more mirrors or reflectors. Often, the light source and the photosensor/alarm circuit will be enclosed in a single unit. A simple reflector is mounted opposite this unit, on the other side of this area to be protected. With this arrangement, connections must be made to only one of the two units. The reflector is entirely passive and self contained. There is no real functional difference in this case. The light source emits a beam of light, which is focused on the reflector, and bounced back to the photosensor. Again, any nontransparent object (or body) coming between the photosensor unit and the reflector will break the light beam and set off the alarm.

Another possible use for a photosensor in a burglar-alarm system is to protect an enclosed, darkened area such as a closet. If the closet door is opened, light from the outside room will spill in and be detected by the photosensor, setting off the alarm. Of course, to provide reasonable security, this system must be set up to guarantee that there will always be sufficient light outside the closet to trigger the alarm when the door is opened. If there is not enough light an intruder can easily defeat the alarm (assuming he or she knows it is there) by just turning out the light in the room before opening the closet door. This application of a photosensor is not a commonly used approach to alarm systems, but it can be quite useful in some circumstances.

Photosensors are semiconductor devices. All semiconductors are photosensitive to some degree. Usually, this sensitivity is undesirable. You don't want the transistors in an amplifier or a radio to change their operation in response to random, uncontrolled changes in the ambient lighting of the outside environment. For this reason, most standard semiconductor components are enclosed in a light-tight housing of some sort. Most transistors and ICs are housed in either a metal can or a dark plastic body.

A photosensor, on the other hand, is specifically designed to respond to light in a predictable way. The semiconductor material is exposed to outside light, usually through a protective, transparent shield of some sort.

One of the simplest types of photosensor is the *photovoltaic cell*, or solar cell. This device is sometimes called a solar battery, although this name isn't strictly correct unless multiple cells are being used together.

Figure 2-17 shows the schematic symbol for a photovoltaic cell. Notice that it closely resembles the symbol used for a standard battery cell. Both types of cells are dc voltage sources. The incoming arrows indicate sensitivity to light. In some sources, the surrounding circle might be omitted from the schematic symbol, because it doesn't really add any information. Including a circle for all photosensitive component symbols is preferred because the circle makes it harder to mistake for an ordinary (non-photosensitive) component.

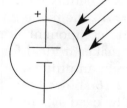

Fig. 2-17 *The photovoltaic cell generates current when light strikes its sensing surface.*

A typical photovoltaic cell is a square or rectangular flat board. On one side of this board, or wafer, is photosensitive, while the other side is inactive. This photosensitive board is quite thin and fairly fragile, so you must be careful in working with such devices. It is rugged enough for practical use, but if it is dropped, bent, or subjected to other mechanical stress, it could easily break or crack.

The photovoltaic cell will have either two wires extending from it or two connection points to add such wires externally.

One of these wires or contacts will be labeled + or positive, and the other will be the − or negative lead. These wires correspond directly to the positive and negative terminals of an ordinary battery cell. As far as the connected circuitry is concerned, there is no difference between a standard battery cell and a comparable array of photovoltaic cells, provided they have the same voltage and current-handling capabilities.

The typical photovoltaic cell produces an output voltage of about 0.5 V, when illuminated. Of course, if the photovoltaic cell is shielded from all light, it won't have any output voltage at all. Assuming there is some light reaching the surface of the photovoltaic cell, its output voltage is nearly constant, regardless of the intensity of the light. Once a little light reaches the cell, the output voltage will rise to about its final value. In other words, either the output voltage is there or it is not there, making the photovoltaic cell act a little bit like a photosensitive switch.

The output current of the cell, on the other hand, is sensitive to the light intensity striking the the photosensitive surface of the cell. The brighter the light, the more current the photovoltaic cell can put out.

The output voltage of photovoltaic cells is also constant with the size of the photosensitive surface, which can vary over quite a range. The larger the photosensitive board, the greater the overall current capacity for a given amount of illumination.

Because the standard output voltage of a photovoltaic cell is 0.5 V, three such devices must be used in series to simulate a standard 1.5 V battery cell, such as a size AA battery.

Technically, the name *photovoltaic cell* is bit of a misnomer, because this component is really a current generator. Current generation makes it ideal for use with transistors, which are basically current amplifiers.

Figure 2-18 shows the circuit for a light-sensitive relay. This circuit can be used as a normally open sensor switch in an alarm system. To use the same circuit in place of a normally closed sensor switch, simply change the switch contacts you use on the relay.

Nothing in this circuit is particularly critical, with one very important exception. Germanium transistors must be used in this circuit. Just about any small-signal NPN germanium transistor should work well in this circuit. The more common silicon transistors will not work. The base-to-emitter voltage of a germanium transistor is only about 0.2 V, so the output voltage from the photovoltaic cell (0.5 V) is high enough to make the base current flow. A silicon transistor, however, has a base-to-emitter

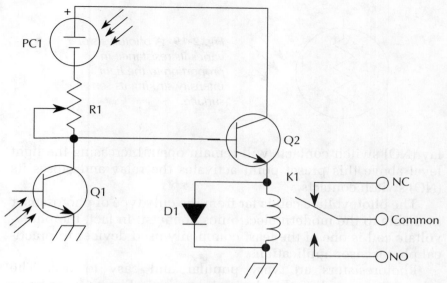

Fig. 2-18 Project 1. Light-sensitive relay.

Table 2-1   Parts list for project 1.
Light-sensitive relay of Fig. 2-18.

Q1	Phototransistor	NPN
Q2	NPN transistor	(2N3904 or similar)
D1	Diode (1N4001 or similar)	
PC1	Photovoltaic cell	
K1	Relay to suit load	
R1	500 kΩ (kilohms) potentiometer	

voltage of about 0.7 V. The 0.5 V output from a single photo-voltaic cell is not sufficient to allow a base current to flow in transistor Q1.

It actually wouldn't be too difficult to adapt this light-activated relay circuit to work with silicon transistors. Instead of a single photovoltaic cell, use two photovoltaic cells in series for a combined voltage of 1.0 V, which is enough to permit the base current of a silicon transistor to flow.

The sensitivity of this light-activated relay is adjustable via the potentiometer in parallel with the photovoltaic cell itself. The sensitivity control should be set so that the relay will operate at the desired light level. If the detected light level is lower than this critical value, the relay will be deactivated, and the re-

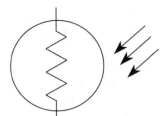

Fig. 2-19 *A photoresistor varies its resistance in proportion to the light intensity striking its sensing surface.*

lay (NO) switch contacts will remain open. Increasing the light level above this preset point activates the relay and closes its (NO) switch contacts.

The photovoltaic cell is far from the only type of photosensor available to the modern electronics hobbyist. In fact, the photovoltaic cell is one of the least commonly used devices in practical photosensor applications.

Photoresistors are very popular and easy to use. The schematic symbol for this device is shown in Fig. 2-19. As far as the electronic circuitry is concerned, a photoresistor is simply a two-terminal potentiometer, or variable resistor. The only difference is that the resistance of this potentiometer is not controlled by a mechanical shaft, but by light intensity. For most photoresistors, the greater the light intensity striking its sensing surface, the lower the resistance.

Unlike the photovoltaic cell, and most other semiconductor components, a photoresistor is a nonpolarized device. That is, it doesn't care which end is positive and which is negative. It can't be wired backwards, because it will work just as well in either direction, just like an ordinary resistor.

A photoresistor can be used in any circuit that uses a standard potentiometer, providing, of course, that light control suits the application at hand.

In some technical literature (especially older material), photoresistors are sometimes referred to as *LDRs,* or light-dependent resistors. The two names mean the same thing. *Photoresistor* is, by far, the preferred term in modern electronics.

A number of other photosensors are also available to the electronics hobbyist and experimenter, duplicating the function of standard semiconductor components with the added feature of photosensitivity. Figure 2-20 shows a photodiode, and Fig. 2-21 shows a phototransistor. Some phototransistors have three leads, like ordinary transistors, but most have just two. The light striking the sensor takes the place of the usual base signal in a phototransistor.

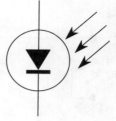

Fig. 2-20 *Another common photosensor is the photodiode.*

Fig. 2-21 *Phototransistors are popular photosensors.*

Another type of photosensor is the LASCR, or light-activated SCR (silicon-controlled rectifier), as shown in Fig. 2-22. This component works in much the same way as an ordinary SCR, except the gate signal is controlled by the light intensity striking the sensor.

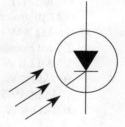

Fig. 2-22 *In a LASCR (light-activated silicon-controlled rectifier), light controls the gate.*

Circuitry using photodiodes, phototransistors, or LASCRs is similar to that using ordinary diodes, transistors, or SCRs, except for the controlling effect of light in photosensors. The operation of the circuit responds directly to the intensity of the light reaching the sensor (or sensors).

Touch sensor

An electronic alarm circuit can even monitor whether or not something has been touched. Several touch-switch circuits have

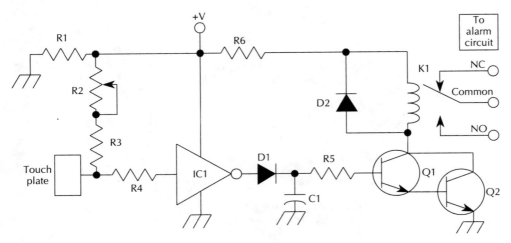

Fig. 2-23 *Project 2. Touch sensor.*

**Table 2-2   Parts list for project 2.
Touch sensor of Fig. 2-23.**

IC1	CD4049 hex inverter
Q1, Q2	NPN transistor (RS2009, GE20, SK3122, ECG128, or similar)
D1	Signal diode (1N4148, 1N914, or similar)
D2	Diode (1N4001 or similar)
K1	Relay SPDT
C1	0.47 µF (microfarad) capacitor
R1	5.6 kΩ ¼ W (watt) 5% resistor
R2	2.5 MΩ potentiometer
R3	3.3 MΩ ¼ W 5% resistor
R4	100 kΩ ¼ W 5% resistor
R5	47 kΩ ¼ W 5% resistor
R6	6.8 kΩ ¼ W 5% resistor

been designed over the years. One that is suitable for this discussion is shown in Fig. 2-23. A suitable parts list for this project is given in Table 2-2.

The object to be protected by this touch sensor circuit should be metallic or of some other electrically conductive material. The metal surface should not be too large. This project is best for protecting relatively small objects. But is can also be used to guard a doorway by sensing when someone touches the doorknob. Of course, the door must have a metal doorknob for this to work. The door should not be metal.

This project will not work out in the wilderness. It depends on the presence of ac power lines in the vicinity. You see, the human body acts like a sort of antenna, picking up the low-level ac hum. This hum signal is transferred to the protected metal object when it is touched, triggering the sensor circuit.

The metal probe is connected to the input of an inverter (IC1). Instead of a dedicated inverter, you could use a spare NAND or NOR gate with the inputs shorted together if you prefer.

Potentiometer R2 is adjusted to bias the circuit so that the inverter output is normally LOW when the metal sensor is not being touched. A trimpot would probably be the best choice for this application. A front-panel control wouldn't make much sense.

If a sufficiently strong hum signal is detected at the input of this circuit, the output of the inverter will be a 60 Hz pulse wave (or 50 Hz in some countries). This signal is treated by a Darlington pair of transistors (Q1 and Q2) to activate the relay (K1). The switch contacts of the relay can be used as a standard sensor switch in virtually any alarm circuit.

You should be aware that while generally effective, this circuit can be fooled. For example, if someone is wearing rubber gloves, there probably won't be sufficient hum pick-up when he or she touches the sensor.

An important restriction with this project is that the sensor circuit must be physically close to the object being monitored. This restriction is necessary because connecting wires can also act as antennae and can pick up strong hum signals, even without being touched. If you must mount the circuit more than a couple of inches from the actual sensor, you are very strongly advised to use a shielded cable of some kind to make the connection. Ground the shield at each end. This shielding will help minimize stray hum pick-up, which interferes with proper operation of the project.

Motion detector

A photosensor also can be used as a motion detector. The D1072 is an example of an LSI (large-scale integration) chip designed specifically for use in motion-detector circuits. A simplified block diagram of D1072 internal circuitry is shown in Fig. 2-24.

The D1072 does not require an external photosensor. It has a built-in photodiode (D1). The rest of circuitry is set up to convert the output of the photodiode for practical motion detection. The exact amount of light falling on the photosensor is irrelevant. No dedicated light beam is required for use with the motion detec-

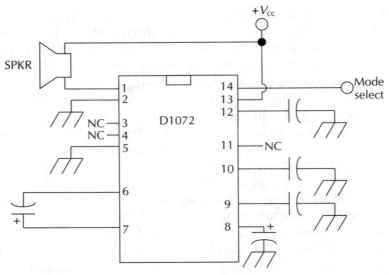

Fig. 2-24 *The D1072 is a motion-detector IC (integrated circuit).*

tor. It responds to the normal ambient lighting in the protected area. Changes in the light level are what is detected by this circuit. If any nontransparent object within the sensor range moves, this movement will inevitably change the light level seen by the photodiode. The new position of the object will almost certainly block more or less of the ambient light reaching the photosensor.

A number of other motion detectors have been designed over the years. Most such circuits require some kind of light transmitter and receiver, and generally they must be very carefully aligned for proper response. The D1072 functions in whatever ambient light happens to be available. Standard transmitter/receiver motion detectors usually require that the transmitted light beam be completely broken for reliable detection of the motion. The D1072 motion detector can respond to lighting changes as small as ±5%. This is obviously a very sensitive motion detector, and it will respond to even slight movements, even of small objects.

Because this device will respond to increases as well as decreases in the sensed light level, it cannot be confused by reflective surfaces. Some other motion-detector circuits can be fooled by a clever and agile intruder carrying a mirror.

The D1072 is not fussy about the ambient lighting level. It can be used under light levels varying over a 1000-to-1 range. The ambient light level can be any value from 0.1 to 100 candlepower. This range should be more than adequate for virtually all applications. As a rough rule of thumb, if there is enough light for you to see the movement, there should be enough light for the D1072 to detect it too. If the area to be protected appears to be well lit, the D1072 will have no problem at all.

The LSI circuitry of this chip is packaged in a clear plastic DIP (dual inline package) housing, with a molded lens mounted over the photodiode. This lens improves the photosensor effective sensitivity at low light levels. Light is gathered by this lens in such a way that a two-foot circle up to eight feet away from the sensor can be reliably monitored.

A typical motion-detector alarm circuit built around the D1072 is illustrated in Fig. 2-25. Any light reaching the internal photodiode (D1) causes the sensor to generate a small voltage. This voltage will vary in step with any fluctuations in the detected lighting level. Notice that the voltage can change in either direction—either increasing or decreasing.

Capacitor C5 (not shown—connected externally to pins 6 and 7) couples this changing voltage to internal amplifiers (A2 and

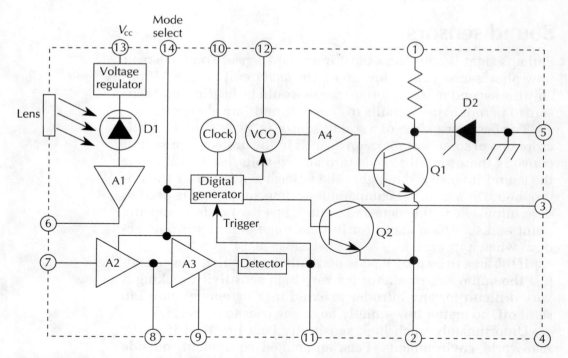

Fig. 2-25 *This is a typical motion-detector circuit built around the D1072.*

A3). Capacitors C5 and C3 (not shown—pin 9) serve as part of a simple filter network to allow the circuit to respond to low-frequency voltage changes (light fluctuations due to motion of an object within the monitored area), but constant voltages (due to unchanging detected light levels) are ignored.

High-frequency signals are significantly attenuated by capacitor C4 (not shown—pin 8), so the circuit will not be falsely triggered by the normal flicker from ac lamps. This flicker is generally invisible to the human eye, but the photodiode can see it.

Amplifiers A1 and A3 precondition the voltage signal to produce a suitable trigger signal for the detector stage. When the voltage (light level) changes more than 5% in either direction, the detector will be triggered, producing a brief burst of tone from the internal digital signal generator. The speaker (not shown) will emit a loud, whopping alarm sound for about 4 to 12 seconds whenever any motion is detected by the sensor. The nominal pitch and the rate of pitch change of this whooping alarm tone are determined by the values of capacitor C1 (pin 12) and C2 (pin 10).

Instead of the simple audible alarm shown here, the output of the D1072 motion detector could be used to drive almost any electrically controllable device or circuit.

Sound sensors

Perhaps sight is a human's most important sense. You have read how photosensors can allow an electronic circuit to "see." Probably the second most important sense would be hearing, and sensors to permit alarm circuits to "hear" sounds are also possible.

The basic principle of a sound sensor is fairly simple. A microphone of some sort picks up sounds in the protected area, and converts these sound signals into analog voltages. The stronger the sound intensity, the higher the voltage generated by the microphone. Some sort of comparator or detector circuit is used to determine when the detected sound level exceeds a specific point and set off an alarm (or initiate some other electronic action) when appropriate.

If the area to be protected is normally fairly quiet, you can adjust the audio sensor circuit for very high sensitivity, making it very difficult for any intruder to avoid making enough noise to set it off, no matter how quietly he or she tries to move.

Unfortunately, such high sensitivity isn't practical in many real-world environments. Pets, automated equipment, outside traffic, or weather sounds could result in numerous false alarms.

But that does not mean that an audio sensor would be useless in an alarm system protecting such an area. A typical application is to place an audio sensor with moderate to low sensitivity near a window that is likely to be broken by an intruder. Most normal sounds will be ignored by the sensor, but the noise of breaking glass will set off the alarm.

In most practical circumstances, audio sensors offer only fair reliability, and they are almost always subject to false triggering. For example, if a truck passing by your home backfires, it could be louder than the sound of breaking glass, so the alarm would be needlessly set off. Many experienced burglars are very good at being as quiet as humanly possible. They might use a glass cutter instead of crudely breaking a window. This is a relatively quiet operation that is not likely to set off the audio sensor alarm.

These problems strongly suggest that it would not be a very good idea to use audio sensors as the primary triggering devices for your alarm system. They can be useful to supplement other types of sensors to add a little extra protection.

A practical audio sensor circuit is illustrated in Fig. 2-26. A suitable parts list for this project appears in Table 2-3. For the most part, the exact component types and component values are not too critical, but if you make any changes, it is certainly a good idea to first breadboard the circuit to make sure it functions

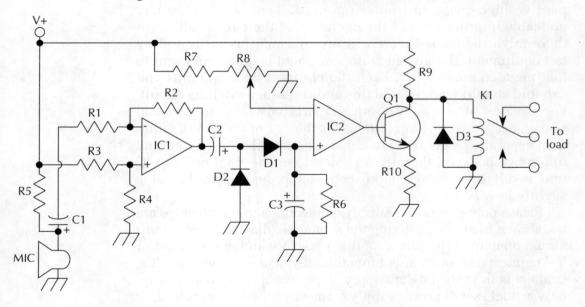

Fig. 2-26 *Project 3. Audio sensor.*

Table 2-3 Parts list for project 3. Audio sensor of Fig. 2-26.

IC1, IC2	Op amp
Q1	NPN transistor (2N3904, Radio Shack RS2009, or similar)
D1, D2	Signal diode (1N4148, 1N914, or similar)
D3	Diode (1N4001 or similar)
K1	Relay to suit load
MIC	Small microphone element
C1, C2	1 μF 25 V electrolytic capacitor
C3	47 μF 25 V electrolytic capacitor
R1	1.2 kΩ ¼ W 5% resistor
R2	680 kΩ ¼ W 5% resistor
R3, R4	47 kΩ ¼ W 5% resistor
R5	2.2 kΩ ¼ W 5% resistor
R6, R9, R10	10 kΩ ¼ W 5% resistor
R7	100 kΩ ¼ W 5% resistor
R8	100 kΩ potentiometer or trimpot

the way you expect it to. Breadboarding is always a good idea for almost any electronic project.

Virtually any standard op amp (operational amplifier) IC will work fine for IC1 and IC2 in this circuit. There is no need for expensive high-grade, low-noise op amps. They won't offer any noticable improvement in the operation of the circuit, although there might be some theoretical improvement as measured by test equipment. But any such improvement is quite irrelevant to the intended application. Even the cheapest op amp chips you can find should work well in this audio sensor switching circuit. For reasons of economy (both in parts cost and in physical space), use a dual op amp IC (such as the 747 or the 1458), rather than separate, single op amp chips. There will be no functional difference between these two choices, but the dual op amp IC will result in a neater, more compact project, probably at a slightly lower cost.

Please note that power supply connections to the op amps are not shown to avoid cluttering the schematic diagram. Every individual op amp chip must have the proper V+ and ground (and/or V−) connections, or it cannot function. If you use two separate ICs, connect both to the power supply. If you use a dual op amp chip, only a single set of power supply connections will be required.

To avoid potential confusion if different op amp devices are used, the pin numbers are not given for the op amps. Pin numbers are different for single op amp chips and dual op amp chips, of course. Check the manufacturer's spec sheet or a standard reference guide for the device you are using.

The actual sensor in this circuit is a small, inexpensive microphone. The circuit was designed for use with a condenser microphone, but other types of microphones should also work, although some might require additional preamplification.

IC1 and its associated components serve as a preamplifier stage, to boost the signal level. You might want to experiment with alternate values for resistors R1 and R2, which set the gain of the amplifier. Use the standard op amp inverting amplifier gain formula:

$$G = \frac{-R_2}{R_1}$$

The negative sign simply indicates the polarity inversion that results from using the inverting input. If the input signal is positive, the output will be negative, and vice versa.

Using the component values suggested in the parts list, the nominal gain of this amplifier stage is set at:

$$G = \frac{-680,000}{1200}$$

$$= -566.67$$

A constant voltage, derived from the circuit supply voltage through a simple voltage-divider string made up of resistors R3 and R4 provides bias for the op amp, so the output voltage is centered around ½ V+, instead of zero (ground potential), as would normally be the case. This permits the op amps in this circuit to use a single-polarity supply voltage. Many standard op amp devices normally call for a dual-polarity power supply, which is more expensive and complex. The simple addition of resistors R3 and R4 make things a lot easier and result in a less expensive and bulky project.

The output signal from IC1 is also rectified by diodes D1 and D2. Capacitors C2 and C3 and resistor R6 help filter out noise from the signal and convert the audio-frequency ac signal into more of a fluctuating dc voltage.

The second op amp stage (IC2) is a simple voltage comparator. The output signal from IC1 is compared to a steady dc voltage from the circuit supply voltage through a simple variable voltage-divider string made up of resistor R7 and potentiometer

R8. The potentiometer acts a sensitivity control for the sound sensor. The setting of this control determines how loud the detected sound must be to trigger the comparator.

Transistor Q1 is a simple amplifier stage to boost the output current of IC2. When the output of IC1 (corresponding to the detected sound level) exceeds the voltage set up by R7 and R8, the comparator (IC2) output goes HIGH, which activates the coil. Diode D3 simply protects the relay coil from possible back EMF spikes.

This sound sensor circuit can act as either a normally open switch or a normally closed switch, depending on which of the relay's switch contacts you use. If it suits your application, you can use the circuit as a sound-activated SPDT, DPST, or DPDT switch, providing the relay has the appropriate switch contacts.

For best results, the supply voltage for this project should be in the +9 to +15 V range. It can be operated for a reasonable period from a heavy-duty or alkaline 9 V transistor battery.

Temperature detectors

Electronic temperature detectors are also available. Obviously, these components convert changes in temperature to proportional electrical changes.

Temperature detectors are much more likely to be used in fire alarms than in burglar alarm systems. It is theoretically possible to design a super-sensitive burglar alarm circuit that responds to the body temperature of an intruder, but this project would be far from a practical project. With currently available components, such an ambitious project would be well beyond the capabilities of virtually all electronics hobbyists.

But a good security system should watch out for more than just intruders. There are other types of risks to your security, and fire is the most obvious and generally one of the most devastating of these.

Complete smoke detectors are widely available today, of course, and are usually quite inexpensive. In many areas, the installation of such smoke detectors are mandatory in public buildings or apartments.

So why would you want to bother with additional fire alarms in your security system? Because smoke detectors, like everything else in this world, are not perfect. There is no question that smoke detectors are generally effective and have helped save countless lives, but they have their limitations. As the name clearly suggests, a smoke detector detects only smoke. Most common household fires smolder and smoke for some time before they burst out into major flames. Detecting smoke from such a fire gives ample warning for all in the building to escape or possibly put out the fire before it does too much damage. But some fires are not very smoky, at least until they have gotten very large. A smoke detector might ignore such a smokeless fire until it is too late.

A temperature detector detects the heat from a smokeless fire long before a smoke detector could sense the same fire. On the other hand, a slow, smouldering fire won't put out much heat until it breaks into flames, so a temperature detector fire alarm cannot give a timely warning of the danger. But such a slow, smouldering fire will almost always emit enough smoke to set off a smoke detector.

For maximum security against the threat of fire, use smoke detectors and temperature detectors together.

There is another important limitation to standard smoke detectors. They are somewhat sensitive to false alarms, especially when mounted near kitchens, as they often are, because the kitchen is one of the most likely places for a fire to start. Many smoke detectors go off everytime the oven is used. The only way to turn it off, or prevent it from going off is to remove the battery. A great many people remove the batteries from their smoke detectors and forget to put them back. Of course, this totally defeats the purpose of the smoke detector. It can't warn you of a fire if it has no power source. If your security system includes one or more temperature detectors in addition to the smoke detector, you'll still be at least partially protected, even if you get careless and neglect to put the battery back in the smoke detector.

Incidentally, ac-powered smoke detectors are not a good idea. One of the most common types of household fires are electrical fires. Such fires start deep within the walls. The fire could easily burn through a wire carrying power to the smoke detector before enough smoke reaches it to set it off. This will neutralize the smoke detector altogether.

Early smoke detectors were of two basic types—a battery-operated smoke detector and an ac-powered smoke detector. The difference was not just in the power supply. These two types of smoke detectors used entirely different principles of operation. It was found, unfortunately after a number of disasters, that the ac-powered type of smoke detector could, under some conditions, actually start a fire itself. Clearly, such a device did not provide very good security. This type of smoke detector has long since been removed entirely from the market, so there is no need to worry about it.

All commercially available smoke detectors are now probably of the dc powered type. If there are a few that use ac power, they almost certainly have an ac-to-dc converter circuit of some sort, and are the same basic type as the more common battery-powered types. But even this design is not a good idea, because of the possibility of an electrical fire disabling the smoke detector before it gets a chance to emit a warning.

Temperature-detector fire alarms can be a useful supplement (not a replacement) for smoke detectors to offer fuller security. Each type of fire alarm is most effective at detecting certain types of fires, so using the two together will reduce the chances of the system being fooled by an unusual type of fire.

Temperature sensors are also widely used in automation and remote-control applications. They can be used to monitor and control furnaces, air conditioners, ovens, and other such equipment. They can also be used to warn of overheating conditions in delicate electronic circuitry.

The simplest type of temperature sensor is the thermocouple. You can make a thermocouple yourself. This device is nothing more than a junction of two dissimilar metals. If such a junction is heated, a voltage proportional to the temperature of the junction will be developed across the two conductors. This is called the *Seebeck effect*, and it is created by the different work functions of the two metals. Of course wires are connected to the two dissimilar conductors of the thermocouple to carry the generated voltage to appropriate detection circuitry.

A similar approach is used in standard mechanical thermostats. Two dissimilar metals are placed back to back. The difference in the rates of expansion and contraction due to changes in temperature cause the two-metal sandwich to bend back and forth, opening and closing switch contacts.

Simple thermocouples and mechanical thermostats would probably be of only limited value in a practical fire alarm. Today, semiconductor temperature sensor components of several types are readily available.

In a sense, a semiconductor component is a sort of crude temperature sensor, because semiconductor materials are quite sensitive to heat. By applying a small forward bias to an ordinary silicon diode, the approximate temperature can be determined by measuring the voltage drop across the diode. This is a rather critical measurement, because the voltages here are very small. Typically, the voltage drop across a silicon diode will change about 1.25 mV (millivolt) or 0.00125 V per degree Fahrenheit, or about 2.24 mV (0.00224 V) per degree Celsius.

Bipolar transistors can make even better temperature sensors than diodes, especially if they are diode connected, as illustrated in Fig. 2-27. The base/emitter voltage is dependent on the collector current and the temperature. By holding the collector current constant (with a constant current source circuit), you can measure the temperature by monitoring the voltage across the base and the emitter of the transistor.

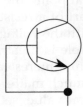

Fig. 2-27 *A diode-connected bipolar transistor can function as a crude but effective temperature sensor.*

A specialized, junctionless semiconductor device for sensing temperature is the *thermistor*. This name is derived from THERMal resISTOR. This suggests that the resistance varies with changes in temperature, which is precisely the case.

There are two basic types of thermistors. A positive-coefficient thermistor resistance increases as the monitored temperature rises. Conversely, a negative-coefficient thermistor lowers its resistance in response to a rise in temperature.

The standard schematic symbol for a thermistor is shown in Fig. 2-28. Notice that this is similar to the symbol used to represent a standard resistor. The letter *T* indicates that this component is temperature sensitive. The parts list will describe the thermistor required in the circuit and indicate whether it is the positive coefficient or the negative coefficient type.

Fig. 2-28 *A thermistor is designed to change its resistance in proportion to the sensed temperature.*

One problem with thermistors in many applications is that the response of this component is not linear, making direct measurement techniques rather inefficient. A thermistor works very well over a relatively limited range—far better than any other type of temperature sensor. For a wide-range thermometer circuit, you need to add some external circuitry to linearize the response of the device.

Fortunately, these linearity problems aren't of much importance for your purposes here. A temperature-detector fire alarm is basically a simple yes/no comparator device. If the temperature is above a critical point, the alarm is triggered. If the temperature is below this critical point, the alarm circuit ignores it. You can use a thermistor as part of a resistive voltage string, comparing the derived voltage with the voltage from a fixed-resistive divider string. The basic principle is illustrated in Fig. 2-29. Notice that because you are really only interested in one specific temperature (or voltage), it doesn't much matter if the sensor is linear or not on either side of the critical value, set by the resistances in the fixed, reference-voltage divider string.

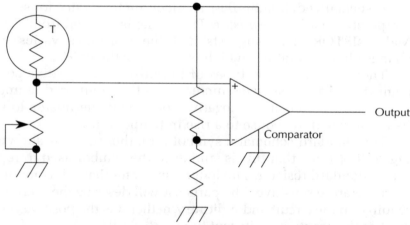

Fig. 2-29 *Thermistors are often used in resistive voltage dividers in comparator circuits.*

Gas sensors

A number of specialized sensor devices are also available, and many are appropriate for use in certain security systems. For example, several gas sensors have appeared on the market. Obviously, such a device could be used in an alarm circuit that warns of a dangerous gas leak.

Gas sensors are almost always rather expensive and difficult to find for a hobbyist. One fairly typical device of this type is discussed below. There is no way to guarantee that this particular product is available to you. If you have an interest in gas sensors or other highly specialized sensors, your best bet is to check the catalogs of the mail order surplus houses that advertise in the back of the hobbyist electronics magazines. You can often find great bargains on discontinued items, and sometimes you will find specialized parts and devices that were never sold directly on the hobbyist retail market.

The Taguchi Gas Sensor, or TGS, is a fairly typical gas sensor that was first made available in the 1980s. This unit can be used to detect the presence and degree of concentration of a wide variety of deoxidizing (potentially poisonous or flammable) gases, including alcohol vapors, carbon monoxide, gasoline vapors, hydrogen, methane, and propane.

The TGS is extremely sensitive to gas concentrations over an impressively wide range. Depending on the external circuitry used with this sensor, it can be used to measure minute concentrations of just a few ppm (parts per million), or the high concentrations that might be found in certain specialized environments, such as within an automobile exhaust pipe.

It is not difficult to design a circuit to use this sensor. The TGS is a resistance-type sensor, acting as a variable resistor whose value is set by the level of concentration of the detected gas. This characteristic means the sensor can easily be used as part of a voltage-divider string in a voltage-comparator alarm circuit. When the presence of too much dangerous gas is detected, an alarm can be set off or an automated exhaust fan turned on to increase ventilation within the protected area.

Hall-effect magnetic sensors

Another specialized type of sensor is the Hall-effect magnetic sensor. This type of device is less directly applicable to most standard security systems, but it can be useful in some specialized applications. For example, many stores today mark their merchandise with a magnetic strip that sets off an alarm when a shoplifter tries to sneak it out the door. (The magnetic strip is deactivated for legitimate paying customers.)

If a current flows through a conductor or a semiconductor under the influence of a magnetic field at right angles to the direction of current flow, a voltage drop is produced. In essence, the effective resistance of the conductor or semiconductor is increased in proportion to the strength of the magnetic field. This is the *Hall Effect*. The verbal description of the Hall effect is a bit of a mouthful, so refer to the rough diagram of Fig. 2-30.

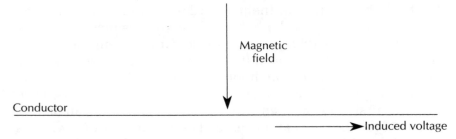

Fig. 2-30 *This is a rough illustration of the Hall effect.*

Hall-effect magnetic sensors can prove useful in a number of automation and remote control applications where a magnetic field of almost any type exists. Any inductor (coil or transformer) produces a magnetic field. This also is true of motors, which of course, use coils.

Like the gas sensors discussed earlier, Hall-effect magnetic sensors are highly specialized devices, used primarily in industrial applications, so they are almost always rather expensive and difficult to find for the hobbyist. The mail order electronics surplus houses are usually your best bet for finding such unusual components.

One fairly typical device of this type is discussed later. There is no way to guarantee that this particular product is available to you.

Sprague Electrical Company has manufactured several Hall-effect magnetic sensors in IC form. Take a quick look at the UGN-3020T Hall-effect switch IC, which is shown in Fig. 2-31. Because this chip has just three leads, it clearly is a fairly easy component to use.

A simplified block diagram of the UGN-3020T is shown in Fig. 2-32. The amplifier boosts the voltage from the actual Hall-effect sensor. When the amplifier output signal exceeds a specific threshold level, the Schmitt trigger stage turns on the output transistor.

Output oscillations are prevented by the built-in hysteresis of the Schmitt trigger stage. If the strength of the monitored magnetic field is very close to the critical threshold level, small random noise components could make the level wobble back and

Fig. 2-31 *The UGN-3020T is a Hall-effect switch in IC form.*

```
 1    2    3
+Vcc GND OUT
```

forth on either side of the triggering point of the Schmitt trigger. Without hysteresis, this wobbling could cause the output to be erratically switched on and off. The hysteresis built into the Schmitt trigger circuit requires the amplifier output voltage to drop fairly significantly below the turn-on level before the Schmitt trigger will snap back off. This greatly improves the stability of the device.

Pressure sensors

The last type of sensor device in this chapter is the pressure sensor. Physical (mechanical) pressure along the Y axis of a crystal generates a voltage across its X axis. This is known as the *piezoelectric effect*. It can be used to electronically sense touch or footsteps and other types of pressure.

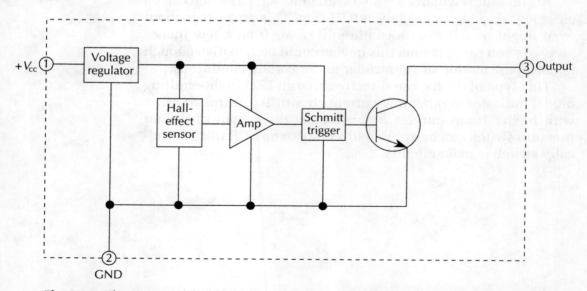

Fig. 2-32 *This is a simplified block diagram of the internal circuitry of the UGN-3020T.*

A variation on this basic principle is used in hybrid piezoresistive IC pressure transducers. Such devices are rapidly replacing older mechanical-type (crystal) pressure sensors in many applications. Again such devices are very specialized and are used mainly in industrial applications, so they might be a little difficult for you to find in small quantities. Check the catalogs of mail order electronics surplus houses.

These hybrid IC pressure sensors are generally smaller and more reliable than their mechanical crystal counterparts. Moreover, they are virtually insensitive to mechanical vibration and offer frequency responses that allow operation right up through the audio frequencies.

Piezoresistive IC pressure transducers are available for a wide variety of pressure ranges. Units have been designed for measuring pressures from 0 to 5000 psig (pounds per square inch—gauge).

Mechanical pressure sensors are not always built around quartz crystals and the piezoelectric effect. A spiral coil of hollow glass, metal, or quartz can be used as a pressure sensor if one end is sealed. The coil winds slightly tighter or unwinds slightly as the pressure of a liquid or a gas within the hollow tube is varied. This physical motion is electronically monitored in a variety of ways. Some hobbyists and experimenters might be able to design and build such pressure sensors themselves.

Air pressure switches are also available. Such a switch can be closed by air pressures as low as 0.02 psig. This pressure is about what might be felt from a gentle puff of air from a few inches away. As you can imagine, this device could be sensitive enough to detect the motion of an intruder under certain conditions.

This type of device can directly drive an LED (light-emitting diode) indicator or other low-current circuit. To control circuitry with higher input current requirements, the output of the air pressure switch can be applied to a relay or an SCR to electronically switch heavier circuits.

❖ 3
Sounding and warning devices

OBVIOUSLY NO ELECTRONIC SYSTEM OF ANY KIND IS OF MUCH use unless it has some sort of output. This is especially true of alarm systems. This chapter considers buzzers, bells, sirens, and other suitable output devices for security alarm systems. Several distinctive alarm sounding projects are presented in this chapter.

In some ways, this chapter is a logical extension of the last one. In both chapters, you consider a class of electronic components known as transducers. A transducer converts one type of energy into some other type of energy. In electronic sensors, it can generally be assumed that one of the types of energy involved will be electrical energy. The sensors discussed in the preceding chapter are input transducers. They convert some other type of energy (mechanical energy, light, or whatever) into electrical energy.

Reasonably enough, output transducers perform just the opposite action. These devices convert electrical energy into some other type of energy. In alarm systems, the vast majority of output transducers convert electrical energy into acoustic energy (sound), but sometimes, the output transducer will convert the electrical signal into photo energy (light).

The output sounding device of an alarm system is intended to serve one or both of the following functions:

- Alert a guard, systems operator, or resident to a potentially hazardous condition, permitting them to take corrective action.
- Frighten off an intruder by letting him or her know, in no uncertain terms, that the intruder has been detected, and help will soon arrive.

An audible alarm of some sort will usually serve these functions best.

Visual indicators

In some cases, an alarm circuit might only give a visual indication, usually at some remote location. This is appropriate when someone, for some reason, wants to catch an intruder in the act and doesn't want to frighten the intruder off with an audible alarm. But this arrangement requires a security guard to continuously watch for the warning light to glow. Such an alarm system would be of limited application for most people.

This is not at all to say that a visual indication device would not be a useful and practical addition to many alarm systems. A common control panel could have several lights to indicate which of several sensors has activated the alarm. This is particularly useful when an alarm system is used to protect a fairly large area or an entire building.

A visual alarm indication device will rarely be very complex. All you need in most cases is an LED, or a small incandescent bulb (like those used in flashlights). The output of the alarm circuit presumedly puts out a voltage of some sort when it is triggered. Simply choose a light-emitting device that works well with the voltage being put out by your circuit. When the LED or lamp receives the appropriate voltage, it will light up. Otherwise (when the alarm has not been triggered) it will remain dark. It is as simple as that.

It is a very, very good idea to check out all lighting devices periodically, especially incandescent bulbs, which can easily burn out without warning. A manual, normally open push-button switch that permits you to temporarily apply the necessary voltage (probably derived directly from the circuit power supply) to the lighting device(s) will probably be all you need.

In most circuits, it is necessary to use a current-limiting resistor in series with an LED. This resistor prevents the LED from attempting to draw more current than it can safely handle and self destructing. The lower the resistance, the brighter the LED will glow when the voltage is applied. If the series resistance is less than about 100 Ω, it probably won't provide sufficient current limiting, so resistors smaller than this should not be used in this application.

At the other extreme, if the series resistance is more than 1 kΩ (1000 Ω) or so, it will probably limit the current too much.

The LED might not light at all. At best, it will glow very dimly and will be barely visible except in a completely darkened area.

Generally speaking, the best values to use for an LED current-limiting resistor are 330 or 390 Ω. These are all standard resistor values, and you should have no trouble finding at least one of these values. If you are building a project that calls for a current-limiting resistor (in series with an LED) of 33 Ω, and you don't have a 330 Ω resistor, but do happen to have a 470 Ω resistor, go ahead and use it. Such a substitution will make little (if any) noticeable difference in the operation of the circuit. (Of course, this is not necessarily true for any other resistors used in the project.)

A variation on the basic alarm system might use a more powerful light as a primary (or more likely, secondary) output device. When the alarm system is triggered, it could turn on additional lights in the appropriate area. A high-intensity flood lamp might be suitable in some cases. Besides helping frighten off an intruder, this could also help you locate the intruder (or other problem condition). After all, it's easier to hide in the dark.

Most practical alarm systems do rely primarily on sounding devices as their output indicators. In most cases, it is more than reasonable to assume that when an alarm system is triggered, it will sound an audible alarm of some kind.

Piezoelectric buzzers

Perhaps the simplest, and often the least expensive alarm sounding device, is the piezoelectric buzzer, or simply the *buzzer*. The name is pretty much self descriptive. When a voltage is applied to a buzzer, it makes a buzzing noise. The sound is usually quite loud, considering the relatively small size of the device. But it is not nearly as loud as most other alarm-sounding devices.

Like some of the pressure sensors discussed in the last chapter, the buzzer relies on the piezoelectric effect. A pressure sensor works because a mechanical stress (pressure) along the Y axis of a crystal produces an electrical signal across its X axis. Similarly, an electrical signal applied across the X axis generates a mechanical stress along the Y axis. In a buzzer, this mechanical stress causes mechanical vibrations which create the distinctive buzzing noise.

Because a buzzer is so simple and direct in its use, most of the alarm circuits discussed throughout this book show a buzzer as the output device. This is just for convenience. A buzzer is an excellent choice for testing alarm projects. But in most practical applications, you will probably want to replace the buzzer shown in the schematic with a louder and more effective alarm-sounding device.

A buzzer is a good alarm indicator if the alarm system just needs to catch someone's attention (within a single room or other fairly limited area) so he or she can take some corrective action. But it will be relatively hard to hear at any distance. A sound sleeper might not be awakened by it. The neighbors are unlikely to summon help if your alarm system goes off and you are not home. And it is hardly likely to scare off an intruder—especially if the buzzer is located where the intruder can't hear it.

But, a buzzer is ideal for testing an alarm system. It won't hurt your ears or give you an instant headache, and it is unlikely to disturb your neighbors.

Bells and sirens

A bell or siren can produce quite a bit of sound when activated by an appropriate voltage. Often, the effect can be quite ear piercing, and can carry a considerable distance.

Such a loud alarm will frighten off all but the most nervy intruders. Anyone in the general area is bound to hear it and can take corrective action or summon help. If you are not home, your neighbors are likely to summon help, either out of neighborliness or out of annoyance at the sound. EIther way, the authorities will probably be notified.

Many commercial alarm bells or sirens are available today. Electromechanical bells were once the norm, but today they seem to be significantly outnumbered by electronic sirens. The latest Radio Shack catalog offers alarm sirens ranging in price from $11 up to $42.

The larger the alarm bell or siren, the louder it will be, and the greater the power required to drive it. Larger (and louder) devices also tend to be more expensive, of course. The appropriate compromise depends on the specific requirements of your individual application and just how much security you need (or want).

In the remainder of this chapter, you will read about some practical electronic siren and other suitable sounding circuits that you can build yourself for your security system. All these circuits are surprisingly loud, considering their relatively low power requirements. They should be plenty loud enough for most practical home-alarm applications. In fact, you might want to add a resistor or potentiometer to limit the volume somewhat.

But if you find the circuitry as shown here doesn't put out sufficient sound levels to suit your intended application, it should be no problem at all to add a simple audio amplifier stage between the sounding circuit and the loudspeaker. Naturally, the loudspeaker used might be hefty enough to safely handle the sound levels involved.

Siren circuit

A powerful siren circuit is illustrated in Fig. 3-1. A suitable parts list for this project is given in Table 3-1. This project is built around the 389, an audio amplifier IC, which includes an NPN transistor array, and it is designed to operate off a fairly low voltage. The three transistors used in this circuit are part of the IC itself.

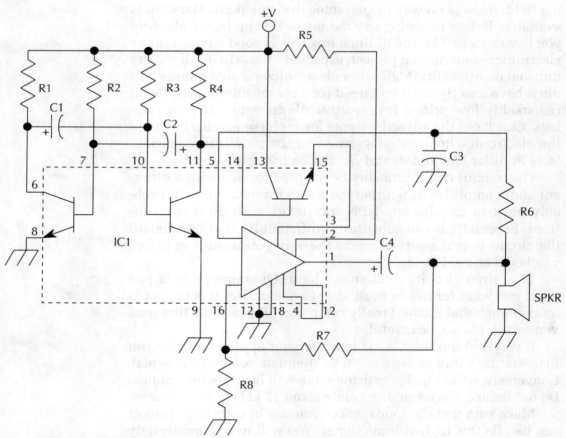

Fig. 3-1 *Project 4. Siren circuit.*

Table 3-1 Parts list for project 4.
Siren circuit of Fig. 3-1.

IC1	389 low-voltage audio power amplifier with NPN transistor array (see text)
C1, C2	10 μF 25 V electrolytic capacitor
C3	0.1 μF capacitor
C4	47 μF 25 V electrolytic capacitor
R1, R4, R7	10 kΩ ¼ W 5% resistor
R2, R3	68 kΩ ¼ W 5% resistor (see text)
R5	33 kΩ ½ W 10% resistor
R6	39 kΩ ¼ W 5% resistor
R8	1 kΩ ¼ W 5% resistor
SPKR	Loudspeaker (see text)

Because electronics is such a rapidly and constantly changing field, there is no way to guarantee that this particular chip is available. Before investing any money in this project, make sure you have a source for the IC lined up. This is good advice for any electronics construction project, especially those that call for any unusual components. Mail order electronics surplus houses will often have exactly what you need (or a reasonable substitute) at remarkably low prices. It is worthwhile to send away for catalogs. Check out the advertisements for such companies in any of the electronics hobbyist magazines on the newsstand, particularly *Popular Electronics* and *Radio-Electronics.*

This circuit could probably be adapted for use with a different audio amplifier IC without too much trouble. You will probably need to use discrete NPN transistors with most substitutions. Especially if you substitute a different IC, first breadboard the circuit to make sure it works the way you want it to before you begin any soldering.

This siren circuit is extremely loud. Of course, this is just what you want for use in most alarm systems, but this project is loud enough that it could really catch you off guard the first time you test it. Please, be careful.

If you find the siren is too loud for your application, you can increase the value of resistor R6 to attenuate some of the signal. Conversely, reducing this resistor value will increase the volume. Do not reduce this resistance below about 12 kΩ (12,000 Ω) or so.

Make sure that the loudspeaker you use in your siren project can handle this high-volume signal. You will need a moderately hefty speaker. A small transistor radio-type speaker will probably be destroyed almost instantly. A power-horn type speaker would probably be a good choice for this type of application.

It probably isn't too important in an alarm system, but if for some reason you aren't satisfied with the pitch of the siren, you can experiment with different values for resistors R2 and R3, and possibly capacitors C1 and C2.

Low-voltage two-tone siren

A continuous-tone siren like the circuit shown in Fig. 3-1 is effective, especially if it is very loud (as the last project certainly is). But generally, a changing tone siren will catch the ear better for a given signal volume. A multitone siren will be harder to ignore in most cases.

A remarkably simple two-tone siren circuit is shown in Fig. 3-2. A suitable parts list for this project is given in Table 3-2.

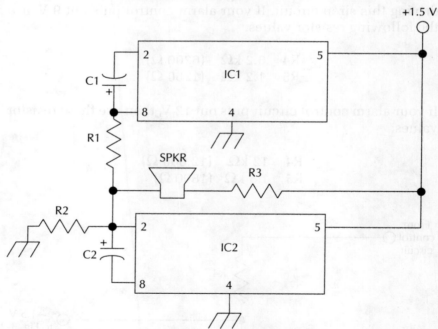

Fig. 3-2 *Project 5. Low-voltage two-tone siren.*

In addition to its very low parts count, one of the big advantages of this project is its very, very low power consumption. It is designed to operate on just 1.5 V, and the current drain is almost negligible.

**Table 3-2 Parts list for project 5.
Low-voltage two-tone siren of Fig. 3-2.**

IC1, IC2	LM3909 LED flasher/oscillator
C1	100 µF 10 V electrolytic capacitor
C2	1 µF 10 V electrolytic capacitor
R1	3.3 k Ω ¼ W 5% resistor
R2	1.8 kΩ ¼ W 5% resistor
R3	68 Ω ¼ W 5% resistor
R4, R5	Optional ¼ W 5% resistors—see text for values and Fig. 3-3 for location

Most alarm control circuits will probably put out a much higher voltage than 1.5 V. Common values 9 and 12 V. This is no real problem. Just add a couple of resistors in series as a simple voltage divider network, as illustrated in Fig. 3-3. This will drop the alarm circuit output voltage to the 1.5 V level suitable for driving this siren circuit. If your alarm-control puts out 9 V, use the following resistor values:

$$R4 \quad 6.2 \text{ k}\Omega \quad (6200 \text{ }\Omega)$$
$$R5 \quad 1.2 \text{ k}\Omega \quad (1200 \text{ }\Omega)$$

If your alarm control circuit puts out 12 V, then use these resistor values:

$$R4 \quad 12 \text{ k}\Omega \quad (12,000 \text{ }\Omega)$$
$$R5 \quad 1.8 \text{ k}\Omega \quad (1800 \text{ }\Omega)$$

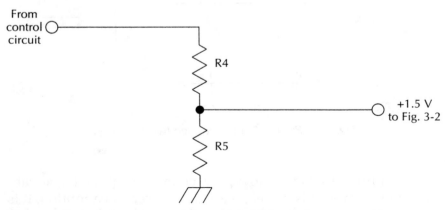

Fig. 3-3 *If your alarm circuit puts out too high a voltage, a simple resistive voltage divider string can drop it down to a usable level.*

Of course, other resistor values with similar ratios will work just as well. If your alarm control circuit puts out some other voltage, you can calculate suitable resistor values using Ohm's law. The supply voltage for this siren circuit is not at all critical. It does not have to be exactly 1.5 V. Anything from about 1.25 V to 2.5 V is quite acceptable as far as the circuitry is concerned.

The two ICs used in this project are LM3909 LED flasher/oscillators. This simple chip is designed mainly for use in LED flasher circuits, but it can also be operated at audio frequencies, as you are doing in this project. IC1 is a low-frequency oscillator that frequency modulates the audio frequency oscillator built around IC2. Because a LM3909 oscillator puts out a square wave signal, the pitch will oscillate back and forth between two discrete tones, at a rate determined by the frequency of the IC1 oscillator. To change this frequency, experiment with alternate values for capacitor C1. The smaller this capacitor, the higher the frequency.

The main audio frequency is controlled by the values of the capacitor C2 and resistor R2. Resistor R1 controls the depth of the two-tone effect, or how far apart the two tone pitches will be.

Resistor R3 limits the volume of the siren. For a louder siren, decrease the value of this resistor. This volume-limiting resistor can even be omitted from the circuit altogether, with the positive end of the speaker connected directly to the circuit supply voltage line. Of course, if you feel the volume is too high for your particular application, you can increase the value of resistor R3.

This two-tone siren is not nearly as loud as the siren project of Fig. 3-1, but it should be loud enough for many practical alarm applications, especially in home installations. It would be more than adequate for use in an apartment, for example, where a super-loud alarm would be real overkill, and a few too many false alarms could get you evicted.

British-type siren

A two-tone alarm sound is much more ear catching and hard to ignore than a continuous tone. It also tends to carry farther.

The circuit shown in Fig. 3-4 produces a "hee-haw" effect similar to the sirens used for British emergency vehicles. It is a very noticeable and effective alarm sound. A suitable parts list for this project is given in Table 3-3, although you are encouraged to breadboard the circuit and experiment with alternative component values, particularly resistors R1 through R4 and capacitors C1 and C4.

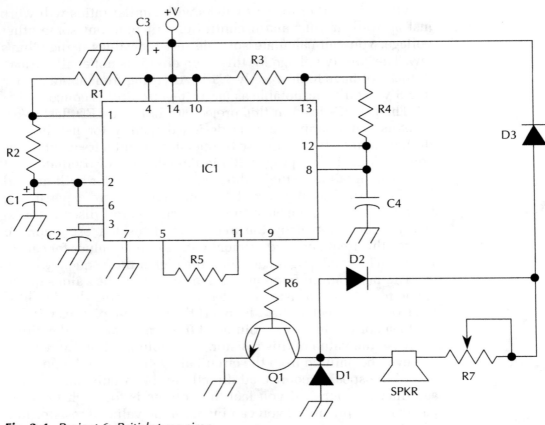

Fig. 3-4 *Project 6. British-type siren.*

**Table 3-3   Parts list for project 6.
British-type siren of Fig. 3-4.**

IC1	556 dual timer (see text)
Q1	NPN power transistor (Radio Shack RS2041, GE19, SK3027, ECG130, or similar)
D1, D2, D3	Diode (1N4001 or similar)
C1	10 µF 25 V electrolytic capacitor
C2	0.022 µF capacitor
C3	330 µF 25 V electrolytic capacitor
C4	0.01 µF capacitor
R1, R3, R5	10 kΩ ¼ W 5% resistor
R2	100 kΩ ¼ W 5% resistor (see text)
R4	33 kΩ ¼ W 5% resistor
R6	120 Ω ¼ W 5% resistor
R7	500 Ω potentiometer (optional)
SPKR	8 Ω loudspeaker

The heart of this circuit is a 556 dual timer IC (IC1), which is the exact equivalent of two 555 chips in a single, convenient housing. If you want to use separate 555 timers or 7555 CMOS (complementary metal-oxide semiconductor) timers, feel free to do so. It's just a matter of correcting the pin numbers. For your convenience, the pin-out diagram for the 556 dual timer IC is shown in Fig. 3-5, and the pin-out diagram for the 555 single timer IC is shown in Fig. 3-6. The 7555 CMOS timer IC has the exact same pin-out as the 555. The only real functional difference between the 555 and 7555 is that the 7555 is slightly more precise, and more significantly, uses noticeably less current than the 555.

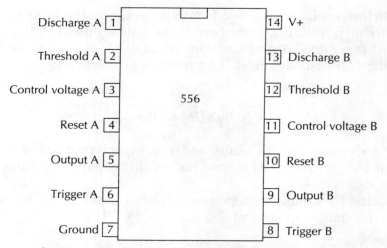

Fig. 3-5 *The 556 is the equivalent of two 555 timer ICs in a single housing.*

Both timers in this circuit are wired in the astable multivibrator mode. In other words, you have two free-running rectangular wave oscillators at work here. Oscillator 1 frequency modulates oscillator 2, producing the two-tone, hee-haw effect. Oscillator 2 puts out one frequency when the output of oscillator 1 is LOW and a second, higher frequency when oscillator 1 output is HIGH.

The output of oscillator 1 (pin 5) is connected to the control voltage input of oscillator 2 (pin 11) through resistor R5. The value of this resistor determines the depth of the hee-haw effect or the pitch difference between the two alternating tones.

Oscillator 1 has a much lower frequency than oscillator 2 to produce an audible hee-haw effect. In fact the frequency of this

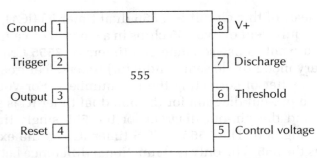

Fig. 3-6 *The 555 timer IC is a popular device used in many electronic projects.*

oscillator is subaudible—too low to be heard by the human ear. The frequency of this control oscillator is determined by the values of capacitor C1 and resistors R1 and R2, according to the standard 555 astable multivibrator frequency formula:

$$F = \frac{1}{(0.693 \ (R_1 + 2R_2) \ C_1)}$$

The resistances are in ohms and the capacitance value is in farads (not microfarads) to give the resulting frequency value in hertz.

Using the component values suggested in the parts list, you get a hee-haw frequency of about:

$$F = \frac{1}{(0.693 \times (10{,}000 + 2 \times 100{,}000) \times 0.00001)}$$

$$= \frac{1}{(0.693 \times (10{,}000 + 200{,}000) \times 0.00001)}$$

$$= \frac{1}{(0.693 \times 210{,}000 \times 0.00001)}$$

$$= \frac{1}{1.453}$$

$$= 0.69 \ \text{Hz (hertz)}$$

There is almost one and a half output pulses from this oscillator per second. To slow down this frequency, increase any of the relevant component values (capacitor C1 or resistor R1 or R2). Similarly, decreasing the value of any or all of these components will increase the hee-haw frequency.

The base frequency of the main audio oscillator (oscillator 2) is set by the formula:

$$F = \frac{1}{(0.693\ (R_3 + 2R_4)\ C_4)}$$

Again, the resistances are in ohms and the capacitance value is in farads (not microfarads) to give the resulting frequency value in hertz.

Using the component values suggested in the parts list, you get a nominal (no modulation) audio frequency of about:

$$F = \frac{1}{(0.693 \times (10{,}000 + 2 \times 47{,}000) \times 0.0000001)}$$

$$= \frac{1}{(0.693 \times (10{,}000 + 94{,}000) \times 0.0000001)}$$

$$= \frac{1}{(0.693 \times 104{,}000 \times 0.0000001)}$$

$$= \frac{1}{0.00072}$$

$$= 1388\ \text{Hz}$$

Sounds at or near 1000 Hz are usually the most audible for most persons, so this frequency is a good choice.

As in the other oscillator, you can select an alternate base audio frequency, if you prefer. To get a lower-pitched sound, simply increase any or all of the relevant component values (capacitor C4 or resistor R3 or R4). Similarly, decreasing the value of any or all of these components will increase the audible pitch of the siren.

The output of oscillator 2 is then fed through resistor R6 to the base of transistor Q1, which acts as an amplifier. Almost any NPN power transistor should work fine. You should be aware that the sound of this siren is very, very loud. Test it with caution.

Potentiometer R7 is an optional volume control. This component can be deleted from the circuit or replaced with a suitably

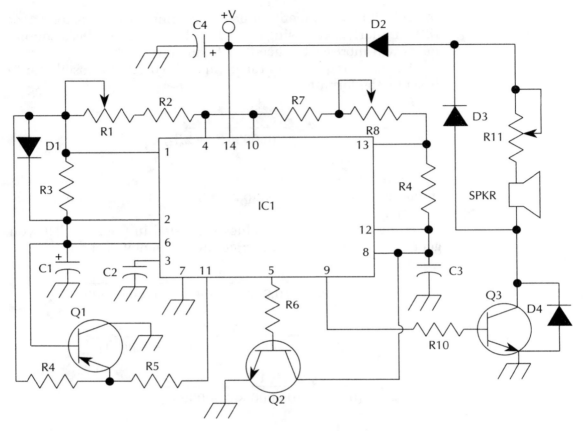

Fig. 3-7 *Project 7. Red-alert siren.*

valued fixed resistor if it is not needed. For many alarm applications, you will want the siren to be as loud as possible, so no volume-reducing resistor at all would be used.

To sound the alarm, just have the alarm control circuit apply
the supply voltage to this siren circuit at the appropriate time. If
power is continuously applied to this circuit, the siren will continuously sound.

Red-alert siren

If you prefer an alarm siren that sounds more high tech and ultra-
modern, you might like the circuit shown in Fig. 3-7. This one produces a "whoop-whoop" sound like the red-alert sirens aboard
spaceships in science-fiction movies and TV shows, such as *Star
Trek*. A suitable parts list for this project is given in Table 3-4.

**Table 3-4 Parts list for project 7.
Red-alert siren of Fig. 3-7.**

IC1	556 dual timer
Q1	PNP transistor (Radio Shack RS1604, GE21, SK3025, ECG159, or similar)
Q2	NPN transistor (Radio Shack RS2009, GE20, SK3122, ECG128, or similar)
Q3	NPN power transistor (Radio Shack RS2041, GE19, SK3027, ECG130, or similar)
D1–D4	Diode (1N4001 or similar)
C1	47 μF 25 V electrolytic capacitor
C2, C3	0.01 μF capacitor
C4	470 μF 25 V electrolytic capacitor
R1, R8	10 kΩ potentiometer
R2, R7	4.7 kΩ ¼ W 5% resistor
R3	27 kΩ ¼ W 5% resistor
R4	4.7 kΩ ¼ W 5% resistor
R5	3.3 kΩ ¼ W 5% resistor
R6	12 kΩ ¼ W 5% resistor
R9	100 kΩ ¼ W 5% resistor
R10	120 Ω ¼ W 5% resistor
R11	500 Ω potentiometer (optional)
SPKR	8 Ω loudspeaker

As in the preceding project, the heart of this circuit is a 556 dual timer IC (IC1), which is the exact equivalent of two 555 chips in a single, convenient housing. If you want to use separate 555 timers (or 7555 CMOS timers), feel free to do so. It's just a matter of correcting the pin numbers. Refer back to the previous project for more information on this substitution.

This circuit works very much like that last one. Once again, the two timers are wired as astable multivibrators, except in this case transistors Q1 and Q2 change the waveform from a rectangle pulse output of each oscillator to a more or less linear ramp.

Optional potentiometer R1 controls the "whoop" rate, and optional potentiometer R8 controls the base frequency of the generated tone. Both of these potentiometers are optional. Potentiometer R1 and resistor can be replaced by a single fixed resistor if you don't want a manual control here. The same is true for potentiometer R8 and resistor R7.

You can also control the whoop rate by changing the value of capacitor C1. Similarly, changing the value of capacitor C3 alters the audio frequency of the siren. Increasing either capacitance will lower the appropriate frequency.

The output of the second oscillator stage in this circuit (pin 9) is fed through resistor R10 to the base of the transistor Q3, which acts as an amplifier. Almost any NPN power transistor should work fine. Be aware that the sound of this siren is very, very loud. Test it with caution.

Potentiometer R11 is an optional volume control. This component can be deleted from the circuit or replaced with a fixed resistor of suitable value if a potentiometer is not needed. For many alarm applications, you will want the siren to be as loud as possible, so no volume-reducing resistor at all would be used.

Be aware that diode D1 and capacitor C4 are very important in this circuit. These components help protect the timer IC (or ICs) from voltage transients that might result from the inductive aspects of the speaker coil.

To sound the alarm, just have the alarm control circuit apply the supply voltage to this siren circuit at the appropriate time. If power is continuously applied to this circuit, the siren will continuously sound.

Protecting your equipment

NOW THAT YOU HAVE TAKEN A LOOK AT THE BASIC PRINCIPLES of the three parts of an alarm system, you are ready to start putting them all together in some practical projects.

Start out relatively small and try protecting some specific pieces of equipment, or objects. You are concerned with four types of protection here:

- Protection from theft of portable equipment.
- Protection from unauthorized use of electrical equipment.
- Protection from brown-outs or black-outs.
- Protection from electrical faults.

The last three, of course, apply only to electrical and electronic equipment. Protection is considered for theft protection for both electrical and nonelectrical objects.

The first two of these four types of equipment protection are forms of security against the actions of the people, and the other two could be considered security against forms of environmental risks. An electrical fault could start a fire or a serious (possibly even fatal) shock hazard. Remember, the best security system is always one that prevents potential disasters before they occur. That is, a security system that keeps intruders out is better than one that simply alerts you when an intrusion has taken place. (Although often, this protection is all you can accomplish in a practical, real-world situation.) Similarly, a heat-sensitive fire alarm or a smoke alarm is great and can save property and lives. But, the seemingly mundane protections against electrical faults here can help prevent an electrical fire from ever getting started, and that is an unquestionable improvement.

Portable object alarm

Everyone has many portable items, many of them quite valuable. Portable items are very convenient, of course, because you can easily carry them with you. Unfortunately, that same portability also make it very convenient for a theif to steal them.

The portable object alarm circuit shown in Fig. 4-1 can be used to protect almost anything from theft—computers, typewriters, small stereos, piles of important papers, TV sets, bicycles, cellular telephones, and many other possessions. This project can also be used to guard door knobs, file cabinets, drawers, and the like. A suitable parts list for this project appears as Table 4-1.

This alarm can be bolted to or chained to what you want to protect, or it can even be set simply on top of the protected object. The goal is to place the alarm so that the protected object cannot be taken or moved without tilting the alarm, which sets it off.

It is recommended that you use a key switch for the alarm disable switch (S1) to aid in foiling clever thieves. This circuit will apply power to an external buzzer or siren circuit (like those discussed in the preceding chapter) when it is triggered. The output voltage will be a little less than +9 V.

**Table 4-1   Parts list for project 8.
Portable object alarm of Fig. 4-1.**

IC1	556 dual timer
IC2	555 timer
Q1	NPN transistor (Radio Shack RS2009, GE20, SK3122, ECG128, or similar)
Q2	PNP transistor (Radio Shack RS1604, GE21, SK3025, ECG159, or similar)
D1	LED
D2	Diode (see text)
C1, C3–C7, C9	0.01 µF capacitor
C2	10 µF 25 V electrolytic capacitor
C8	4.7 µF 25 V electrolytic capacitor
R1, R5, R6	10 kΩ ¼ W 5% resistor
R2, R7	1 MΩ (megohm) potentiometer
R3	330 Ω ¼ W 5% resistor
R4	1 kΩ ¼ W 5% resistor
R8	390 Ω ¼ W 5% resistor
S1	SPST key switch
S2	Mercury switch
B1, B2	9 V batteries

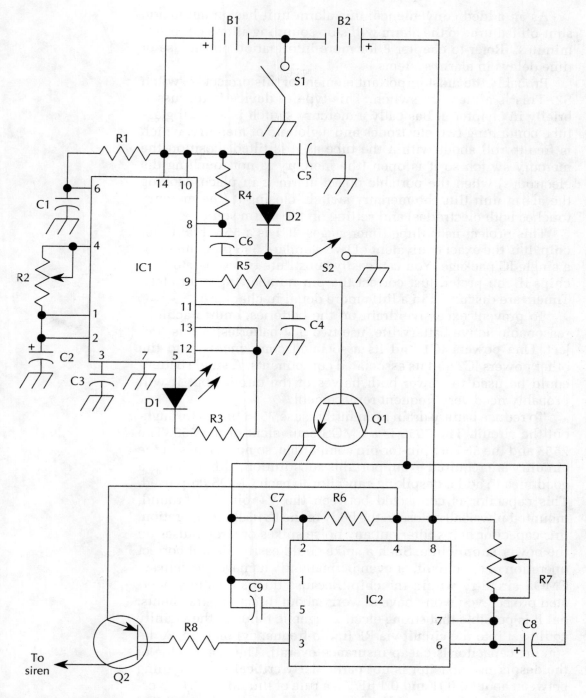

Fig. 4-1 Project 8. Portable object alarm.

As an added convenience, this alarm unit has an automatic shut-off feature, so the alarm will stop sounding after a couple of minutes. (Refer to chapter 8 for more information on the use of time delays in alarm systems.)

Probably the most important element of this project is switch S2. This is a mercury switch. This type of device is discussed briefly in chapter 2. Basically a mercury switch is a small glass tube containing two electrodes and a globule of mercury, which is free to roll about within the tube as it is tilted. Position the mercury switch so it is open (the mercury is not touching the electrodes) when the portable object alarm is in place. Moving the alarm unit tilts the mercury switch, closing it (the mercury touches both electrodes) and setting off the alarm sound.

This project uses three timer stages. IC1 is a 556 dual timer chip. It is the exact equivalent of two standard 555 type timers in a single IC package. You can easily substitute two separate 555-chips if you prefer. Just correct the pin numbers appropriately. Timers are discussed in a little more detail in chapter 8.

To prevent excessive drain on the batteries, and to achieve reasonable active battery life, use two 9 V batteries in this project. One powers IC1 and its associated components, and the other powers IC2 and its associated components. A single battery could be used to power both halves of the circuit, but it will probably need very frequent replacement.

To reduce battery drain even further, use 7555 timers throughout the circuit. The 7555 is a CMOS equivalent of the 555. The 7555 and the 555 are pin-for-pin compatible, so no changes in the circuitry are required to support this substitution, although it is a good idea to add a despiking capacitor to each CMOS chip used. This capacitor is connected between the V+ pin and ground, mounted physically close to the body of the IC itself. In operation, this capacitor helps filter out any noise spikes or stray pulses on the power supply line. Such a spike could easily disrupt correct operation of the circuit, or even permanently damage the delicate CMOS circuitry within the chip. Because this is a battery operated project, you won't have to worry about direct line transients, but it is possible that strong electromagnetic fields in the vicinity could get into the circuit via RF (radio-frequency) pick up. A despiking capacitor is cheap insurance overall. The exact value of the despiking capacitor is not particularly critical. Use anything between about 0.001 and 0.1 μF. As a rule of thumb, a 0.01 μF capacitor is generally considered the standard choice for a CMOS protecting despiking capacitor.

There is probably no direct CMOS replacement for the 556 dual timer, although such a device is sure to appear on the market before long. This doesn't really present any problem, because a 556 chip is simply the equivalent of two separate 555 ICs, so it can be replaced with a pair of 7555 chips.

All three of the timers used in this circuit are used as monostable multivibrators. One half of IC1 sets up the delay time between the time the circuit is turned on and when it becomes armed. This gives the legitimate operator adequate time to turn it on and off via the key switch (S1) without falsely setting off the alarm. This delay period is set by potentiometer R2. A screwdriver-adjusted trimpot is advisable in this application. If you prefer, you can replace this potentiometer with a fixed resistor of suitable value. The second half of IC1 is the actual sensing/trigger circuit.

Finally, IC1 turns on the external siren or buzzer for a preset period of time. When this monostable multivibrator times out, the alarm sounding device turns off. Assuming the portable object alarm has been returned to its proper position, it will be automatically reset and ready to detect another attempt to disturb the protected property.

The alarm-on period can be changed via potentiometer R7. A screwdriver-adjusted trimpot is again advisable in this application. Of course, if you prefer, you can replace R7 with a fixed resistor of suitable value.

There is one very special requirement for this circuit to function as designed. Diode D2 can't be too good. This diode should have some measurable leakage when reverse biased, so it acts like a very high resistance. A standard 1N4148 or 1N914 diode probably will not work in this application, because it is not leaky enough.

You can easily find a leaky diode with an ohmmeter. At worst, you can add a large value trimpot (several megohms) in parallel with this diode, and calibrate the circuit for proper operation. If the diode is not leaky enough, or is open, the triggering of the alarm will be very erratic.

LED D1 indicates that the portable object alarm has been turned on and will soon be armed and ready to go off if disturbed. The purpose here is to let the legitimate user know that the circuit is in its arm-delay phase. This LED and its current-limiting resistor (R3) can be omitted from the circuit if you prefer. In this case, connect the output of the first timer stage (pin 5 of IC1) directly to the input of the next timer stage (pins 12 and 13 of IC1).

Enclose the project in a relatively secure housing of some sort, so it cannot be opened without setting off the alarm. A key switch is almost essential for disarming switch S1. At the very least, this switch should be well hidden and disguised.

Battery power is virtually essential for this project. If ac power is used, all but the most idiotic of potential theives should be able to figure out that they can disable the alarm simply by unplugging it. This would reduce the project effectiveness to that of a glorified paper weight.

Snoop detector

If you aren't really concerned with actual theft, the last project might be a bit of overkill. But what if you suspect someone has been getting too nosy and has been snooping into your personal papers or something along those lines?

The circuit shown in Fig. 4-2 will let you know if any unauthorized snooping has been done in your absence. A suitable parts list for this project is given in Table 4-2.

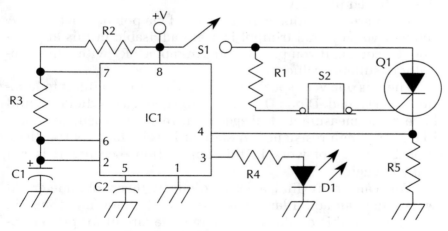

Fig. 4-2 *Project 9. Snoop detector.*

As you can see, this is a relatively simple project. A 7555 CMOS timer IC is called for in the parts list, because of its low power consumption. But you can directly substitute a standard 555 timer chip if you prefer. The 555 and the 7555 are pin-for-pin compatible, and no changes in the circuitry are required to support such a substitution.

**Table 4-2 Parts list for project 9.
Snoop detector of Fig. 4-2.**

IC1	7555 CMOS timer (or 555 timer)
Q1	Low-power SCR (Radio Shack RS1067 or similar)
D1	LED
C1	10 μF 25 V electrolytic capacitor
C2	0.01 μF capacitor
R1	10 kΩ ¼ W 5% resistor
R2	33 kΩ ¼ W 5% resistor
R3	47 kΩ ¼ W 5% resistor
R4	470 Ω ¼ W 5% resistor
R5	1 kΩ ¼ W 5% resistor
S1	SPST key switch
S2	Normally closed push-button switch

The requirement for the SCR (Q1) used in this project are far from critical. Almost any low-power SCR should work just fine, but first breadboard the circuit, just to be sure.

The secret of this project is in how it is housed. The project should look like a harmless paper weight, or some innocuous device that just happens to be sitting on top of the papers (or whatever) to be protected. The normally closed push-button switch (S2) is mounted on the bottom of this device, so it is held open while the project is sitting in place, but if it is lifted up, the switch contacts will close, turning on the SCR and turning on the oscillator (IC1) which flashes the LED (D1). Setting the project back down reopens the switch, but does not turn off the SCR or extinguish the LED. This can only be done by reset switch S1. A key switch or a well-hidden or disguised switch should be used here.

The flash rate of the LED, when the snoop detector project has been triggered is determined by the values of resistors R2 and R3 and capacitor C1. If for some reason you want a different flash rate, just change any or all of these component values. Using the values suggested in the parts list, the flash rate will be about 0.6 Hz.

This project, as shown here, does not set off an audible alarm. If the LED is hidden, the intruder might not even be aware that the snooping has been detected. But when you come back and see the lit LED, you will know your privacy has been invaded, and perhaps it is time to take greater security precautions.

This project is quite simple, inexpensive, and easy to build and use, but it is very effective in detecting unauthorized snooping.

Power-use monitor

The circuit shown in Fig. 4-3 will tell you if someone has been using a piece of electrically powered equipment without authorization. The culprit will not be alerted to that fact that his or her illicit use of your equipment has been detected. A suitable parts list for this project is given in Table 4-3.

The ac input of this circuit is wired in parallel with the primary of the protected equipment power transformer, after its power switch. Notice that this involves opening the case of the protected equipment. Alternately, you can wire a standard ac plug to the power-use monitor circuit and plug it into the same

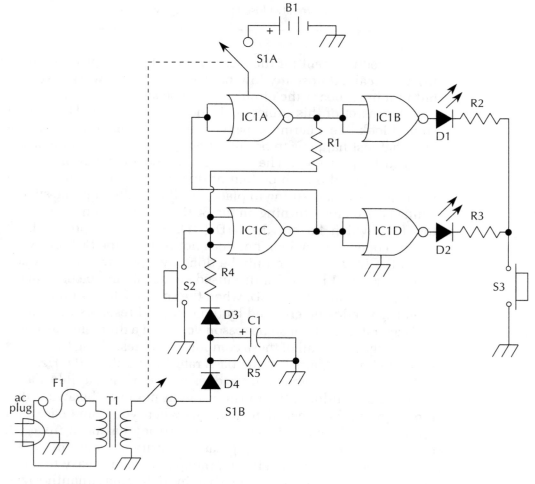

Fig. 4-3 *Project 10. Power-use monitor.*

Table 4-3 Parts list for project 10.
Power-use monitor of Fig. 4-3.

B1	9 V battery
IC1	CD4001 quad NOR gate
D1, D2	LED
D3, D4	Diode (1N4002 or similar)
C1	2.2 μF 25 V electrolytic capacitor
R1	220 kΩ ¼ W 5% resistor
R2, R3	470 Ω ¼ W 5% resistor
R4	10 kΩ ¼ W 5% resistor
R5	180 kΩ ¼ W 5% resistor
T1	Power transformer 120 Vac: 6.3 Vac
F1	0.5 A fuse (see text)
S1	DPST switch
S2, S3	Normally open SPST switch
ac plug	Three prong

socket as the equipment to be monitored, preferably with a cube tape, or a power strip, or something similar. The results might be a little less reliable using this method. Fortunately, it is easy enough for you to check out how well the power-use monitor works with your particular equipment. Just arm the monitor circuit before using the equipment yourself and see if it reliably indicates your usage.

The power-use monitor is powered by closing DPST switch S1. Notice that this switch has two sections. One applies ac power from the transformer (T1) to the input, and the other section feeds dc battery power to the digital gates.

A DPST switch is called for as S1. Actual DPST switches are relatively rare, and therefore can be more expensive than they really need to be. A more common DPDT switch will work just as well. Just leave one end of each set of contacts open, and don't worry about it. The switch will function in exactly the same way as a DPST switch.

The ac signal is rectified and crudely filtered by diodes D3 and D4, capacitor C1, and resistor R5. R4 is a current-limiting resistor to protect the input of the CMOS gates. This ac signal is present only when the monitored equipment is in use (that is, receiving power). When the ac signal is present, the input of gate IC1C sees a logic HIGH, otherwise it sees a logic LOW.

When you first turn on the power-use monitor, before there is any ac input, briefly close push-button switch S2. This resets the flip-flop comprising the four gates of IC1. Now, if you press push-button switch S3, you will see that LED D1 is lit and LED D2 is dark.

When the monitored equipment is powered up, an ac signal will pass through transformer T1 to apply a HIGH signal at the input of the flip-flop, triggering it to change states. As far as the person illicitly using your equipment can tell, the power use monitor circuit isn't doing anything at all. There is no visual or audible indication of its operation. But the flip-flop has been set, and it will remain set, even if the monitored equipment is now turned off, removing the ac signal from the circuit.

Now, when you return, you can press push-button switch S3 again. When you see that LED D2 is now lit and LED D1 is dark, you will know that the monitored equipment has been used in your absence. You can then take whatever action seems appropriate to your specific situation. Pushing push-button switch S2 will reset the flip-flop so the circuit will return to its original condition.

It would probably be a good idea to conceal the LEDs and push-buttons S2 and S3. If a curious intruder presses S3, he or she might figure out the purpose of the monitor circuit. And, because S2 resets the circuit, and erases the evidence, you definitely don't want the intruder to deliberately or accidentally close this switch.

Different colored LEDs for D1 and D2 will make the results more clearly visible and will limit the possibility of confusion.

Because ac power flows through this circuit, it is vital to use all appropriate precautions. Make sure everything is well insulated. Use a plastic or other nonconductive housing for the project. Do everything you can to eliminate the possibility of anyone ever touching any of the conductors in the circuit. Please, don't take any chances on creating a shock or fire hazard.

Power-failure alarm

For some equipment, such as computers running continuous programs, it is critical that power not be interrupted. But power failures do occur. When a power failure happens with such critical equipment, you want to know about it as soon as possible so you might be able to do something to correct the situation.

The circuit shown in Fig. 4-4 is a power-failure alarm. When ac power is interrupted for any reason, the circuit switches over to battery power, and the alarm sounds. A suitable parts list for this project is given in Table 4-4.

This project is also a very useful antitheft alarm for any ac-

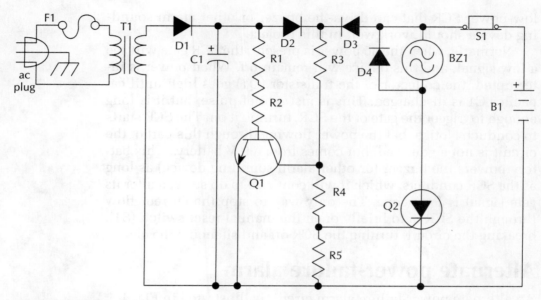

Fig. 4-4 *Project 11. Power-failure alarm.*

**Table 4-4 Parts list for project 11.
Power-failure alarm of Fig. 4-4.**

Q1	NPN transistor (RS2009, GE20, SK3122, ECG128, or similar)
Q2	Low-power SCR (Radio Shack RS1067 or similar—see text)
D1–D4	Diode (1N4001 or similar)
T1	Power transformer 120 Vac: 12 Vac
C1	330 µF 25 V electrolytic capacitor
R1	10 kΩ ¼ W 5% resistor
R2	2.2 kΩ ¼ W 5% resistor
R3	27 kΩ ¼ W 5% resistor
R4, R5	1 kΩ ¼ W 5% resistor
BZ1	Buzzer
B1	9 V battery
S1	Normally closed SPST push-button switch (reset)
ac plug	Three prong

powered equipment. When the protected device is unplugged, the circuit will sense a power failure and sound the alarm.

This circuit is pretty straightforward overall. As long as ac power is applied, the secondary of the transformer (T1) puts out 12 Vac, which is rectified by diode D1 and capacitor C1. This signal is applied (through resistors R1 and R2) to the base of transistor Q1, which controls the gate of an SCR (Q2). Almost any low-power SCR that can drive the buzzer or other alarm sounding device should work well in this project.

Normally, when the ac power is present, the SCR gate will see a low signal, and this device will remain off. When power is interrupted, the collector of the transistor (Q1) goes high until capacitor C1 is discharged. This is just a brief pulse, but it is long enough to trigger the gate of the SCR, turning it on. The SCR starts to conduct. Notice that the power flowing through this part of the circuit is not ac derived, but comes from a 9 V battery., This battery powers the buzzer (or other alarm sounding device) as long as the SCR conducts, which it will continue to do so even after its gate signal is long gone. The only way to stop the current flow through the SCR is to briefly open the manual reset switch (S1), breaking the circuit, turning the SCR off and silencing the alarm.

Alternate power-failure alarm

An alternate power-failure alarm circuit is illustrated in Fig. 4-5. A suitable parts list for this project is given in Table 4-5.

An unusual feature of this power-failure alarm project is that it does not include a battery. So how does the alarm function when the power is interrupted? Capacitor C1 stores up a substantial charge while the circuit is receiving normal ac power. If this power is interrupted, the relay is deactivated, closing the lower set of switch contacts, which permits the stored voltage in capacitor C1 to drain off through the piezoelectric buzzer and resistor R3. Both capacitor C1 and resistor R3 should have very large values, so the time constant will be relatively long. The parts values suggested in Table 4-5 should be sufficient for the buzzer to sound for a good half minute or so before the capacitor is discharged.

Do not use a larger alarm sounding device than a piezoelectric buzzer with this particular project. A hefty siren or bell could draw too much current for the stored charge on the capacitor to drive.

When ac power is present, the relay (K1) is activated. This means the upper set of switch contacts in the relay (as shown in the schematic) will be closed, and the lower set of switch contacts will be open.

The ac voltage is rectified by a full-wave rectifier network made up of diodes D1 through D4. Resistor R2 and zener diode D5 drop this rectified voltage down considerably. This reduced pseudo-dc voltage is used to charge the capacitor (C1). Typically,

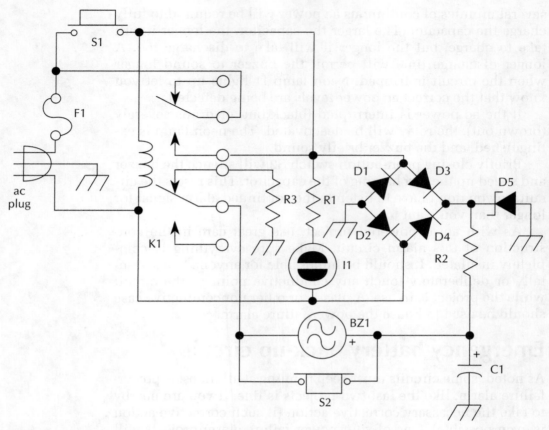

Fig. 4-5 *Project 12. Alternate power-failure alarm.*

**Table 4-5   Parts list for project 12.
Alternate power-failure alarm of Fig. 4-5.**

D1–D4	Diode (1N4003 or similar)
D5	5.1 V zener diode
C1	470 μF electrolytic capacitor (see text)
R1, R2	180 kΩ ½ W 10% resistor
R3	2.2 MΩ ½ W 10% resistor (see text)
K1	120 Vac relay with DPDT switch contacts
F1	1 A fuse
BZ1	Buzzer
I1	NE-2 neon lamp
S1, S2	Normally open SPST push-button switch
ac plug	Three prong

several minutes of continuous ac power will be required to fully charge the capacitor. The larger the capacitor, the longer it will take to charge, but the longer it will take to discharge too. A longer discharge time will permit the buzzer to sound longer when the circuit is tripped. Neon lamp I1 lights up to let you know that the correct ac power levels are being detected.

If the ac power is interrupted (black out, or drops severely (brown out), the relay will be deactivated. The neon lamp is extinguished, and the buzzer briefly sound.

Briefly closing push-button switch S2 will silence the buzzer and speed up the discharging of the capacitor. This resets the circuit, so you don't have to listen to the continued alarm signal for longer than you want to.

As with an ac-powered project, use great care in the construction of this alarm circuit. Make sure everything is completely insulated. It should be impossible for anyone to accidentally or deliberately touch any conductive point in the circuit while the project is in use. A plastic or other nonconductive case should be used to house the power-failure alarm.

Emergency battery back-up circuit

As noted, some circuits must keep running at all times. A power-failure alarm, like the last two projects is fine, if you are nearby to take the necessary corrective action (if such corrective action is even possible). One of your power failure alarm projects will let you know if a power failure occurred during your absence, but it won't do anything at all about the fact that the equipment was not running for some period of time. In some cases, this might be just a more or less minor inconvenience. Under other circumstances, it could be a real disaster. But what can you do about it?

One solution to the problem of ac power outages is to use battery power for all continuously operated devices. Of course, it will then be necessary to check and probably replace the batteries fairly frequently, especially if the equipment in question draws a substantial amount of current. Batteries tend to die at the most inconvenient moments. Naturally, if the battery voltage drops too low, your equipment will stop running. Continuous battery powered operation of all essential equipment can rapidly get very expensive, not to mention the inconvenience of having to frequently replace the batteries, which will probably require shutting down the equipment for at least a couple of minutes.

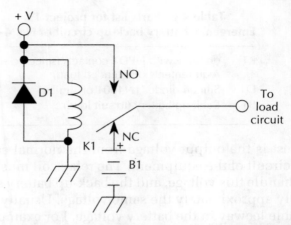

Fig. 4-6 *Project 13. Emergency battery back-up circuit.*

This emergency battery back-up project, shown in Fig. 4-6, does a lot to combine the best of both worlds. The load device is normally powered from an ac power supply of some sort. It is assumed that a power supply circuit converts the ac household voltage to a lower dc voltage. If this voltage is interrupted for any reason, the load will automatically be switched over to a back-up battery. As soon as the main ac power supply is back in action, it will take over again, and the back-up battery will be automatically disconnected. Battery life is maximized by the fact that current is drawn from the battery only when it is absolutely necessary to do so. As long as the ac household voltage is available, it will be used to operate the load equipment, and the battery will just sit there waiting. As far as the battery is concerned, it is sitting unused on a shelf.

For large systems, you might want to wire this project to supply emergency battery power to those stages that are absolutely necessary, while other stages (especially displays which generally consume relatively large currents) are permitted to go dead until the ac supply voltage is restored. For example, in a computer system, the battery back-up could drive just the RAM (random-access memory) memory circuits so essential data is not lost, but any displays or perphial equipment is permitted to shut down during the ac power black out. These devices will be brought back on line when the ac power is restored.

A suitable parts list for this emergency battery back-up project is given in Table 4-6. As you can see, this is a very simple project. The relay and battery are selected to suit the necessary dc voltage used by the equipment, which will serve as the load. The voltage

**Table 4-6   Parts list for project 13.
Emergency battery back-up circuit of Fig. 4-6.**

K1	dc relay with DPDT contacts (select to suit requirements of intended load)
D1	Silicon diode (1N4001 or similar)
B1	Back-up battery (to suit load)

of interest is the output voltage from the normal ac-to-dc power supply circuit of the equipment. The relay coil must obviously be able to handle this voltage, and the back-up battery should be able to supply approximately the same voltage. Usually there is some reasonable leeway in the battery voltage. For example, a standard output voltage for many ac-to-dc converters is 6.3 V. A 6 V battery (a standard value) will probably do just fine.

Use the heftiest batteries you can find, especially if frequent or long ac power outages are a significant possibility. A heftier battery will be able to supply more current for a longer period of time. AA or AAA batteries would probably go dead very quickly unless the load device is very small and quite modest in its current consumption.

Diode D1 is included as cheap insurance to prevent possible damage to the relay coil due to back-EMF, a common problem in relay circuits. Almost any standard silicon diode should work well here.

The relay switch contacts should be of the SPDT type. Of course, a DPDT relay can be used, just ignore one set of switch contacts. Or you could hook up two of these circuits in parallel to simultaneously supply emergency back-up battery power to two different circuits or stages within a larger system. This way, one set of batteries won't have to do too much work.

Usually, when ac power is present, the relay will be activated. This means the NO contacts will be closed, and the NC contacts will be held open. The load device is connected to the common switch contact. As long as the relay is activated, the dc output of the ac powered supply circuit is fed directly to the load device, which operates normally.

If ac power is lost for any reason, the dc voltage applied to the relay coil will disappear, and the coil will be deactivated. The NO contacts will open up, and the NC contacts will close, connecting the battery to the load device, which will continue to operate, even though its power source has been changed.

When the ac power has been restored, the input voltage to

this circuit reappears, and activates the relay once more. The back-up battery is disconnected from the load device, and the dc voltage from the ac driven power supply is re-connected.

For your convenience, a summary of the connections to the relay switch contacts follows:

Relay switch contact	Connected to
NO	ac-driven power source
Common (center)	Load device (V+)
NC	Back-up battery (B1)

Be aware that a relay, being a mechanical switching device, requires a finite period of time to switch its contacts from one position to the other. This means there will be a brief fraction of a second when neither the NO contacts nor the NC contacts are closed. For this instant, the load device will not receive any power. In most applications, this won't make any noticeable difference in the continuous operation of the load device. But a few circuits are very, very sensitive even to brief power outages. For example, some computer memory circuits can be completely erased if the supply voltage is removed even for a fraction of a second. This tended to be more of a problem with early designs. Most modern designs, and commercial equipment, will include a large capacitor or something similar on the same board as such critical circuitry. The voltage stored in the capacitor will be able to keep the circuit sufficiently powered during the relay switching time.

But you can't expect miracles from such a simple and rather crude circuit as this. This project is not intended to replace a $500 uninterruptable power supply. (Many of these devices cost a lot more than $500.) But in many applications, this project will be perfectly adequate and will do a great job, without your laying out the big bucks for a commercially manufactured uninterruptable power supply unit.

Current limiters

For any electronic circuit or other electrically powered device to function, it obviously needs to receive electrical power. Moreover, the power it receives must be the correct amount. If the supplied power level is too low, the circuit or device will not function correctly or reliably, if at all. But too much power can be even more of a problem. If excessive power is applied to an electronic circuit, some of its components are likely to be damaged or destroyed. Usually the most expensive components are the very ones that are the most sensitive to such damage too. Similar over-power damage can be done to other nonelectronic electrically powered devices.

If you want to consider your electrical and electronic equipment truly secure, then you must consider electrical security. Electrical power, as you know, is measured in units called *watts*, and is equal to the product of the current and the voltage. That is;

$$P = IE$$

where *P* is the power in watts, *I* is the current in amperes, and *E* is the voltage in volts.

The voltage part is relatively easy to control in most cases. A voltage source generally puts out a fixed voltage, and that's that. For example, a typical battery cell puts out 1.5 V. This voltage might vary over time, due to conditions within the voltage source itself. For example, a fresh battery might actually put out 1.65 V, but an old battery due for replacement might be putting out only 1.05 V or so. But excessive over-voltage conditions are not likely, and there is no way for the load circuit or device to induce an over-voltage, no matter what defect it might develop. A 1.5 V battery is not going to put out 8.37 V, no matter what.

Similarly, an ac-driven power supply might put out too low a voltage, due to a power brown out, but an over-voltage, although possible, is relatively unlikely. This rather slim possibility can easily be reduced to negligible proportions with a zener diode or a voltage regulator IC.

But when you consider current, the situation is more complex. The load circuit or device, in effect decides how much current it will draw from the power supply. As long as the power supply can handle the current demands of its load, it will supply them, no matter if they are dangerously excessive.

The problem is due to the effects of Ohm's Law, which defines the interrelationships between voltage, current, and resistance:

$$I = \frac{E}{R}$$

where *I* is the current in amperes, E is the voltage in volts, and R is the resistance in ohms.

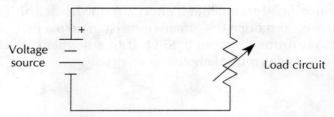

Fig. 4-7 *In effect, the load circuit looks like a resistance across the power supply output.*

In effect, the load circuit or device looks like a resistance across the power supply output, as illustrated in Fig. 4-7. This load resistance might vary under different operating conditions.

As an example, assume a typical electronic circuit (it doesn't matter what it does) that normally presents an average impedance (ac resistance) of about 500 Ω to the +9 V power supply. The current drawn by this circuit will average about:

$$I = \frac{9}{500}$$
$$= 0.018 \text{ A}$$
$$= 18 \text{ mA (milliampere)}$$

But this hypothetical circuit might have a couple of special operating modes, which change the effective input resistance as seen by the power supply. In mode A, the input impedance is reduced to 400 Ω, so the current flow is increased to:

$$I = \frac{9}{400}$$
$$= 0.0225 \text{ A}$$
$$= 22.5 \text{ mA}$$

In mode B, the effective input impedance of the load jumps up to 750 Ω, so the current drawn from the power supply is reduced to:

$$I = \frac{9}{750}$$
$$= 0.012 \text{ A}$$
$$= 12 \text{ mA}$$

Increasing the resistance decreases the current and vice versa. Now, what would happen if a defect forms in the load circuit? Specifically, consider a short circuit. By definition, a short circuit would reduce the effective resistance to a very low value. Assume it drops down to 0.25 Ω. If this happens, the load will try to draw a current of about:

$$I = \frac{9}{0.25}$$

$$= 36 \text{ A}$$

$$= 36,000 \text{ mA}$$

It is not likely that the more sensitive components in the load circuit will be able to withstand this heavy current. But the power supply will try to supply it, even though the power supply itself might be damaged in the process. In addition, for ac-powered circuits, such conditions can create dangerous electrical shock and fire hazards. It should be clear that some sort of current limiting is often essential to provide electrical security.

The simplest type of current limiting is the common fuse. A fuse is basically just a thin, specially composed wire contained in a protective housing. Any wire heats up as current passes through it. The greater the current flow, the more heat will be produced. The fuse wire, or *filament* is designed for a very specific melting temperature. This temperature is reached when the current passing through it exceeds a specific limit. The filament melts, and the circuit is broken, stopping all further current flow until the fuse is replaced.

You should never replace any fuse with one of a higher rating. Doing so will defeat the purpose of the fuse. For example, assume you have a piece of equipment with a 0.5 A fuse. If you replace this fuse with a 1 A unit, a current of 0.75 A could easily pass through, and this might be sufficient to damage some of the components in the supposedly protected circuit. Probably one of the essential (and probably expensive) components will blow to "protect" the fuse. Clearly, this wouldn't do you any good.

If several fuses of the specified value blow immediately or soon after being replaced, something is seriously wrong with the load circuit or possibly the power supply circuitry. Locate and correct the fault before trying to operate the equipment again. Never bypass the fuse, even temporarily. Excessive current can do its destructive work in the blink of an eye. Many people have put a penny in the fusebox and many, admittedly, have gotten away with it through pure dumb luck. But many others who tried this stupid trick were rewarded with an electrical fire, or a painful, harmful, or even fatal electrical shock. It is **NEVER** worth the risk! **NEVER** defeat the purpose of any fuse. Doing so would just be courting disaster.

A slightly more sophisticated form of current limiting is the circuit breaker. This is an electromechanical device that physically opens a switch, stopping current flow, when the current passing through it exceeds a specific maximum level. The advantage of a circuit breaker over a fuse is that the blown fuse must be physically replaced. A popped circuit breaker can be manually reset just by pressing a button. Otherwise, the principles involved are the same.

Fuses and circuit breakers do a pretty good job against gross defects, but because they depend on mechanical action to open up the circuit and stop current flow, it takes a finite amount of time to operate. In some cases, enough excessive current can get through to damage or destroy a delicate component before the fuse or circuit breaker opens up.

When dealing with very sensitive or critical electronic or electrical equipment, an electronic current-limiting circuit is often very desirable. Because this subject is really just peripheral to this book, just quickly glance at a few typical current limiter circuits without going into much detail about them.

The circuit shown in Fig. 4-8 regulates the output current to 1 A. The parts list for this simple project is given in Table 4-7. The actual current limit can be altered by selecting different values for resistor R1.

A precision current-limiter circuit is shown in Fig. 4-9, with

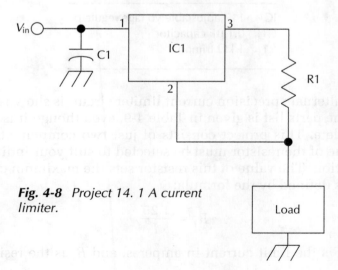

Fig. 4-8 *Project 14. 1 A current limiter.*

**Table 4-7 Parts list for project 14.
1 A current limiter of Fig. 4-8.**

IC1	117 adjustable voltage regulator
C1	0.1 µF capacitor
R1	1.2 kΩ 2 W 10% resistor

the parts list in Table 4-8. Potentiometer R1 is used to calibrate the circuit. A screwdriver-adjust trimpot makes the most sense here. A front-panel control would probably be ridiculous for most applications. (Although this might be appropriate and useful on a power supply on an experimenter's or technician's workbench.) For maximum precision, a 10-turn trimpot is strongly recommended for use in this circuit.

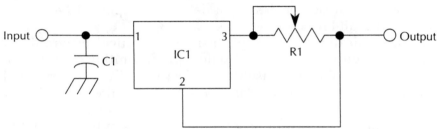

Fig. 4-9 *Project 15. Precision current limiter.*

**Table 4-8 Parts list for project 15.
Precision current limiter of Fig. 4-9.**

IC1	117 adjustable voltage regulator
C1	0.1 µF capacitor
R1	1 kΩ trimpot

An alternate precision current limiter circuit is shown in Fig. 4-10. The parts list is given in Table 4-9, even though it is rather incomplete. This project consists of just two components, and the value of the resistor must be selected to suit your individual application. The value of this resistor sets the maximum current level, as defined by the formula;

$$R_1 = \frac{1.25}{I}$$

where I is the limit current in amperes, and R_1 is the resistance

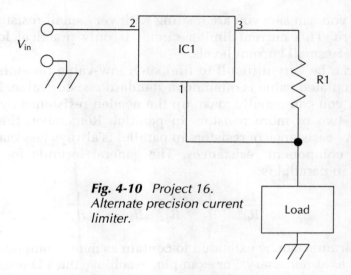

Fig. 4-10 *Project 16. Alternate precision current limiter.*

Table 4-9 Parts list for project 16. Alternate precision current limiter of Fig. 4-10.

IC1	LM317 1.2- to 37-V regulator
R1	see text

value in ohms. Run through a few quick examples. For a limit current of 0.25-A, use a resistor with a value equal to approximately;

$$R_1 = \frac{1.25}{0.25}$$

$$= 5 \ \Omega$$

For a limit current of 0.1 A (100 mA), a suitable resistor value would be:

$$R_1 = \frac{1.25}{0.1}$$

$$= 12.5 \ \Omega$$

Finally, if you want to limit the current to 0.65 A (650 mA), use a resistor with a value of about:

$$R_1 = \frac{1.25}{0.65}$$

$$= 1.32 \ \Omega$$

As you can see, you are dealing with very small resistor values here. This current limiter circuit is only practical for use with very small current levels.

It can be very difficult to find such low-value resistors, and the calculated value is often not a standard resistor value. Fortunately, you can usually make up the needed resistance by combining two or more resistors in parallel. Remember, the total effective resistance of resistors in parallel is always less than any of the component resistances. The general formula for resistances in parallel is:

$$\frac{1}{R_t} = \frac{1}{R_1} + \frac{1}{R_2} + \frac{1}{R_3} \; ... \; + \frac{1}{R_n}$$

This formula can be extended to contain as many component resistances as necessary. For example, to achieve the 5 Ω resistance called for in one of your examples, you can use two 10 Ω resistors in parallel:

$$\frac{1}{R_t} = \frac{1}{10} + \frac{1}{10}$$

$$= 0.1 + 0.1$$

$$= 0.2$$

$$R_t = \frac{1}{0.2}$$

$$= 5 \; \Omega$$

As a second example, you can come very close to the 12.5 Ω value you need for a limit current of 0.1 A if you use two 100 Ω resistors, two 47 Ω resistors, and a 62 Ω resistor in parallel:

$$\frac{1}{R_t} = \frac{1}{100} + \frac{1}{100} + \frac{1}{47} + \frac{1}{47} + \frac{1}{62}$$

$$= 0.01 + 0.01 + 0.0213 + 0.0213 + 0.0213 + 0.0161$$

$$= 0.0787$$

$$R_t = \frac{1}{0.0787}$$

$$= 12.7 \; \Omega$$

This is 0.2 Ω too high, but component tolerances could account for as much error. When in doubt, plug the parallel resistance value back into the original limit current equation:

$$R_1 = \frac{1.25}{I}$$

$$I = \frac{1.25}{R_1}$$

$$= \frac{1.25}{12.7}$$

$$= 0.0985 \text{ A}$$

That is very, very close to the desired limit current value of 0.1 A.

For your convenience, the pinout diagram for the LM317 adjustable voltage-regulator IC used in this project is shown in Fig. 4-11. Although this device looks like a power transistor, it is really an integrated circuit. The output voltage is taken from an electrical connection made directly to the case of the device. No separate pin is provided for this purpose.

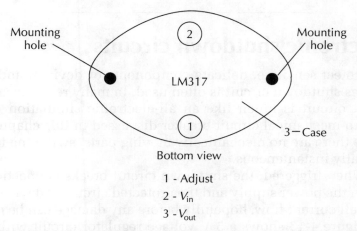

Fig. 4-11 *The LM317 adjustable-voltage regulator IC is used in Project 16.*

The circuit shown in Fig. 4-12 is a current-limited voltage regulator. Depending on the setting of the potentiometer (R2) the output voltage can be anything from 1.2 V up to 20.0 V, with very good regulation and a minimum load current of 4 mA (0.004 A). A suitable parts list for this project is given in Table 4-10.

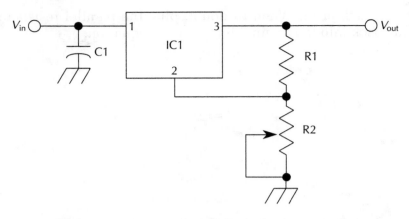

Fig. 4-12 *Project 17. Current-limited voltage regulator.*

Table 4-10 Parts list for project 17.
Current-limited voltage regulator of Fig. 4-12.

IC1	LM117 adjustable voltage regulator
C1	0.1 µF capacitor
R1	1.2 kΩ 1 W 10% resistor
R2	25 kΩ trimpot

Electronic shutdown circuits

To protect sensitive, delicate components or devices, and electronics shutdown circuit is often used. In many respects, a shutdown circuit is much like an all-electronic simulation of the electro-mechanical circuit breaker discussed in this chapter. Because there are no mechanically moving parts, switching time is virtually instantaneous.

When triggered, the shutdown circuit breaks connection between the power supply and the protected circuit or device, stopping all current flow, hopefully before any damage can be done.

Figure 4-13 shows a 5 V voltage regulator circuit with electronic shutdown. A suitable parts list for this project appears as Table 4-11.

The input voltage to this circuit can be anything ranging from +7 to +35 V. The output voltage will always be a well-regulated +5 V, making it ideal for use with TTL (transistor-transistor logic) circuits.

A logic signal on the base of transistor Q1 activates the shutdown function. This transistor acts like a simple electronic

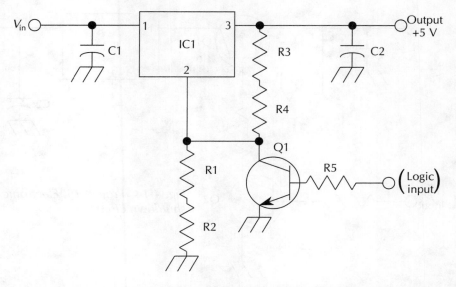

Fig. 4-13 *Project 18. 5 V regulator with electronic shutdown.*

**Table 4-11   Parts list for project 18. 5 V
regulator with electronic shutdown of Fig. 4-13.**

IC1	LM117 adjustable voltage regulator
Q1	NPN transistor (2N2219, Radio Shack RS2030, GE18, SK3024, or similar)
C1, C2	0.1 μF capacitor
R1	680 Ω ½ W 5% resistor
R2	39 Ω ½ W 5% resistor
R3	220 Ω ½ W 5% resistor
R4	22 Ω ½ W 5% resistor
R5	1 kΩ ½ W 5% resistor

switch, shunting the voltage regulator output to ground, detouring from the normal output (that is, the protected load.)

A higher-power electronic shutdown circuit is shown in Fig. 4-14. The table for this project is given in Table 4-12.

The input voltage for this circuit is nominally about +20 V. This input is regulated to +15 V at the output. This voltage regulator can put out up to 1.0 A of current.

A logic signal on the base of Q2 activates the shutdown function, cutting off the input to the voltage regulator (IC1).

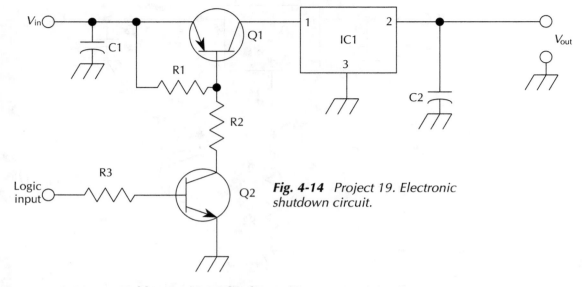

Fig. 4-14 *Project 19. Electronic shutdown circuit.*

Table 4-12 Parts list for project 19. Electronic shutdown circuit of Fig. 4-14.

IC1	LM340 series voltage regulator
Q1	PNP transistor (2N6107 or similar)
Q2	NPN transistor (2N4969, Radio Shack RS1617 or similar)
C1	0.22 µF capacitor
C2	0.1 µF capacitor
R1	470 Ω ½ W 10% resistor
R2	360 Ω 1 W 10% resistor
R3	1 kΩ ¼ W 10% resistor

Event-failure alarm

In some electronic systems, it is vital that certain events occur at more or less regular intervals. For example, a pulse must be sensed once a second. If the expected event doesn't occur, the operator must be notified so the situation can be looked into and corrected.

The circuit shown in Fig. 4-15 is an event-failure alarm circuit. The parts list for this project appears as Table 4-13.

The input signal to this circuit must be conditioned so that the expected recurring event appears as a brief grounding pulse. That is, when the event is not occurring, this signal should be HIGH, going LOW only during the expected event. Functionally,

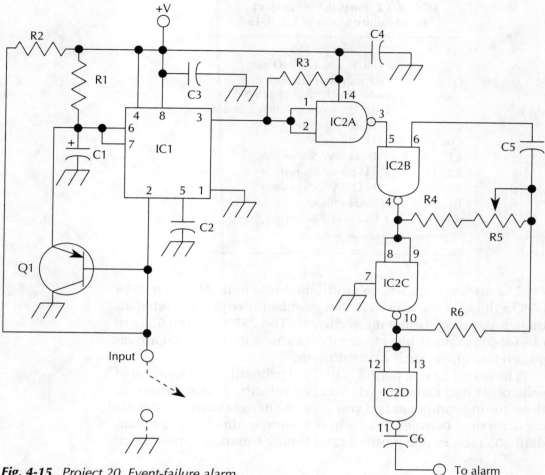

Fig. 4-15 *Project 20. Event-failure alarm.*

the input works like a simple switch shorting pin 2 of IC1 to ground. In fact, the event can be a simple closure of a mechanical or electronic switch. This input is held normally HIGH through resistor R2, so pin 2 of IC1 will see a HIGH signal unless the input forcibly brings it down to ground potential.

After one event has been detected, the next must occur before the monostable multivibrator (IC1 and its associated components) times out, or the external alarm will be triggered. The output circuitry (IC2 and its associated components) is self latching. The actual alarm-sounding device can be a piezoelectric buzzer, or one of the siren circuits presented in chapter 3, or something similar.

**Table 4-13 Parts list for project 20.
Event-failure alarm of Fig. 4-15.**

IC1	7555 timer (or 555)
IC2	CD4011 quad NAND gate
Q1	PNP transistor (2N2907, Radio Shack RS2023 or similar)
C1	10 μF 25 V electrolytic capacitor*
C2–C5	0.01 μF capacitor
C6	0.047 μF capacitor
R1	330 kΩ ¼ W 5% resistor*
R2, R3	4.7 kΩ ¼ W 5% resistor
R4	2.2 kΩ ¼ W 5% resistor
R5	100 kΩ trimpot
R6	1 MΩ ¼ W 5% resistor

*Timing component—see text.

The critical monostable multivibrator is built around a 7555 CMOS timer. A standard 555 can be substituted if you prefer, although it will consume more current. The 7555 and the 555 are pin-for-pin compatible, so no modifications in the circuit are required to support such a substitution.

The actual timing period is defined primarily by the values of resistor R1 and capacitor C1. You can substitute other values for these timing components if you want to change the maximum acceptable time between events to suit your application. The standard 555 monostable multivibrator timing equation applies here:

$$T = 1.1R_1C_1$$

Using the component values suggested in the parts list, the maximum acceptable time period between events is:

$$T = 1.1 \times 330{,}000 \times 0.00001$$
$$= 3.63 \text{ seconds}$$

If the next event isn't detected within 3.63 seconds after the last event, the alarm will be sounded.

To increase the maximum acceptable time between events, increase the value of either resistor R1 or capacitor C1, or both. Conversely, reducing the value of either or both of these timing components will reduce the circuit timing period.

A typical application for this project might be to monitor objects coming down an automated conveyor belt. Each object is detected by a light-sensitive optical sensor as it passes by, breaking a light beam, as shown in Fig. 4-16. The sensor circuitry is designed so that it goes LOW when the light beam is broken by a passing object. This signal is fed to the event failure alarm circuit. If one or more of the objects has been removed from or fallen from the conveyor belt, or is missing for any other reason, the event-failure alarm will be triggered, alerting you to the problem.

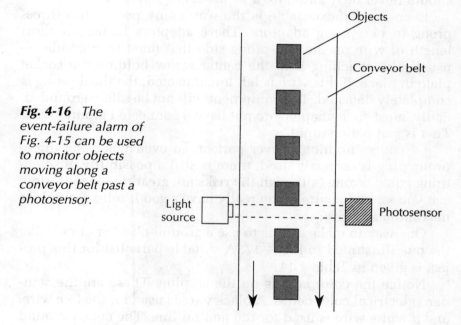

Fig. 4-16 *The event-failure alarm of Fig. 4-15 can be used to monitor objects moving along a conveyor belt past a photosensor.*

Safe-ground tester

Perhaps the greatest risk when working with any sort of electrical equipment comes from improper or insufficient grounding. A poor or interrupted ground is an open invitation to equipment damage, fire, and electrical shock.

To ensure good electrical grounding, many pieces of electrical equipment come with three-prong ac plugs. The added third prong carries no active current—it is a ground connection. With few exceptions, the equipment will work without any connection to this ground prong, and many people try to defeat the purpose of the grounding prong to fit the plug into a two-prong socket. The two-prong socket was once the norm and is still common in many areas. Three-prong extension cords are still relatively rare and unnecessarily expensive. It is often possible to force a three-prong plug into a two-prong extension cord socket, with the third prong sticking out over the edge. This is very commonly done. Yes, the equipment will usually work just fine, and there probably won't be any problems most of the time. But if something does go wrong, the results could be disasterous—to your equipment, to your home, and even to yourself and your loved ones. This sort of abuse significantly increases risk and should never be resorted to. It is just asking for trouble.

Even more inexcusable is the way many people use three-prong to two-prong adaptors. These adaptors include a short length of wire on the two-prong side that must be grounded—usually by attaching it to the center screw holding the socket plate in place. If this wire is left unconnected, the third prong is completely defeated. The equipment will not be safely grounded. Sadly, most such adapters do not have a connected ground wire. That is just plain stupid.

Of course nothing is ever perfect, so even when the three-prong plug is correctly used, there is still a possibility of something going wrong (although the risks are greatly reduced). How can you know for sure if you really have a good, solid ground for maximum security?

One way to make sure is to use a ground-checker circuit like the one illustrated in Fig. 4-17. A suitable parts list for this project is given in Table 4-14.

Notice the color coding on the ac plug. These are the standard electrical color codes. A black wire is used for the live wire, and a white wire is used for the neutral line. The center ground is usually green or brown.

Similarly, different metals are used for the two main prongs in the ac socket. The silver side (A in the schematic) is the live (black) wire connection. The neutral (white) wire connection is made to the brass side of the socket (B in the schematic).

Switch S1 is a DPST switch. Do not use two separate SPST switches. Both switch sections must always be operated in unison. Because true DPST switches are generally rather difficult to find, it will probably be easiest to use a DPDT switch and simply leave the unneeded extra contacts disconnected.

"Switch" S2 is not a switch at all. It is a circuit breaker. The parts list suggests a circuit breaker rated for 10A. In some applications, you might want to change this value to suit the equipment being protected by this project. If you increase the

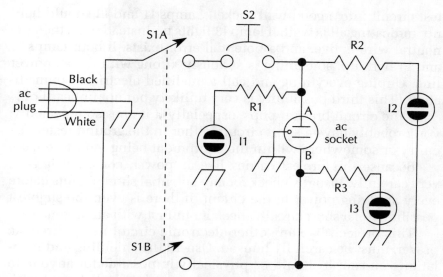

Fig. 4-17 *Project 21. Safe-ground tester.*

**Table 4-14   Parts list for project 21.
Safe-ground tester of Fig. 4-17.**

I1, I2, I3	NE-2 neon lamp
S1	DPST switch (see text)
S2	Circuit breaker (10 A) (see text)
R1, R2, R3	47 kΩ ½ W 10% resistor
ac plug	Three prong
ac socket	Three prong

current rating, you might have to use higher wattage resistors in the circuit.

You could use a fuse and holder in place of the circuit breaker, but changing fuses would probably be a nuisance in this application. A circuit breaker can be reset by pressing a small button, which is less fuss and bother and almost certainly less expensive over the long run.

Standard neon lamps are used as the indicator devices in this project. Do not try to substitute LEDs. They will almost certainly be quickly destroyed.

This safe-ground tester project is quite simple to use. Plug the equipment to be monitored into the project socket and plug the test circuit into a good wall socket. Lamps I1 and I2 should light up, indicating all is well. If lamp I3 lights up instead of I1, then the neutral wire is live, and a potential error exists. If both lamps I1 and I3 light up, something is seriously wrong with the ac power line. Unplug everything and call a qualified electrician immediately. (This third possibility is very unlikely but not unheard of.)

If the circuit breaker pops, especially if it does so repeatedly, you probably have a short circuit, either in the ground tester circuitry or somewhere within the equipment being monitored.

Because this project carries live ac power, construct it very, very carefully. Visually check for any potential short circuits before every applying power to the circuit. If there is even the slightest possibility of a short circuit, check it out first with an ohmmeter.

This project, like any other electronic circuit using direct ac power, must be carefully housed. Use all the shielding and insulation you can. It should be physically impossible for anyone to deliberately or accidentally touch any conductor that can possibly be part of the circuit at any point. Even a connection that isn't supposed to be live could become unexpectedly (and dangerously) live under certain fault conditions. Please, don't take any chances. It's not worth cutting corners.

Blown-fuse alarm

Sometimes it isn't always obvious right away when a piece of equipment stops working due to a blown fuse. Perhaps the equipment normally operates intermittently. It is not being triggered, or is dead? Some equipment gives no direct indication of operation. If indicator lights exist, they might not be informative enough, especially in critical applications.

The circuit shown in Fig. 4-18 will let you know right away when a fuse has been blown, by flashing an LED as an alarm. You don't have to watch over the equipment continuously. This project will do that for you. Just glance at it occasionally, or keep the equipment in your sight, and this circuit will alert you when you need to take action (replace the fuse and trace out the problem, if necessary). A blinking LED is much more eye catching and visible than a continuously lit LED. A suitable parts list for this project is given in Table 4-15.

Nothing is terribly critical in this circuit. Resistors R8 and R9 and capacitor C1 determine the flash rate of the LED when the alarm is activated. You might want to experiment with alternate component values here. Don't make the flash rate too fast, or the

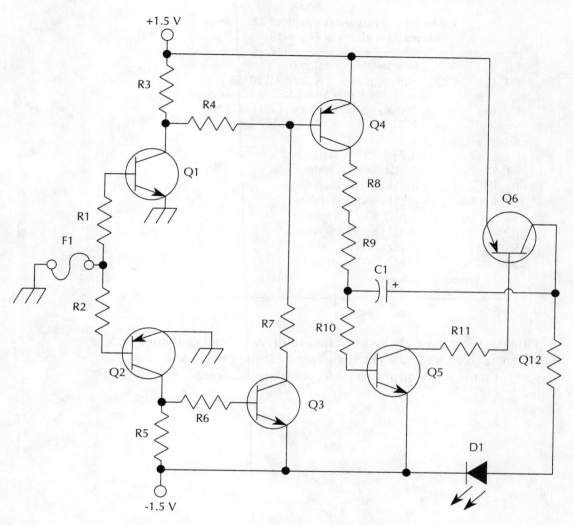

Fig. 4-18 *Project 22. Blown-fuse alarm.*

LED will appear to be continuously lit, decreasing the advantage of added visibility offered by the blinking indicator.

Because of the fairly large resistance required, two resistors (R8 and R9) are used in series. If appropriate to your desired flash rate and parts availability, you can combine these two resistors into a single unit.

Fuse F1 is the original-equipment fuse being monitored by this project. The exact fuse value is irrelevant as far as this alarm circuit is concerned—the fuse value is determined by the equipment being protected by that fuse.

**Table 4-15   Parts list for project 22.
Blown-fuse alarm of Fig. 4-18.**

F1	Fuse being monitored (see text)
Q1, Q3, Q4, Q5	NPN transistor (2N3094, GE20, SK3122, ECG128, Radio Shack RS2009 or similar)
Q2, Q6	PNP transistor (2N3906, GE21, SK3025, ECG159, Radio Shack RS1604, or similar)
D1	LED
C1	2.2 µF 25 V electrolytic capacitor*
R1, R2	1 MΩ ¼ W 5% resistor
R3, R5	100 kΩ ¼ W 5% resistor
R4, R6, R7	10 kΩ ¼ W 5% resistor
R8	1 MΩ ¼ W 5% resistor*
R9	680 kΩ ¼ W 5% resistor*
R10, R11	1 kΩ ¼ W 5% resistor
R12	39 Ω ¼ W 5% resistor

*Timing component—see text.

This circuit can easily be modified to drive an external audible alarm such as a piezoelectric buzzer or some other sounding device, if that is more appropriate to your application.

Electronic combination locks

YOU KNOW THAT ONE WAY TO PROTECT PORTABLE POSSESSIONS or equipment from theft or unauthorized use is to use a lock. There are two basic types of locks—key locks and combination locks.

A key lock requires a specially cut key to turn its tumblers and open the lock. In electronics there is something similar in the key switch. This is a mechanical switch that can only be operated with a key, similar to your house keys or car keys. Most commercial key switches available to the electronics hobbyist are of the SPST types, but other, more complex switching arrangements are possible. Key switches are often used in industrial equipment. One good source for key switches for the hobbyist is discarded or obsolete equipment sold by electronics surplus dealers, often for amazingly low prices. These key switches are exactly the same as the ignition in your car. They also can be used in electronic equipment to prevent unauthorized persons from turning on the protected equipment or from performing certain operations. Such key switches are often used on cash registers. A "clerk" key enables the basic functions of the cash register so the clerk can ring up sales. But special functions such as returns, voided sales, and clearing the register memory require the use of a "master" key that can turn the key switch to additional positions.

The other basic type of mechanical lock is the combination lock. A series of numbers must be entered in the correct sequence via a rotating dial to open the lock.

In this chapter you look at a few electronic equivalents to the mechanical combination lock. There are two basic ways an electronic combination lock can be used. Such a circuit can restrict operation of a protected piece of electronic equipment (or certain functions of such equipment) much like the use of a key switch. An electronic combination lock circuit also can control a solenoid that physically moves some sort of physical latching device. The protected item (which does not have to be an electronic circuit) cannot be removed without opening the lock, just as with an ordinary mechanical combination lock.

The chief advantage of a combination lock is that there is no key to lose. But keep a written record of the combination somewhere, so you aren't faced with disaster if you forget it.

The combination is entered by pushing a series of push buttons in the correct sequence. Pressing an incorrect button, or pushing the right buttons in the wrong order, will often disable the lock for some period of time to discourage potential intruders from trying combinations at random until they get lucky.

In use, the circuitry for an electronic combination lock must be securely housed. An intruder who is knowledgeable in electronics should not be able to open up the case and disable the circuit. Ideally, the guts of the circuit should not be accessible without opening the lock, which can only be done by entering the correct combination.

Latching electronic combination lock

An electronic combination lock doesn't necessarily have to be a very complex and sophisticated circuit to give good security. Obviously, the longer the combination is (the more numbers required in the sequence), the harder it will be for an intruder to guess the correct combination and gain unauthorized entry. A large number of code switches, and a fairly long combination might have millions of possible combinations, with only one combination that will successfully open the lock. Great security, but it can also be a major nuisance for any legitimate user of the system. Do you really want to hassle with a 25-switch keypad and remember a seven- or eight-step combination? Long combinations are especially bothersome if the protected system is something you have to access frequently. Do you really need that much security?

After all, if there are just a couple thousand possible combinations, the odds are very good that an intruder won't guess the correct sequence. And it will still take quite a bit of time and patience to try every possible combination to find the right one. Is an intruder likely to be that determined to get past your electronic lock? Probably not.

For most common applications, the electronic combination lock circuit shown in Fig. 5-1 will probably offer plenty of security at minimal cost. A suitable parts list for this project is given in Table 5-1.

The coded keypad for this electronic combination lock project consists of just seven switches. You can easily add more dummy switches in parallel with S4 through S7 if you choose. A three-digit combination is required to release the lock. The physical placement of the active switches and the dummy switches on the keypad will determine the actual combination "numbers". Choose an arrangement that has meaning to you and is easy to remember but will be unobvious to any intruder.

Switches S1, S2, and S3 are the active combination switches in this circuit. Switches S4 through S7 are dummy switches to make the keypad more complex, permitting more false entries. Pressing any of the dummy switches will negate the current combination, and will disable the circuitry for almost 30 seconds. The circuit will ignore any further combination entries during this time-out period. Even if the correct combination is entered during this time, it will be ignored by the circuit. This will help frustrate and discourage any potential intruder who is trying to guess the combination.

Don't be too obvious in your choices for the combination. Be sneaky. For example, don't use the first three digits of your phone number; instead, use the second, fourth, and sixth digit of the phone number. Don't use your birthdate—that is usually the first thing an informed intruder is likely to try because so many people have used birthday combinations. If you must use a birth

Table 5-1   Parts list for project 23.
Latching electronic combination lock of Fig. 5-1.

Q1, Q3	PNP transistor (SK3004, ECG102, GE-2, or similar)
Q2	SCR (select to suit load—see text)
D1–D3	diode (1N4001 or similar)
K1	9 V relay with contacts to suit load
K2, K3	9 V miniature dc relay (5000 Ω coil)
C1	33 μF 25 V electrolytic capacitor
C2	100 μF 25 V electrolytic capacitor
R1, R2	1 kΩ ¼ W 5% resistor
R3	100 kΩ ¼ W 5% resistor
S1–S7	SPST normally open push-button switch
S8	SPST key switch

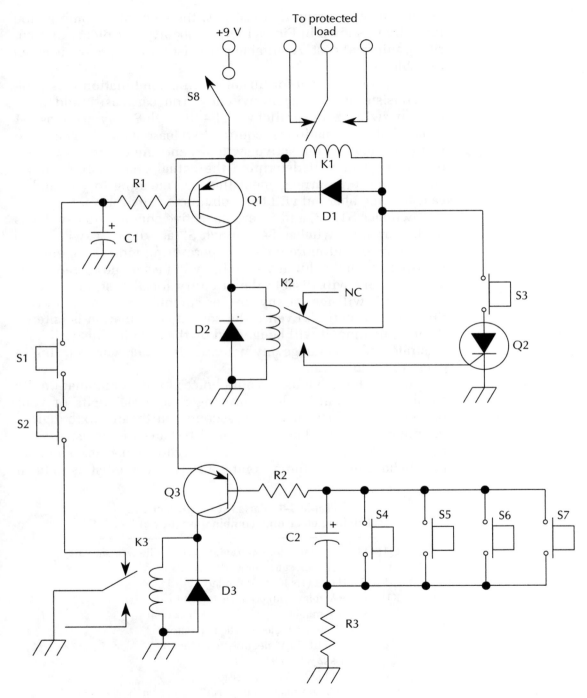

Fig. 5-1 *Project 23. Latching electronic combination lock.*

date, at least scramble the digits. For example, if your birthday is April 17, don't use 417 or 174 as the combination. Reverse the numerical order—714 or 471. Even better, put the month in middle of the date—147. Be creative. The first idea that comes to your mind as a good mnemonic for the combination will probably be too obvious. Try something a little more devious, but try something that only you can easily remember.

A three-digit combination might not seem too tough to crack, but it would require the aspiring intruder to have plenty of time and patience. To further complicate matters for the intruder, the sequence for the combination is not S1 then S2, then S3, as with most other electronic combination lock circuits. Switches S1 and S2 must be closed simultaneously. Closing just one or the other won't help. Pressing S1 then S2 also won't accomplish anything at all. Notice that these two normally open switches are in series. This means that to complete the circuit, both of these switches must be closed together. To release the lock, you must press S1 and S2 together, then press S3. Pressing any of the dummy switches (S4 through S7) will disable the circuit for almost half a minute, so the intruder will have to wait and then start all over. No one is likely to want to try out every possible combination, even with this simple combination lock circuit.

The exact transistor types used in this circuit aren't too critical. Almost any low-power PNP transistor should work. Both transistors should be of the same type number. If there is any doubt over whether a specific type of transistor will work, please first breadboard the circuit before you start soldering. That is always a good idea for any electronics project anyway.

Switch S8 might be considered optional in this project, but using it is a very good idea. This switch is a simple power switch for the circuit. It permits you to disable the locking circuit when you need to. Unexpected things can always go wrong, so there should be some way to manually bypass the electronic lock.

Obviously, it should not be possible for any intruder to operate this switch, or the entire project will serve no real purpose at all. Use a locking key switch, or conceal the switch carefully. If you are using this electronic combination lock project to protect a room or storage area, such as a garage door, you could put the manual override switch (S8) within the protected area, so the potential intruder can't get to it. Whether or not this is possible or appropriate will depend on the nature of your specific application.

To use or test the project, switch S8 must be closed so the circuitry can receive the power it needs to operate. To test the project once you've built it, you might want to first temporarily re-move relay K1 and its protective diode (D1) from the circuit and replace them with a small lamp that can handle the 9 V supply voltage used in this project.

Simultaneously depress push buttons S1 and S2 and watch relay K1 to make sure that it closes. You should hear a small click, and you might be able to actually see the relay internal switch contacts move. (The physical construction of some relays might block your view.) If in doubt, you can check out the conti-nuity of K2 relay contacts with an ohmmeter or continuity tester. Like any other switch, when the normally open relay contacts are open (deactivated), you should get an infinite (or near infi-nite) resistance reading. Closing these switch contacts (activating the relay) should drop the resistance reading down to zero or very close to it.

With some relays, it might be necessary to use a pair of nee-dle-nose pliers to gently bend the metal tab the armature spring is connected to, so that the relay contacts will be positioned properly for correct operation. If you do this, be very, very care-ful. Do not force or break the tab, or you will have to replace the entire relay.

It is usually best to operate a relay in an upright position. In other positions, you might eventually get some unreliability problems. With some relays, such problems will show up right away. Others will seem to work fine for a while, then they'll stop working as the contacts slip from the correct positions.

If relay K2 does not respond, the first thing to check is that you actually pressed the correct buttons. Trace your wiring very carefully. It is quite easy to make a mistake here.

If you still have problems with this portion of the circuit, re-move power from the circuit and double check all your wiring one more time. You can't double check the connections too many times in any electronics project. Are all of the solder joints clean and shiny? If one or more joints looks dull or gritty, you might have a bad solder joint. Resolder any suspect connections.

Assuming there is no problem in the construction of the cir-cuit, and you have correctly pressed S1 and S2 together, if the re-lay still doesn't activate, the most likely trouble spots are a bad transistor (Q1) or a bad relay K2.

Once activated by switches S1 and S2, the relay should re-main activated for only about a couple of seconds. To extend this time period, you can experiment with larger values for resistor R1 and capacitor C1, especially the capacitor.

Once this portion of the circuit has been demonstrated to function correctly, your next step in the testing procedure is to try the complete combination. Press S1 and S2 together, then press S3. The lamp should light up. If it does not, and there is no problem with the circuit wiring or the entered key sequence, then the most likely culprit is the SCR (Q2). It certainly should be getting a sufficient gate voltage if relay K2 has been activated. (Make sure you are actually using the relay normally open contacts and not the normally closed contacts.) Use a voltmeter to make sure the SCR is conducting. If not, check the manufacturer's specification sheet for the SCR you are using. Is 9 V a sufficient gate voltage? It certainly should be for almost any low-power SCR, but you might run across an oddball exception.

Unless you happen to have a defective or inappropriate SCR, the test lamp should light up without any problem when the correct combination (S1 and S2, then S3) is entered.

The next step in the testing procedure for this project is to make sure the dummy switches disable the combination lock properly. Press S1 and S2 together, then press any of the dummy switches (S4 through S7). Relay K3 should be activated. Trace out any potential problems in the same manner as described for the Q1/K2 portion of the circuit. While this relay is activated, pressing switch S3 should not accomplish anything. The lamp (in place of relay K1) should not light up. The circuit should ignore these switches, and relay K2 should remain deactivated.

This relay (K3) should be held activated for a period of approximately 30 seconds, and then it should automatically deactivate itself. To experiment with different timing periods, you might want to try different component values for resistors R2 and R3 and capacitor C2.

This completes the testing procedure for the electronic combination lock project. Remove the test lamp and replace relay K1 and diode D1, as shown in the original schematic. House the project appropriately, and you're ready to put the circuit to work protecting your property.

Nonlatching electronic combination lock

Your next project is a somewhat more sophisticated electronic combination lock circuit. Unlike the previous project, the output of this circuit does not latch itself, and therefore no manual reset procedure is required. The circuit will automatically reset (relock) after a brief timing period.

For convenience and greater clarity, the schematic diagram for this project is divided into two sections, in Fig. 5-2 and Fig. 5-3. Four connections are made between these two circuits—the power supply connections (V+ and ground), and the two points marked A and B in the diagrams. Connect the two A points together and the two B points together. A suitable parts list for this project is given in Table 5-2.

Notice that this circuit uses several TTL integrated circuits. These devices demand a tightly regulated power supply of exactly +5 V (within 0.5 V in either direction). An incorrect supply voltage will result in erratic operation at best, and is very likely to result in permanent damage to one or more of the ICs in the circuit.

The combination is entered via four normally open push-button switches (S1 through S4), which feed clock pulses into a string of four JK type flip-flops (IC1 and IC2). There are two flip-flops on each 74107 IC. You could easily extend the project for a longer combination by adding more flip-flop stages like the ones shown in Fig. 5-2.

There are also six dummy switches (S4 through S10). Pressing any of these dummy switches resets all of the flip-flop stages, cancelling out any previous correct entries. Notice that this CLEAR signal is carried from Fig. 5-2 to Fig. 5-3 as line B.

The Q outputs of the four flip-flops are combined through the gates of IC3 and IC4. A truth table for this gating network is given in Table 5-3. Notice that this network is essentially a four-input NAND gate. Such NAND gates are available in dedicated IC form, but they tend to be difficult to find and rather expensive, so use standard two-input gates. If you prefer, you can replace IC3 and IC4 with a single four-input NAND gate device. Other than eliminating capacitor C4, there will be no other changes in the circuitry to accommodate this modification. The project will function in exactly the same way.

The output of this gating network is carried over from Fig. 5-2 to Fig. 5-3 via line A. Signal A triggers a monostable multivibrator (IC5). The output (pin 6) of this chip goes HIGH for a time period determined by the values of resistor R5 and capacitor C6. During this time period, transistor Q1 is switched on, activating relay K1, "opening" the lock. When the monostable multivibrator times out, the transistor switches off, deactivating the relay. The lock automatically "relocks" itself.

The Q (not Q) output of the monostable multivibrator (IC5, pin 1) is fed back to line B to clear all the flip-flops.

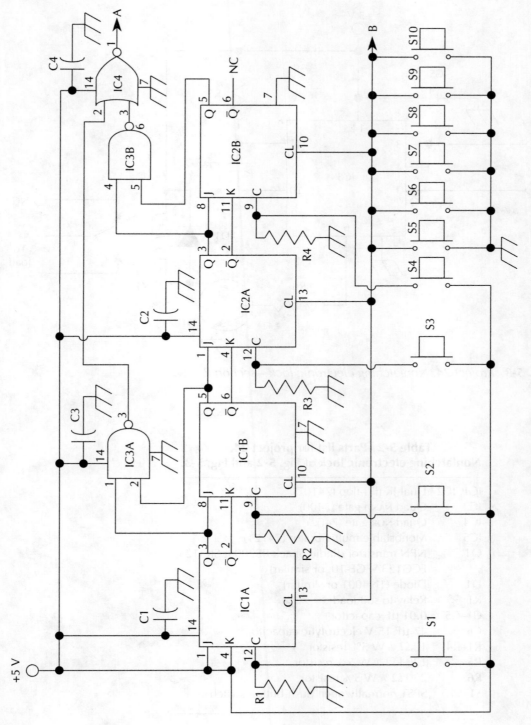

Fig. 5-2 *Project 24. Nonlatching electronic lock—section A.*

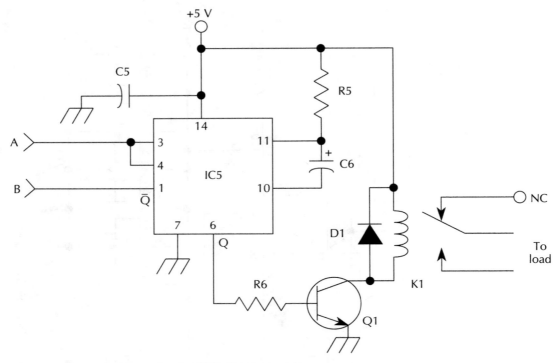

Fig. 5-3 *Project 24. Nonlatching electronic lock—section B.*

**Table 5-2 Parts list for project 24.
Nonlatching electronic lock of Fig. 5-2 and Fig. 5-3.**

IC1, IC2	Dual JK flip-flop (74107)
IC3	Quad NAND gate (7400)
IC4	Quad NOR gate (7402)
IC5	Monostable multivibrator (74121)
Q1	NPN transistor (Radio Shack RS2009, SK3124, ECG123A, GE-10, or similar)
D1	Diode (1N4001 or similar)
K1	Relay to suit load
C1–C5	0.01 μF capacitor
C6	47 μF 15 V electrolytic capacitor
R1–R4	1 kΩ ¼ W 5% resistor
R5	120 kΩ ¼ W 5% resistor
R6	220 Ω ¼ W 5% resistor
S1–S10	SPST normally open push-button switch

**Table 5-3 Truth table for the preset,
preclear, and clocked inputs of a JK flip-flop.**

Inputs		Outputs	
Preset	**Preclear**	**Q**	**Q̄**
0	0	Disallowed state	
0	1	1	0
1	0	0	1
1	1	Determined by clocked inputs	

Inputs			Outputs	
J	**K**	**Clock**	**Q**	**Q̄**
0	0	N	No change	
0	0	T	No change	
0	1	N	No change	1
0	1	T	0	
1	0	N	No change	
1	0		1	0
1		T	No change	
1	1	N	Output states reverse	
		T	(0 becomes 1 and 1 becomes 0)	

To operate this combination lock, first briefly depress any of the dummy switches (S5 through S10) to ensure that all of the flip-flop stages are cleared. At this time, the Q outputs of all of the flip-flop stages will be LOW. Each Q output is connected to the J input of the next stage. Because this signal is now LOW, flip-flops IC1B, IC2A, and IC2B will more of less ignore any key presses.

Refer to the JK flip-flop truth table given in Table 5-3. The next step of the combination is to briefly press and release switch S1, which applies a clock pulse to IC1A, causing it to toggle its outputs. Its Q output goes HIGH (and its Q [not Q] output goes LOW), permitting the next stage (IC1B) to respond to a clock pulse when switch S2 is briefly depressed. Now, this flip-flop Q output goes HIGH. S3 and S4 are then depressed in sequence to activate flip-flops IC2A and IC2B.

Pressing switches S1 through S4 in order will result in all four Q outputs going HIGH, causing the gating network to trigger the monostable multivibrator, opening the lock.

Pressing these switches out of sequence simply confuses the flip-flops, and the lock does not release. If any of the dummy switches (S5 through S10) is depressed at any time within the combination sequence, the flip-flops are all reset back to the beginning (Q output LOW) states. The combination must be started over from the beginning to work the lock.

Additional dummy switches can easily be added in parallel with the ones shown here if you desire.

❖ **6**

Intrusion detection

WHEN MOST PEOPLE THINK OF SECURITY ALARMS, WHAT THEY have in mind is the burglar alarm or intrusion detector. Such an alarm system is triggered whenever someone or something is detected entering or moving within the protected area.

Several practical intrusion-detector projects are presented and discussed in this chapter. For the most part, these circuits are relatively simple but quite effective and reliable. Any of these simple control circuits can be used as the heart of a rather sophisticated, customized alarm system.

To keep the schematics as simple as possible, the sensor switches in these intrusion detector projects are shown as simple push-button switches. Of course, these push-button switches can be replaced by some other appropriate sensor device or circuit, as described in chapter 2. In most cases, the only real restriction is whether the desired sensor device provides the correct switching action (normally open or normally closed), as called for by the alarm-control circuit.

Similarly, the output device of these intrusion-detector alarms is shown as a piezoelectric buzzer in the schematics, only because this is usually the simplest choice. You can replace the buzzer in any of these projects with an alarm bell or siren or one of the alarm-sounding circuits presented in chapter 3. Almost any circuit that generates a clearly audible sound can be substituted. The only real restriction is that the control circuit output voltage must match the requirements or limitations of the sounding device or circuit.

In practical terms, this restriction usually isn't too great. If the alarm control circuit puts out too high a voltage, it can easily be dropped down to the desired level with a simple voltage-divider string, made up of a couple simple resistors. Use Ohm's Law to determine the appropriate resistance values.

If you run up against a situation where the output voltage from the alarm control circuit isn't high enough to drive the desired sounding device, you might be able to overcome the problem by adding a suitable amplifier stage to boost the voltage as necessary, or the output signal from the control circuit could operate a relay that switches a higher voltage.

There is plenty of room for modifications and customization of any of these intrusion-detector projects. The circuits presented here are really just starting points that you can use to create the ideal intrusion-detection system to suit your own individual needs.

Super-simple panic-button burglar alarm

A very, very simple burglar alarm circuit is illustrated in Fig. 6-1. A suitable parts list for this project is given in Table 6-1.

Switches S1 though S3 are all normally open (NO) momentary-action switches. Briefly closing any one of these switches

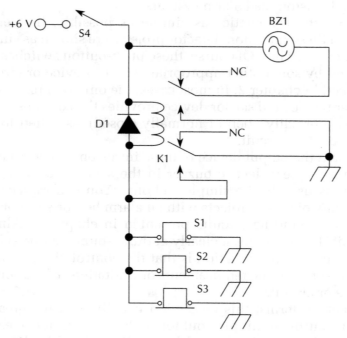

Fig. 6-1 *Project 25. Super-simple panic-button burglar alarm.*

Table 6-1   Parts list for project 25.
Super-simple panic-button burglar alarm of Fig. 6-1.

D1	Diode (1N4001 or similar)
K1	6 V relay with DPDT contacts
BZ1	6 V buzzer
S1, S2, S3	Normally open SPST push-button switch
S4	SPST switch (key switch recommended—see text)

triggers the relay, causing the buzzer (BZ1) to sound. The second set of switch contacts in this DPDT relay are wired to make the relay self latching. Once activated, the relay will remain activated, even if the triggering switch (S1, S2, or S3) is released and permitted to open again. The buzzer will continue to sound until power switch S4 is opened, shutting down the alarm circuit. This is the only way to deactivate the relay in this circuit.

At a minimum, hide or disguise switch S4 in some way, or any intruder can easily override the alarm very quickly. For maximum protection, use a lock-key switch for S4. Without the key, the triggered alarm can not be turned off. Of course, it is assumed that the electricity is enclosed in some sort of reasonably secure housing, or it can be disabled simply by yanking out the wires.

Any normally open (NO) switching devices can be used for triggering switches S1 through S3. Although three switches are shown here, you can easily add more in parallel with these.

For automated intrusion detection, normally open switching generally isn't too desirable. The switch can be effectively disabled, simply by cutting the wire connecting it to the circuitry. As far as the alarm circuit is concerned then, the switch never closes, so the alarm is never triggered. But in some cases, such as a switch on the inside of a closed door or window, a normally open switching arrangement will do fine and will probably be a little less expensive and easier to wire than a normally closed switching system would be.

Pressure switches under a rug or mat can be used in some applications. The most likely use of this alarm circuit, however, will be as a panic button. Ordinary normally open push-button switches are used. They are mounted in convenient, but not too visible locations. If you are menaced by an intruder, you can secretly press one of the hidden buttons, triggering the alarm.

Of course, testing this alarm circuit is certainly as easy as it could possibly be. Just briefly depress one of the panic-button switches, and the buzzer should start sounding, unless there is something wrong with your circuit. To shut the alarm off, you will need to disconnect the power from the circuit (via key switch S4) for a moment. Closing this switch repowers and rearms the alarm circuit.

Super-simple burglar alarm with NC switching

Simple and inexpensive burglar alarm circuits can be built using normally open (NO) switching. Such a circuit typically is simpler overall than a comparable alarm circuit utilizing normally closed (NC) switching. Normally open switches are generally easier to find and are slightly less expensive than normally closed switches of similar quality. So why would anyone want to bother with a burglar alarm circuit with normally closed switching?

The answer is simple—normally closed switches do a better job and provide better security than normally open switches in a practical burglar alarm.

A simple burglar alarm system with normally open switching is illustrated in block diagram form in Fig. 6-2. Closing the normally open switch completes the circuit and permits the alarm to sound. But what if an intruder first cuts a wire connected to the normally open sensing switch to the alarm circuitry? There will always be an open circuit. The switch will be ignored and the intruder can do anything without setting off the alarm, because the alarm circuit "thinks" it still sees a safe, open switch.

Now, consider what happens if normally closed switching is used in a similar system, as illustrated in the block diagram of Fig. 6-3. In this case, the switch circuit must be closed and complete to prevent the alarm from sounding. Opening the normally

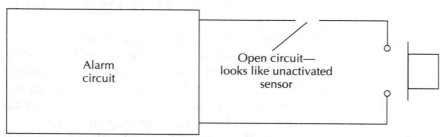

Fig. 6-2 *A burglar alarm system using normally open switches can be defeated by cutting the connecting wires.*

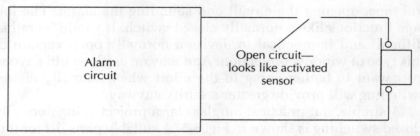

Fig. 6-3 *A burglar alarm system using normally closed switches will be set off if a connecting wire is cut.*

closed switch breaks the circuit and triggers the alarm. If an intruder tries cutting a connecting wire, the effect is exactly the same as if the sensing switch was opened—the circuit is broken, and the alarm goes off. A burglar alarm circuit with normally closed switching cannot be defeated by cutting a connecting wire between a sensing switch and the alarm circuit.

Also, some types of intrusion switches naturally take a normally closed form. For example, a common way to protect a window is to use foil tape, as shown in Fig. 6-4. Normally, this foil tape completes the circuit and acts like a closed switch. If an intruder breaks the window, he or she will also break some of the

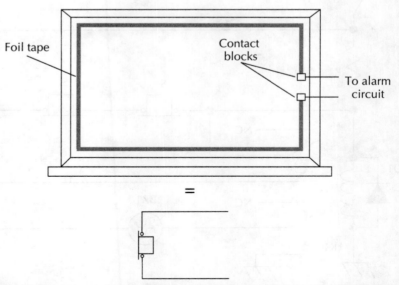

Fig. 6-4 *Foil tape, used to protect a window naturally acts like a normally closed switch.*

foil tape, opening the circuit and sounding the alarm. The foil tape functions like a normally closed switch. It would be rather difficult and impractical to devise a normally open version of this type of window protection. And why on earth would anyone ever want to bother going to the effort when normally closed switching will provide greater security anyway?

A simple, but practical burglar alarm project using normally closed switching is shown in Fig. 6-5. A suitable parts list for this simple project is given in Table 6-2.

Although three normally closed switches (S2 through S4) are shown here, you could eliminate one or two or add more in series with the switches shown in the schematic diagram. Whenever any one of the series normally closed switches is opened, the alarm is triggered. This alarm circuit is self latching. That is, reclosing the switch once the alarm has been triggered will not shut down the alarm. To silence the buzzer (BZ1) and reset the circuit, switch S1 must be opened to remove power from the circuit. For true security, this reset switch should be a locking switch that can be opened only with a key. At the very least, hide

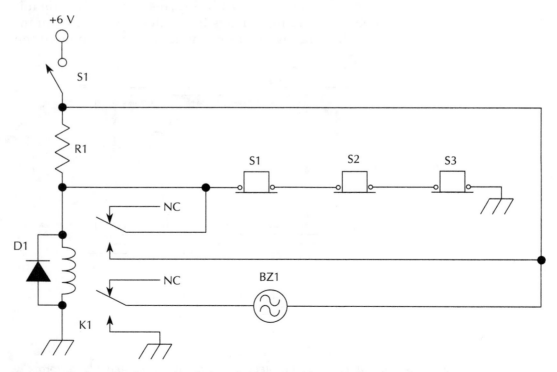

Fig. 6-5 *Project 26. Super-simple burglar-alarm with normally closed switching.*

Table 6-2   Parts list for project 26.
Super-simple burglar alarm (Fig. 6-5) with NC switching.

D1	Diode (1N4001 or similar)
K1	6 V relay with DPDT contacts
BZ1	6 V buzzer
S1	SPST switch (key switch recommended)
S2, S3, S4	Normally closed SPST push-button switch (or other)
R1	1 MΩ ¼ W 5% resistor

the reset switch in an unobvious place, preferably as inaccessible to any intruder as you can manage.

When all the sensing switches are closed (that is, in their normal positions), the upper end of the relay coil is held at ground potential through the switches. Because both sides of the relay coil are more or less at ground potential, the relay is deactivated. The buzzer is silent, and nothing much happens in the circuit.

Now, when any one of the series normally closed switches is opened, the circuit from the upper end of the relay coil to ground is broken. The circuit supply voltage (+6 V) is now fed to the upper end of the relay coil through resistor R1. The exact value of this resistor is not particularly critical, but it should be rather large, so the positive supply voltage is effectively out of the circuit when all of the switches are closed, providing a direct path to ground. This resistor prevents short circuiting of the power supply.

This positive voltage activates the relay, and its normally open switch contacts close. The upper set of switch contacts in the schematic diagram are used to self latch the relay. This switch connects the upper side of the relay coil directly to +V, keeping it activated as long as power is continuously applied to the circuit.

The second set of relay switch contacts apply the supply voltage to the buzzer (BZ1), causing it to sound. Notice that if the triggering switch is reclosed, the relay will remain activated, and the alarm will continue to sound. The only way to turn it off is to open reset switch S1 for a moment.

This burglar alarm project is very crude, and should not be relied upon in any application requiring serious security. It is included here primarily for educational purposes. The basic concepts and principles used here will also be used in the more sophisticated burglar alarm projects discussed in this chapter.

Simple low-power burglar alarm

The burglar alarm with normally closed switching circuit of Fig. 6-5 is functional but very limited. It is intended primarily as a demonstration circuit to illustrate the basic principles involved.

An improved normally closed switch burglar alarm circuit is shown in Fig. 6-6. A suitable parts list for this project is given in Table 6-3.

One major advantage of this circuit is its very low current consumption. This is a particularly important feature if battery power is used, which should generally be the case for most burglar alarm systems. If ac power is used, an intruder can disable it by cutting off power at the fuse box or simply unplugging the circuit. A battery-operated burglar alarm system will also continue

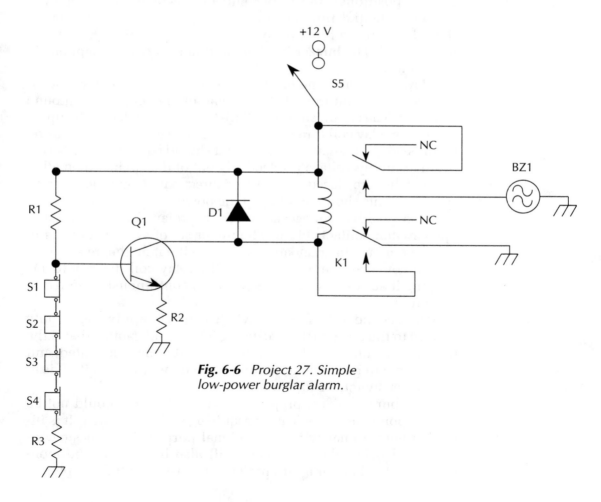

Fig. 6-6 *Project 27. Simple low-power burglar alarm.*

**Table 6-3 Parts list for project 27.
Simple low-power burglar alarm of Fig. 6-6.**

Q1	NPN transistor (GE20, SK3122, ECG108, Radio Shack RS2009, or similar)
D1	Diode (1N4001 or similar)
K1	12 V relay with DPDT contacts
BZ1	12 V buzzer
S1–S4	Normally closed SPST push-button switch (or other)
S5	SPST switch (key switch recommended)
R1	12 kΩ ¼ W 5% resistor
R2, R3	1 kΩ ¼ W 5% resistor
	Optional addition for Fig 6-7:
S6	Normally open SPST push-button switch

to function even in a power black out. Of course, you must check the condition of the batteries periodically to make sure they aren't dead when the alarm is really needed. Notice that this circuit calls for +12 V power supply.

In its normal waiting mode, this circuit draws only about 1 mA (0.001 A) of current. Of course, when the alarm is set off, more power will be consumed, primarily by the buzzer (BZ1) or other sounding device.

Although four normally closed switches (S1 through S4) are shown here, you could eliminate one or two, or add more in series with the switches shown in the schematic diagram.

Whenever any one of the series normally closed switches is opened, the alarm is triggered. This alarm circuit is self latching. That is, reclosing the switch once the alarm has been triggered will not shut down the alarm. To silence the buzzer (BZ1) and reset the circuit, switch S5 must be opened to remove power from the circuit. As in the earlier project of this type, to achieve maximum security, this reset switch should be a locking switch that can only be opened with a key. At the very least, hide the reset switch in an unobvious and relatively inaccessible (to the intruder) place. Of course, the location of the reset switch (and the key) should be relatively convenient for you.

When all the sensing switches are closed (that is, in their normal positions), the base of the transistor (Q1) is biased to hold the relay coil in a deactivated state. In some cases, better and more reliable operation can be achieved if the value of resistor R3 is reduced, or this component can be eliminated altogether. While the transistor is biased in this way, the buzzer (BZ1) remains silent and nothing much happens in the circuit.

Now, when any one of the series normally closed switches is opened, the bias voltage on the base of the transistor is changed so that it now applies sufficient power across the relay coil to activate the relay.

At this time, the normally open relay switch contacts close. The lower set of switch contacts in the schematic diagram are used to self latch the relay. This switch connects the upper side of the relay coil directly to ground, keeping it activated as long as power is continuously applied to the circuit.

The second (upper) set of relay switch contacts apply the supply voltage to the buzzer (BZ1), causing it to sound. Notice that if the triggering switch is now reclosed, the relay still remains activated, and the alarm continues to sound. The only way to turn it off is to open reset switch S1 for a moment.

The particular transistor type used in this circuit is not too critical. Many common, low-power NPN transistors should work fine, in addition to the general-purpose devices suggested in the parts list for this project.

A variation on this project is illustrated in Fig. 6-7. Added is a normally open panic-button switch (S6). If desired, additional normally open switches can be added in parallel with S6.

When this normally open switch is momentarily closed, the collector of the transistor (Q1) is forced to ground, activating the relay. As in the other version of this project, the relay is wired to be self latching. Releasing the normally open switch and permitting it to reopen will not turn the alarm back off. That can only be done via locking switch S5.

Sophisticated burglar alarm systems often use both normally open and normally closed switches for different purposes, to maximize the protection offered by the alarm circuitry.

Portable security alarm

It is not too difficult to install a burglar or intrusion alarm in a fixed location, such as a house. Chapter 7 gives you more details on how to do this.

But what if you travel a lot? Just how secure is your hotel room? Could somebody get in during the night?

And how can you protect portable equipment, such as a laptop computer, or a personal stereo? These items can be quite expensive, and a major hassle to lose, but they can be very tempting targets to light-fingered thieves.

The circuit shown in Fig. 6-8 can address both of these types

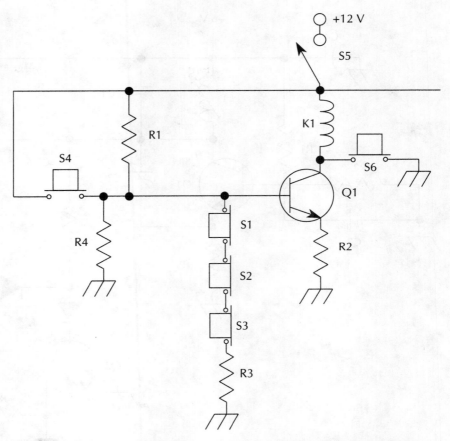

Fig. 6-7 *This variation of the circuit of Fig. 6-6 features a panic button.*

of portable security problems. A suitable parts list for this project is given in Table 6-4.

The protected item must have a metallic case or handle, which is the most likely place for it to be touched. For example, if you are securing the door to your hotel room, the circuit should be connected to the doorknob. Ideally, the door itself should be wood, or some other nonconductive material. The project will work with a metallic door, but it might be more difficult to adjust the sensitivity to prevent false triggering.

The door must have a metallic doorknob. If the doorknob is made of plastic or glass, this project won't work. In a pinch, you could cover a plastic or glass door knob with aluminum foil, which is connected to the alarm circuitry. If anyone touches the doorknob (or tries to remove the foil) while the alarm circuit is activated, the alarm will sound. As shown here, the actual alarm

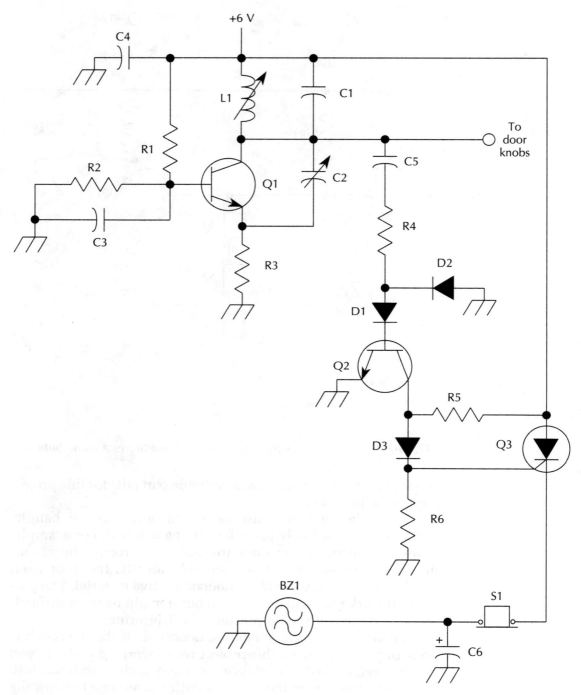

Fig. 6-8 *Project 28. Portable security alarm.*

**Table 6-4   Parts list for project 28.
Portable security alarm of Fig. 6-8.**

Q1	NPN transistor (GE10, SK3124, ECG123A, Radio Shack RS2009, or similar)
Q2	NPN transistor (GE20, SK3020, Radio Shack RS2016, or similar)
Q3	SCR 30 V, 800 mA (minimum ratings) (Radio Shack 276-1067 or similar)
D1, D2	Diode (Radio Shack 276-1123 or similar)
D3	Diode (1N4148, 1N914, or similar)
L1	15 μH (microhenry) adjustable RF coil
C1	47 pF (picofarad) mylar or silvered mica capacitor
C2	365 pF trimmer capacitor
C3, C4, C5	0.047 μF capacitor
C6	47 μF 25 V electrolytic capacitor
R1	47 kΩ ¼ W 5% resistor
R2	10 kΩ ¼ W 5% resistor
R3, R6	1 kΩ ¼ W 5% resistor
R4	470 Ω ¼ W 5% resistor
R5	6.8 kΩ ¼ W 5% resistor
S1	Normally open SPST push-button switch
BZ	6 V buzzer

is a small electrical buzzer (BZ1), but you could substitute almost any other type of alarm indication device that you choose, provided it can be driven by the project 6 V power supply.

There is plenty of leeway for using different transistors in this circuit than the ones suggested in the parts list. First breadboard the circuit to make sure your selected transistors will work properly in this project. Some won't, especially for Q1.

Transistor Q1 and its associated components makes up an oscillator circuit. The output of this oscillator is rectified by diodes D1 and D2 before being applied to transistor Q2. This transistor serves essentially as an electronic switch. Normally, the collector of transistor Q2 holds the gate of Q3, an SCR, at a level near ground potential (0 V). Of course, this keeps the SCR shut off, and nonconducting, so no voltage reaches the buzzer (BZ1), and it remains silent.

Notice that there is an external connection point at the output of the oscillator (Q1). The doorknob or the metallic case or handle of the equipment to be protected is connected to this point. There is no risk of electrical shock at this point in the circuit, especially if batteries are used for the power supply.

The human body can act as a capacitor. This phenomenon is often referred to as *hand capacitance*, though, strictly speaking, the effect is not at all limited to the hands. In this particular application, you are probably only concerned with hands anyway.

If someone touches the protected doorknob (or whatever), their hand capacitance will detune the oscillator circuit, effectively killing its output signal. This causes transistor Q2 to switch off. The gate of the SCR (Q3) is no longer held at ground potential through Q2. Instead, a positive voltage, from the power supply, is fed to the gate through resistor R5 and diode D3. This causes the SCR to turn on and start conducting. This feeds the supply voltage to the buzzer (BZ1), making it sound.

What happens if someone briefly touches the protected doorknob, then immediately lets go? It won't do them any good, no matter how fast their reflexes might be. The buzzer will continue to sound until the circuit is reset. Once it has been turned on, an SCR will continue to conduct, even if the gate signal is removed. The only way to turn it off is to break the current flow from anode to cathode.

The alarm circuit can be reset by momentarily opening switch S1. This must be a normally closed type switch. It is open, only as long as the push button is being depressed. Just a quick press will be sufficient to reset the alarm circuit.

For a hotel door protection alarm, there is no way for any intruder to disable the alarm. The circuit board is placed on the inside of the door, and connected to the inside doorknob (usually). All an intruder outside the door can do is touch the outside doorknob, which triggers the alarm. You must be inside the room to get to the reset button.

Notice that this particular alarm project will not protect your hotel room when you are not there. You must be inside the protected room yourself to use this alarm circuit.

If you are using this circuit to protect a piece of portable equipment, you will need to hid and protect the reset and the circuitry in some way. Often you can open up the case of the equipment to be protected and have enough room inside to add this alarm circuit. Hide the reset switch in some spot where it is not obvious and you can get at it conveniently when you need to. In some applications, you might want to replace the momentary-action push-button switch with a locking switch that requires a key to change its position. It will take a few seconds longer to reset the alarm in this case, but it will offer far greater security.

It should be fairly obvious that there would be no point in using a lock switch for the reset button if you are using this project to protect a hotel room door as described above. The intruder can't get to the reset button anyway (at least, not without the alarm sounding for a while first), so it doesn't much matter if an intruder needs a key or not to turn off the circuit.

In most cases, there will be a direct electrical connection between the inside doorknob and the outside doorknob, but it is advisable to check this out in each individual case. If the two doorknobs are shorted together, you can connect the circuit to the inside doorknob, and no one outside the room will even know your door is protected unless they try to get in. An easy way to connect the alarm circuit to a doorknob is to hang it from a wire loop. The wire loop must be in direct contact with a metallic part of the doorknob assembly.

But what if there is no electrical connection between the inside and outside doorknobs for some reason? Or, what if you have to wrap a plastic or glass doorknob with aluminum foil, as mentioned earlier? In this case, you will have to pass a connecting wire through the doorway to make the connection between the doorknob and the alarm circuit. After all, it wouldn't make very much sense to protect only the inside doorknob, when you're already on that side of the door. Because only a thin single wire is needed here, it can easily go through the crack between the door and the door jam. Just go ahead and close the door on the wire. The wire should only be heavy enough to ensure that it won't easily break. Do not use insulated wire. At least, remove all insulation on the part of the wire that appears on the outside of the door.

Of course, anybody out in the hall can then see that your door is somehow protected. This might give you a little extra security. The potential intruder might decide it isn't worth the risk of trying to get into your room.

Yes, someone could easily cut the wire. But, to do so, they would have to touch it. If the wire is uninsulated, this will have the same effect as touching the doorknob—it sets off the alarm. Then, if the wire is cut, it doesn't make any difference at all to the circuit.

As you can see, you get quite a bit of security with a relatively simple and inexpensive circuit. But don't expect miracles. This project is far from fool proof. If the intruder is wearing gloves, especially heavy gloves, this is likely to mask the hand capacitance and prevent the alarm from sounding. Also, there might be other ways to get into your room, without touching the protected doorknob.

Still, this project will tend to discourage most casual prowlers and intruders. Most of the time, it would be natural for a potential intruder to first try the doorknob in case you foolishly left the room unlocked. This will set off the alarm. Because hotel rooms are used by so many people, few intruders would be likely to wear gloves to avoid leaving fingerprints. It would probably be an unnecessary precaution for them. So this alarm probably will help keep you protected and help you sleep a little better when staying in a strange hotel or motel.

Calibrating this circuit might be a little tricky. You can adjust either coil L1 or trimmer capacitance C2. You'll find it easiest to adjust the capacitor. Try adjusting the trimmer capacitor a small amount, then touch the external connection point with your fingertip to see if the alarm sounds. If not, adjust the trimmer capacitor a little further. Try to set the trimmer capacitor so a light touch just barely sets off the alarm—moving the trimmer capacitor back a little will make the circuit ignore the same type of touch. This way, the circuit will be less likely to be prone to anything false triggering. The ideal sensitivity will depend on your individual application. You'll simply have to experiment. This calibration procedure is rather picky (as most calibration procedures are), but it is not really difficult.

Two-way SCR alarm controller

One common limitation with most alarm controller circuits is that any given circuit uses either just normally open switching or just normally closed switching. Different types of switching sensors might be suitable for different purposes. For maximum protection, you might want to use both normally open and normally closed sensors in a single alarm system.

Figure 6-9 shows a quick-and-dirty solution. This circuit is rather crude, but it is very simple to build, and it is very inexpensive. A suitable parts list for this project is given in Table 6-5.

The basic circuitry shown here could easily be expanded upon to include more features to suit the individual requirements of your intended application. As shown here, this project is a stripped-down, bare-bones alarm control.

The key to the operation of this project is in the two SCRs (Q1 and Q2). One SCR (Q1) is controlled by the normally open sensor switches, and the normally closed sensor switches control the second SCR (Q2).

Remember, an SCR will not conduct from anode to cathode

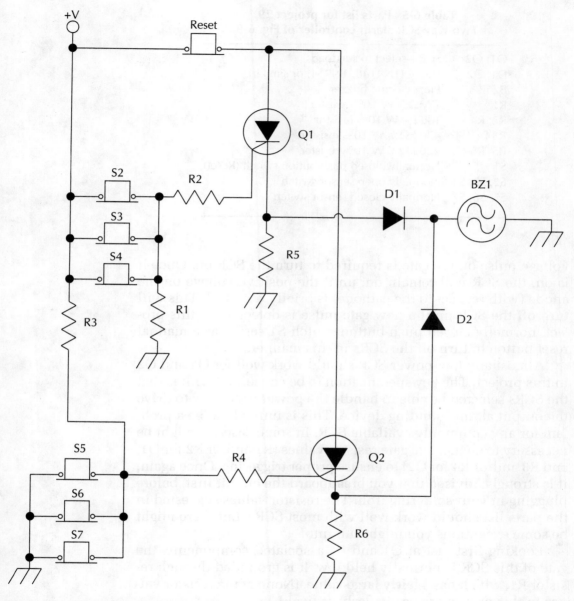

Fig. 6-9 Project 29. Two-way SCR alarm controller.

until it detects a sufficient voltage pulse on its gate. When one of the sensor switches is activated, it feeds a trigger voltage to the gate of its SCR. Once it has been turned on, the SCR will continue to conduct, even if the gate voltage is removed. Only a brief

**Table 6-5 Parts list for project 29.
Two-way SCR alarm controller of Fig. 6-9.**

Q1, Q2	SCR—select to suit load
D1, D2	Diode (1N4148, 1N914, or similar)
BZ1	Piezoelectric buzzer
R1	1 MΩ ½ W 10% resistor
R2, R4	1 kΩ ½ W 10% resistor
R3	470 kΩ ½ W 10% resistor
R5, R6	220 kΩ ½ W 10% resistor
S1	Normally closed push-button switch (Reset)
S2, S3, S4	Normally open sensor switch
S5, S6, S7	Normally closed sensor switch

voltage pulse on the gate is required to turn the SCR on. Once it is on, the SCR will remain on, until the positive voltage on the anode (with respect to the cathode) is briefly removed. This will turn off the SCR until a new gate pulse is detected. In this project, normally closed push-button switch S1 serves as a manual reset button to turn off the SCRs in this manner.

Almost any low-power SCR should work well for Q1 and Q2 in this project. The key specification to be concerned with is that the SCRs selected be able to handle the power necessary to drive the output alarm sounding device. This is unlikely to be a problem for any commonly available SCR. In some cases, it might be necessary to change the gate resistor values (R1 and/or R2 for Q1, and R3 and/or R4 for Q2) to ensure proper triggering. Once again, it is strongly advised that you breadboard the circuit first, before plugging in your soldering iron. The resistor values suggested in the parts list should work well with most SCRs, but there might be some exceptions you might run into.

Looking first just at Q1 and its associated components, the gate of this SCR is normally held low. It is grounded through resistor R1, which has a fairly large value. (None of the resistor values in this project are particularly critical.)

When any one (or more) of the normally open sensor switches (S2–S4) is closed, it feeds the circuit supply voltage to the SCR gate through resistor R2. This should be more than sufficient to turn on Q1. The SCR starts to conduct, causing a voltage to appear at the junction of the Q1 cathode and resistor R5. This voltage (which is just slightly below the circuit supply voltage) is fed to the piezoelectric buzzer BZ1 (or other alarm sounding device), causing it to sound. The buzzer will continue sounding until the circuit is manually rest by briefly opening the reset switch (S1). Additional normally open sensor switches can be added in parallel with those shown in the schematic.

The second SCR (Q2) operates in a similar manner. As long as all of the normally closed sensor switches (S5–S7) are left closed, the SCR gate will be grounded. Opening any one (or more) of the sensor switches breaks the connection to ground, and the supply voltage coming through resistor R3 will be applied to the gate of Q2, turning the SCR on. When all of the sensor switches remain closed, this voltage is shunted directly to ground through the switches.

Once SCR Q2 is turned on, it works just like Q1. A voltage appears at the junction of the Q2 cathode and resistor R6. This voltage is once again fed to the piezoelectric buzzer BZ1 (or other alarm sounding device), causing it to sound. As before, the buzzer will continue sounding until the circuit is manually reset by briefly opening the reset switch (S1). Additional normally closed sensor switches can easily be added in series with those shown in the schematic.

The two SCRs are wired in parallel with one another. This could be a problem if both are turned on at the same time, as could happen if an intruder activates more than one sensor switch. The positive voltage out from the Q2-R6 junction will be fed back to the cathode of Q1, more or less limiting the difference in the SCR anode and cathode potentials. This will turn off the SCR. The positive voltage form the Q1-R5 junction will similarly tend to turn off Q2. Diodes D1 and D2 are included in the circuit to prevent such problems. The output voltage from each SCR can reach the buzzer (or other alarm sounding device) through a forward-biased diode, but the voltage from the opposite SCR faces a reverse-biased diode, and therefore cannot get through.

Time delays and disabling the alarm system

THERE IS ONE IMPORTANT FEATURE THAT IS STILL LACKING FROM most of the alarm projects presented so far. A practical alarm system will usually feature some sort of time-delay feature. A time-delay feature is not really essential, but it is almost always a very desirable addition to any practical alarm system.

The time delay is used as an aid in disabling the alarm system. There must be some way to disable any practical alarm system. You almost certainly don't want the alarm to be set off every time you or some other family member, employee, or friend legitimately enters the protected area. Once you turn on the alarm system protecting your home, how do you get out, and then back in again without setting off the alarm?

Alarm-disable switches

The simplest solution is to mount some sort of arm/disarm (enable/disable) switch outside the protected area. But that could make illegal entry too easy for an intruder. At the very least, use a locking switch in this type of application. A locking switch requires the use of a key to change the position of the switch and enable or disable the alarm system. But the lock mechanisms in most key switches are rather simple and relatively easy to pick. Such a locking switch will probably keep out casual intruders, but it offers only minimal security against serious burglars. It is a good idea to hide or disguise the enable/disable switch as much as possible.

Using an electronic combination lock for the enable/disable switch for your alarm system would offer significantly better security, because a specific series of switches must be pressed in the correct order to activate the switch. And there are no physical keys to lose or be stolen. But you do have to remember the combination. Be careful about writing the combination down, because anyone who finds that piece of paper will be able to get past your intrusion detector system. Electronic combination lock circuits are discussed in chapter 5.

For maximum security, don't give the potential intruder access to the lock circuitry, at least, not until the intruder has already breeched the protected area, and presumedly set off the alarm. For example, you might mount the switch panel for the electronic combination lock on an exterior wall beside the front door, as shown in Fig. 7-1. It would be best to inset the switch assembly into the wall, if possible. House the switches as securely as possible, as discussed in chapter 8. But there is always a chance that a smart or determined intruder could still find a way to open the case. You can foil such efforts by not enclosing the actual lock circuitry in that case. All the intruder should find in this case is the actual switches used to manually enter the combination. A cable of wires leads off into the protected area where all of the actual circuitry is housed. If you can run this cable through the wall, it would provide the best security. You will only need to drill one fairly small hole to accommodate a single, multiwire cable. Because these wires carry only low power signals, the individual wires can have a thin gauge, so you don't need a thick, heavy cable.

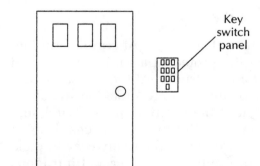

Key switch panel

Fig. 7-1 *The switch panel for an electronic combination lock can be mounted by the front door.*

Yes, the intruder could cut any or all of the wires in this cable, but in this case, it won't do any good at all. Doing so will simply make it impossible to enter the combination to disable the alarm system. That will make it inconvenient for someone later legitimately entering the area—they'll have to set off the alarm, but it won't get the potential intruder in. The intruder must set off the alarm to get into the protected area.

Use an individual pair of wires from each switch. Make all connections at the opposite end of the cable. You don't want to give the intruder any clues to the correct combination. For example, if the intruder opens the switch panel and sees that several of the switches are wired in parallel as shown in Fig. 7-2, he or she will know that these are almost certainly dummy switches, and not part of the correct combination. Eliminating these dummy switches significantly reduces the number of possible combinations, greatly improving the intruder's odds of guessing the correct combination.

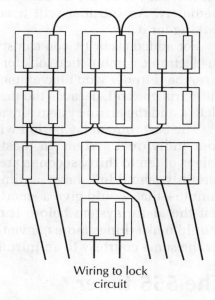

Fig. 7-2 *If an intruder can open the switch panel of an electronic combination lock, he or she might be able to get some clues to the correct combination if the switch wiring is visible.*

Wiring to lock circuit

The advantage of a time delay

Most practical alarm systems include a time delay feature of some sort. When an intrusion is detected by one (or more) of the sensor switches, the alarm control circuit will remember this event, even if the sensor switch is immediately returned to its normal state, but the circuit won't act on the detected intrusion (sound the alarm) for a few moments. If the alarm system is not disabled within this time delay, the alarm will sound. In most cases, it will continue to sound even if the disable switch is used, until a separate manual reset switch is pressed.

With such a time-delay feature, the enable/disable switch can be within the protected area. When someone legitimately enters the protected area, they will have a few seconds to disable the alarm system, before the alarm is sounded. Similarly, a time delay also gives you a chance to leave the area yourself after arming the alarm system.

Now, you obviously don't want an intruder to come in and immediately disable the alarm system during this time delay. This means the delay time period should be kept as short as reasonable. It is also a good idea to hide or disguise the disable switch in some way. But keep it in a conveniently accessible location. A person legitimately entering the protected area will know right where the disable button is, so they can go to it immediately. An intruder will have to waste some valuable time looking for it.

For added security, you can still use a locking switch, or even an electronic combination lock for the alarm disable switch. In this case, the intruder won't have time to pick or break the lock before the alarm goes off, because the protected area has already been violated, and the alarm system already "knows" he or she is there.

The best time-delay period will depend on many variables in your individual system. In most practical alarm systems, time delays of ten to thirty seconds are the most commonly used. You certainly shouldn't have a time delay longer than about a minute—that would give a smart intruder too much time to defeat the alarm system before it can do its job. The time delay should make things more convenient for you, but it shouldn't offer the same courtesy to an intruder.

The 555 timer

Any time there is an electronic function involving a definite time period of some sort, the 555 timer IC comes into the picture. Other timer ICs are available, but the 555 is unquestionably the most popular, and most widely available to electronics hobbyists and experimenters. It is also quite inexpensive and reasonably precise.

Although the 555 might not be suitable for some highly critical applications requiring precision timing, it is more than adequate for your purposes here. Does it really matter if the delay time is 28 seconds or 31.5 seconds, instead of exactly 30 seconds?

Because the 555 is such a good choice for time-delay applications, and is so widely available, it will probably be used more frequently than all other alternatives put together. It is certainly worthwhile to spend a little time here getting to know this handy device a little bit better.

The pin-out diagram for the 555 timer IC is shown in Fig. 7-3. This IC is housed in a standard eight-pin DIP (dual in line package) housing. External resistors and capacitors are used to set the timing values.

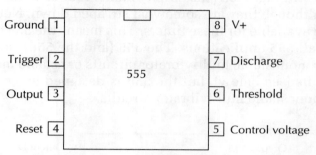

Fig. 7-3 *The 555 is a handy and popular IC for many timing applications.*

A popular variation of the 555 timer is the 556 dual timer. This chip is the equivalent of two independent 555 type timers in a single IC package. The pin-out diagram for the 556 dual timer IC is shown in Fig. 7-4. Notice that the only pins the two timer sections have in common are the power supply pins (pin 7—ground and pin 14—V+). Otherwise, the two timer sections

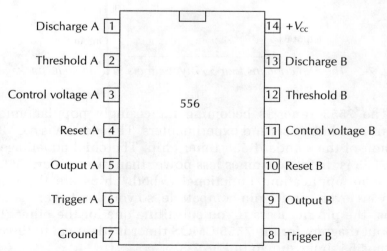

Fig. 7-4 *The 556 is the equivalent of two 555s in a single housing.*

are fully independent of one another, and they can be used just as if they were separate 555 timer chips. The 556 can be used in any circuit calling for one or two 555 chips. You will have a correct for the differing pin numbers, but other than that, there will be on changes in the circuitry.

Another variation of the basic 555 timer is the 558 quad timer IC, shown in Fig. 7-5. This chip contains four separate 555 type timers, although they are somewhat stripped down. Not all functions are available for these timers. This means the 558 cannot be used in all 555 applications. The 555 (and the 556) can be used in either monostable multivibrator circuits or astable multivibrator circuits (see below), but the 558 is designed exclusively for use in monostable multivibrator circuits.

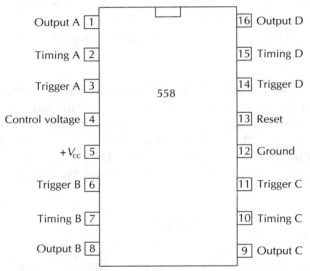

Fig. 7-5 *The 558 contains four 555-type timers in a single IC package.*

The 7555 timer is becoming increasingly popular among electronics hobbyists and experimenters. This device is a CMOS version of the standard 555 timer chip. The chief advantage of the 7555 is that it consumes less power than the standard 555 in the same application. Functionally, both chips are the same. They are even pin-for-pin compatible, so you don't even have to adjust the pin numbers if you substitute one for the other. The pin-out diagram for the 7555 CMOS timer is identical to the one for the 555 timer shown in Fig. 7-3.

For your convenience, the pin numbers for the 555 and its

variants are listed and compared in Table 7-1. Notice that some pin functions are marked * (for not applicable) for the 558 quad timer chip. Circuits using these pin functions cannot be built with the 558, at least not without extensive changes in the circuitry.

Table 7-1   Substituting a 555, a 556, or a 558 is usually just a matter of correcting the pin numbers.

Function	555	556		558			
		A	B	A	B	C	D
Ground	1	7	/	12	/	/	/
Trigger	2	6	8	3	6	11	14
Output	3	5	9	1	8	9	16
Reset	4	4	10	13	/	/	/
Control voltage	5	3	11	4	/	/	/
Threshold	6	2	12	*	*	*	*
Discharge	7	1	13	*	*	*	*
V_{CC}	8	14	/	5	/	/	/

/ = Same pin used for entire chip (see section A).
*= Function not available on 558.

Multivibrators

The 555 timer (and its variations) is designed specifically for use in multivibrator circuits. A multivibrator circuit has two possible output levels. The output of a multivibrator is always either HIGH or LOW. No intermediate output values are possible. There are three basic types of multivibrator circuits—the monostable multivibrator, the bistable multivibrator, and the astable multivibrator. In each case, the name suggests the function.

The monostable multivibrator circuit has one stable output state. The prefix *mono* means one. This type of circuit is rather like a momentary-action switch. It can be either normally HIGH or normally LOW, corresponding to normally closed and normally open switches. For convenience, assume that the normal state of a hypothetical monostable multivibrator circuit is LOW. The output of this circuit will remain LOW indefinitely until an appropriate trigger pulse is detected at the input of the circuit. As soon as this trigger pulse is detected, the monostable multivibrator output goes HIGH. The output remains HIGH for a specific time period, depending on the specific component values used in the circuit. After this time period is over (the circuit has *timed out*), the output reverts to its normal LOW state.

The operation of a typical monostable multivibrator circuit is illustrated in Fig. 7-6. Notice that the length of the trigger pulse is irrelevant, and it has no effect on the length of the output pulse. In most cases, the only limitation on the trigger pulse is that it be shorter than the output pulse. In some monostable multivibrator circuits, a too-long trigger pulse will cause the circuit to be immediately retriggered as soon as it times out, starting a new timing period. Other monostable multivibrator circuits are designed to ignore a trigger pulse that is held too long. A monostable multivibrator circuit is often referred to simply as a *timer circuit.*

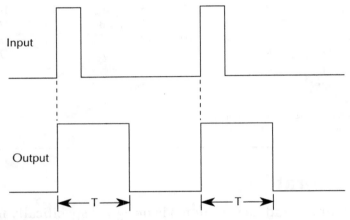

Fig. 7-6 *The output of a monostable multivibrator produces one fixed-length output pulse each time it receives an input pulse.*

A bistable multivibrator circuit has two stable states. The prefix *bi* means two. Either output state can be held indefinitely (assuming power is continuously applied to the circuit, of course). Each time a trigger pulse is detected at the input of this circuit, its output reverses its output state, going from LOW to HIGH or from HIGH to LOW.

The operation of typical bistable multivibrator circuit is illustrated in Fig. 7-7. Notice that there is one complete output cycle for every two complete input (trigger pulse) cycles. That is, two input pulses equal one output pulse. For this reason, the bistable multivibrator is often referred to as a *frequency divider.* This type of multivibrator is also considered a simple type of electronic memory, because it "remembers" the last state it was set for.

Finally, the astable multivibrator circuit has no stable output state at all. The prefix *a* means no or none. Unlike the mono-

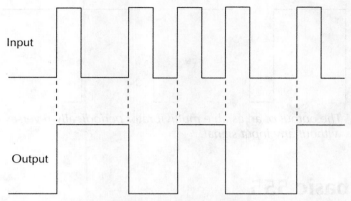

Input

Fig. 7-7 *The output of a bistable multivibrator reverses its state each time it receives an input pulse.*

stable multivibrator and the bistable multivibrator, the astable multivibrator does not have a trigger input, or any kind of input at all. As long as power is continuously applied to an astable multivibrator circuit, its output will continuously oscillate back and forth between the HIGH and LOW states, as illustrated in Fig. 7-8. The length of time each output state will be held is determined by timing periods set by specific component values within the circuit. The HIGH and LOW output times are not necessarily equal in practical astable multivibrator circuits. In fact, such symmetry is not even possible in a standard astable multivibrator circuit built around the 555 timer IC.

Notice that basically an astable multivibrator circuit is just a type of rectangular-wave generator. If the HIGH and LOW times are equal, then the output signal is in the form of a square wave.

The 555 timer IC is designed for use in monostable multivibrator and astable multivibrator circuits. A bistable multivibrator circuit cannot be built around the 555.

For your purposes here, you are only interested in monostable multivibrator circuits. If you look through the projects in other chapters in this book, you often see the 555 in both its monostable and astable modes. But for a time-delay function, you need a monostable multivibrator. When the sensor switch detects an entry to the protected area, a trigger pulse is fed to the monostable multivibrator. If the system is not disabled before the multivibrator circuit times out, the alarm will be sounded. It is just as simple as that.

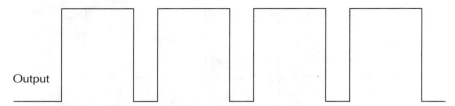

Output

Fig. 7-8 *The output of an astable multivibrator periodically reverses its state without any input signal.*

The basic 555 monostable multivibrator circuit

The 555 timer (and its relatives) is very easy to use. They can be used in a practical circuit with only a handful of external components. In most 555 timer circuits, only a few external capacitors and resistors are required in addition to the timer chip itself.

The basic circuit for using the 555 timer as a monostable multivibrator is shown in Fig. 7-9. As you can see, this is a very simple circuit, requiring just three external passive components in addition to the 555 IC—two capacitors and one resistor.

As a matter of fact, capacitor C2 is often optional. It is included to prevent possible stability problems from leaving the

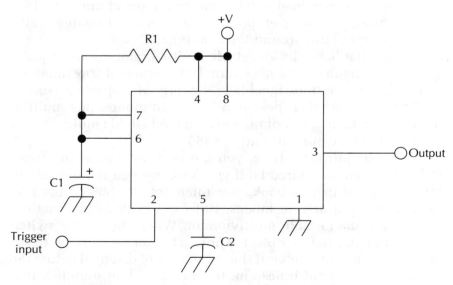

Fig. 7-9 *This is the basic 555 monostable multivibrator circuit.*

voltage control input (pin 5) floating. In many practical applications, there will be no noticeable stability problems without this capacitor, but it is virtually impossible to predict just what circuit is likely to be subject to such problems and under what circumstances. Tracking down stability problems can be very difficult and very frustrating. The circuit will just act strangely sometimes, while behaving itself perfectly at other times. This simple bypass capacitor is just cheap insurance against such problems. It is a good idea to include the stability capacitor in any 555 circuit that does not use the voltage-control input (which is the case in most common applications for this chip).

The exact value of stability capacitor is not critical and will not have any noticeable effect on circuit operation. In most cases, a 0.01 μF is used for this function. Some technicians prefer using a 0.1 μF capacitor, probably because they usually have a lot of capacitors of this value handy. Anything from 0.005 to 0.1 μF will do fine.

The important components in this circuit are capacitor C1 and resistor R1. These are the timing components. Their value determines the length of the monostable multivibrator output pulse.

This circuit responds to a LOW trigger pulse. The trigger input (pin 2) should normally be held HIGH. Pulling this pin LOW via an external signal will trigger the multivibrator. The 555 timer internal circuitry is designed to pull this trigger input pin HIGH when it is left floating (no signal applied to it). In some applications, the circuit might function more reliably if an external pull-up resistor is used too.

The output (pin 3) of the basic 555 monostable multivibrator is normally LOW. When the timer is triggered, the output goes HIGH for a specific timing period determined by the values of capacitor C1 and resistor R1. When the circuit times out, the output goes LOW again.

The timing formula for this simple monostable multivibrator circuit is not complex or difficult to use:

$$T = 1.1(R_1 C_1)$$

where T is the timing period (in seconds), R_1 is the value of the timing resistor (in ohms), and C_1 is the value of the timing capacitor (in farads). The 1.1 constant is defined by the internal circuitry of the 555 timer IC.

Some electronics hobbyists and technicians prefer to express the resistance in megohms (1 megohm=1,000,000 Ω), and the capacitance in microfarads (1 microfarad=0.000001 farad). Be careful not to confuse the units used. It must be either ohms with farads or megohms with microfarads—never megohms with farads or ohms with microfarads. To avoid confusion, stick to the standard ohms and farads units.

Either of these components can be selected from a wide range of values. For reliable operations of this monostable multivibrator circuit, keep the value of resistor R1 within the range of about 10 kΩ (10,000 Ω) to 10 MΩ (10,000,000 Ω). Similarly, the minimum value for capacitor C1 is 100 pF (0.0001 μF or 0.000000001 F), and the maximum value for this component is 1000 μF (0.001 F). The abbreviation *pF* stands for picofarad.

The larger the values of the timing components, the longer the timing period of the monostable multivibrator. For example, if you use the smallest acceptable component values (R_1=10 kΩ, C_1=100 pF), the timing period is:

$$
\begin{aligned}
T &= 1.1(R_1 C_1) \\
&= 1.1(10000 \times 0.000000001) \\
&= 1.1 \times 0.000001 \\
&= 0.0000011 \text{ s (second)} \\
&= 0.001 \text{ ms (millisecond)} \\
&= 1.1 \text{ } \mu\text{s (microsecond)}
\end{aligned}
$$

At the opposite extreme, if you use the maximum acceptable component values (R_1=10, C_1=1000 μF), the timing period is:

$$
\begin{aligned}
T &= 1.1(10000000 \times 0.001) \\
&= 1.1 \times 10000 \\
&= 11,000 \text{ s} \\
&= 183.333 \text{ min (minutes)} \\
&= 3 \text{ h (hours)}, 3.333 \text{ min}
\end{aligned}
$$

As you can see, the basic 555 monostable multivibrator circuit is capable of operating over an impressively wide range. In most practical applications, it will be used somewhere between these extremes of its range. For example, a typical 555 monostable multivibrator circuit might use a 220 kΩ (220,000 Ω) resistor for R1 and a 33 μF (0.000033 farad) capacitor for C1. In this case, the timing period is:

$$
\begin{aligned}
T &= 1.1(220000 \times 0.000033) \\
&= 1.1 \times 7.26 \\
&= 7.986 \text{ s}
\end{aligned}
$$

You might as well round this off to 8 s. Component tolerances are very likely to account for at least that much error. The precision of the timing period will be dependent on the tolerance of the specific timing components used in the circuit. If both the resistor and the capacitor have, for example, tolerances of 20%, the final value might be off from the calculated value by as much as 40%. It makes good sense to use low-tolerances components whenever possible.

If great precision is required in your particular application, you can replace timing resistor R1 with a small fixed resistor in series with a trimpot, which can be adjusted to calibrate the monostable multivibrator circuit for precisely the desired timing period. Such precision probably won't be necessary in a time delay for an alarm system.

In designing a system, you will probably know the desired time value and will need to determine the appropriate component values. This is easy to do by rearranging the basic timing equation. Arbitrarily select a likely value for capacitor C1, then solve for the value of resistor R1, using this modified formula:

$$R_1 = \frac{T}{1.1C_1}$$

If this calculation results in an inconvenient, oddball resistance value, or one outside the acceptable range for the 555 (10 kΩ to 100 MΩ), simply select a different capacitance value and try again. As you gain experience with type of circuit, you will quickly get a sense of what an appropriate capacitance value will be for any given timing range.

For a time delay in an alarm system, a good timing period might be about 25 s. This doesn't have to be precise. It could be 19 s or 32 s for all you care. But as an approximate figure, use 25 seconds. This will give you quite a bit of flexibility in rounding off while performing the equations. Try using a 50 µF (0.00005 F) capacitor for C1. What value do you need to use for resistor R1?

$$R_1 = \frac{25}{(1.1 \times 0.00005)}$$

$$= \frac{25}{0.000055}$$

$$= 454,545.45 \ \Omega$$

This is pretty close to a standard 470 kΩ (470,000 Ω) resistor.

You can double check the effect of this rounding up by re-using the original timing equation. Ignoring the effects of the component tolerances, the actual timing period of your hypothetical monostable multivibrator circuit will be changed to:

$$T = 1.1(R_1 C_1)$$
$$= 1.1(470{,}000 \times 0.00005)$$
$$= 1.1 \times 23.5$$
$$= 25.85 \text{ s}$$

That is certainly close enough for your intended application in an alarm system. That extra second (not quite a second actually) will hardly be of any practical help to an intruder trying to defeat our alarm system. There won't be any realistic reduction in the overall security of your system.

Of course, in a practical circuit, the component tolerances might make the actual timing period somewhat longer or shorter than the calculated value. This is not likely to be of much significance in most alarm system applications.

Timed touch switch

Figure 7-10 shows a simple practical application for the basic 555 monostable multivibrator circuit, which might be useful as a specialized sensor in an intrusion-detector alarm system. What you have here is a timed touch switch. A suitable parts list for this project is given in Table 7-2.

It is very, very important that you power this project (and any other touch-switch circuit) from batteries only. If you use ac power, (even an ac-to-dc converter), there is always the possibility of a short circuit (perhaps even a fluke short) feeding ac power to the touch plate. This could give someone a painful and possibly even fatal electrical shock. Please, use battery power only. Don't take foolish chances.

Normally the 555 trigger input (pin 2) is held HIGH through pull-up resistor R2. This large-value resistor might not always be necessary. This circuit sometimes works just fine without the external pull-up resistor, and sometimes it doesn't. Adding this component to the circuit improves the reliability. The exact value of this resistor isn't too critical, as long as it is large.

When someone touches both touch plates, his or her body completes a circuit to ground, putting a LOW signal on the trigger input. The touch plates should be small metallic plates. Two

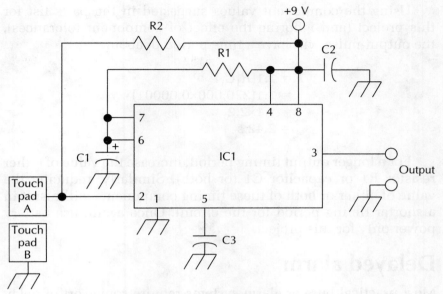

Fig. 7-10 Project 30. Timed touch switch.

**Table 7-2   Parts list for project 30.
Timed touch switch of Fig. 7-10.**

IC1	555 timer
C1	10 µF 25 V electrolytic capacitor*
C2	0.1 µF capacitor
C3	0.01 µF capacitor
R1	220 kΩ ¼ W 5% resistor*
R2	1 MΩ ¼ W 5% resistor
Touch plates	Metallic plates—see text.

*Timing component—see text.

small pieces of unetched copper-clad circuit board will work well. The plates should be placed so they can be bridged with a fingertip. In an alarm system, they should be arranged so an intruder is likely to inadvertently touch both plates at once.

The LOW signal on the trigger pin activates the monostable multivibrator. The output goes HIGH for a period of time determined by the values of resistor R1 and capacitor C1, just as in the basic monostable multivibrator circuit discussed in this chapter.

Capacitor C2 also adds to the overall stability of the circuit. Again, the exact value of this component is not particularly critical.

Using the component values suggested in the parts list for this project (and ignoring the effect of component tolerances), the output pulse will have a time period of about:

$$T = 1.1(R_1 C_1)$$
$$= 1.1(220{,}000 \times 0.00001)$$
$$= 1.1 \times 2.2$$
$$= 2.42 \text{ s}$$

For a longer output timing period, increase the value of either resistor R1 or capacitor C1 (or both). Similarly, reducing the value of either or both of these timing components will result in a shorter timing period for the circuit. Once again, use battery power only for this project.

Delayed alarm

Most practical burglar alarm systems require some sort of delay feature. An alarm without any delay can offer you warning if you are within (or near) the protected area, but if you want to go out, you'd have no way to set the alarm without setting if off yourself when you leave. And even if you did manage to get out, you couldn't get back in without setting off the alarm.

If there is a delay between when the alarm circuit is turned on and when it is actually activated, you can turn it on and have a chance to get out the door before triggering the alarm. Similarly, a short delay between the time one of the sensor switches is set off and the time when the alarm actually sounds, legitimate entrants into the area can hit the alarm's reset button before it goes off. The sensor switch does not have to be continuously activated during this period. Even a very, very brief pulse will be detected by the circuit. It will simply wait a moment after sensing an intrusion before it turns on the actual alarm sounding device, unless the reset button is depressed, deactivated the alarm.

Obviously, placement of the alarm system reset button is rather critical. It must be fairly convenient to get to, so anyone legitimately entering the protected area will have ample time to reset the alarm system before it goes off. But the reset switch should not be readily visible or obvious. After all, you don't want an intruder to be able to find the reset button and disable the alarm system before it can do its job.

Delays of 30 seconds to about a minute are usually more than sufficient. Longer delay times would probably give a clever intruder too much time to figure out how to defeat the alarm system.

A simple, but effective delayed alarm circuit is illustrated in Fig. 7-11 and 7-12. Parts lists for these circuits are given in Tables 7-3 and 7-4. Another feature of this alarm system is its ability to pinpoint just where the intrusion is taking place. This circuit is shown in two parts for convenience and to maximize flexibility of the system. The sensor circuit (Fig. 7-11) is repeated for each sensor switch (or group of sensor switches). Each sensor circuit can monitor several normally closed switches (in series with S1), but they will all be considered a single sensor by the location identification circuitry.

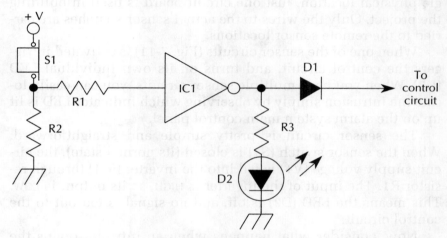

Fig. 7-11 Project 31. Delayed alarm—sensor circuit.

**Table 7-3 Parts list for project 31.
Delayed alarm—sensor circuit of Fig. 7-11.**

IC1	⅙ CD4049 hex inverter
D1	Diode (1N4148, 1N914, or similar)
D2	LED
R1	1 kΩ ¼ W 5% resistor
R2	10 kΩ ¼ W 5% resistor
R3	470 Ω ¼ W 5% resistor
S1	Normally closed momentary-action SPST switch

(Repeat up to five times—see text.)

The main, central control circuit is shown in Fig. 7-12. This circuit only has to be built once. Multiple sensor circuits can be fed into this single control circuit. Use five sensor circuits with each control circuit. The control circuit could probably handle more sensor circuits, but there is a very practical reason to use five sensor circuits. This project uses the CD4049 hex inverter IC, which contains six inverter stages. The control circuit uses one inverter section, and each sensor circuit also uses one inverter stage. Therefore, one control circuit and five sensor circuits equals six inverters, or one complete CD4049 chip.

No power supply connections are shown to the inverters in Fig. 7-11. This is because a single CD4049 chip is assumed. The power supply connections for the entire IC are shown in Fig. 7-12.

Notice that all of the actual circuitry in this project is one single physical location. Just one circuit board is used in building the project. Only the wires to the actual sensor switches are carried to the remote sensor locations.

When one of the sensor circuits (Fig. 7-11) is activated it triggers the control circuit, and turns on its own individual LED (D2). When you have multiple sensor circuits, you can easily locate the intrusion simply by observing which indicator LED is lit up on the alarm system main control panel.

The sensor circuit is pretty simple and straightforward. When the sensor switch (S1) is closed (its normal state), the circuit supply voltage (V+) is fed into the inverter (IC1) through resistor R1. The input of the inverter is HIGH, so its output is LOW. This means the LED (D2) is off, and no signal is fed out to the control circuit.

Now, consider what happens when an intruder opens the sensor switch. When this happens, the input to the inverter is shorted to ground through resistors R1 and R2. The input of the inverter sees a LOW signal, so its output goes HIGH, turning on the LED, and transmitting a trigger signal to the control circuit.

Notice that if the sensor switch is reclosed, the output of the inverter will go LOW again, extinguishing the LED and dropping the output signal to the control circuit back to ground potential.

The exact values of resistors R1 and R2 are not particularly critical, but R2 should have a moderate to large value. The 10 kΩ (10,000 Ω) value suggested in the parts list for the sensor circuit (Table 7-3) is about the minimum. If you decide to use a different resistance value, fine. Just make it larger, not smaller.

The value of R1 should be relatively small, no more than about 2.5 kΩ tops, but at least 500 Ω. The 1 kΩ (1000 Ω) value recommended in the parts list is really just about ideal.

Finally, resistor R3 is just a current-limiting resistor to protect the LED (D2). The smaller this resistance, the brighter the LED will glow when the inverter output goes HIGH. The LED could be damaged if this resistor is smaller than about 200 Ω. If the resistance of this component is made larger than about 1 kΩ (1000 Ω) or so, the LED will glow too dimly to be clearly visible, defeating its purpose. Generally 330 to 470 Ω provide the best choice for LED current-limiting resistors.

Now, turn your attention to the control circuit portion of this delayed alarm system project, which is shown in Fig. 7-12. The suggested parts list for this section of the project is given in Table 7-4. As you can see, this part of the circuit is a bit more complex than the individual sensor circuits.

When a HIGH signal is received from one or more of the sensor circuits, SCR Q1 is turned on. The system main security breach indicator (LED D1) is turned on. Unlike the individual sensor circuit LEDs, this LED will continue to glow until the system is reset

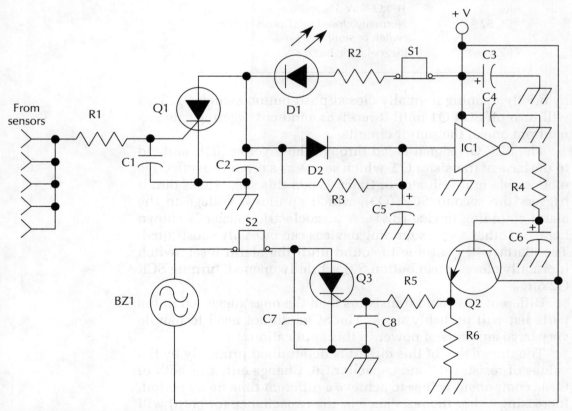

Fig. 7-12 *Project 31. Delayed alarm—control circuit.*

**Table 7-4   Parts list for project 31.
Delayed alarm—control circuit of Fig. 7-12.**

IC1	⅙ CD4049 hex inverter
Q1	SCR (Radio Shack RS1067 or similar)
Q2	NPN transistor (2N3904, Radio Shack RS1617, or similar)
Q3	SCR (S4006L or similar)
D1	LED
D2	Diode (1N4001 or similar)
C1, C2, C7, C8	0.1 µF capacitor
C3	1000 µF 25 V electrolytic capacitor
C4	0.01 µF capacitor
C5	100 µF 25 V electrolytic capacitor
C6	4.7 µF 25 V electrolytic capacitor
R1	1 kΩ ¼ W 5% resistor
R2, R5	470 Ω ¼ W 5% resistor
R3	100 kΩ ¼ W 5% resistor
R4	4.7 kΩ ¼ W 5% resistor
R6	10 kΩ ¼ W 5% resistor
S1, S2	Normally closed SPST push-button switch or similar
BZ1	Piezoelectric buzzer

by briefly opening normally closed push-button switch S1. This will turn off SCR Q1 until it receives another triggering gate signal from one of the sensor circuits.

The SCR ON signal is fed through the inverter (IC1) and fed to the base of transistor Q2, which serves as a crude, but effective monostable multivibrator or timer. When this stage times out, it triggers the second SCR (Q3), which applies a voltage to the alarm sounding device (BZ1). A piezoelectric buzzer is shown here, but other alarm sounding devices can be easily substituted. The alarm will continue to sound until the alarm reset switch (normally closed push button S2) is briefly opened, turning SCR Q2 off.

Different SCRs and transistors than the ones suggested in the parts list will probably work. The SCRs do not need to handle very large amounts of power in this application.

The time delay of this circuit is determined primarily by the values of resistor R4 and capacitor C6. Change either or both of these component values to achieve a different time delay period. Increasing either the resistance or the capacitance (or both) will result in a longer time delay period.

Light sensor for the delayed alarm

The circuit shown in Fig. 7-13 could be used as a substitute for the standard sensor circuit (Fig. 7-11) used in the last project. This is a light sensor circuit.

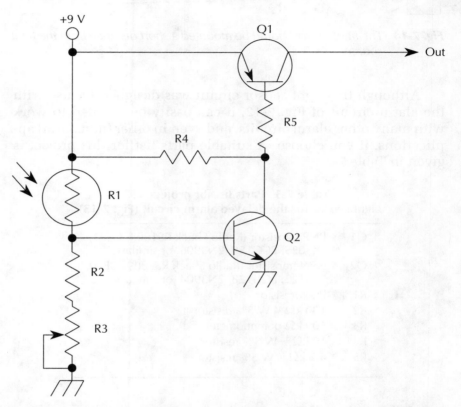

Fig. 7-13 *Project 31. Light sensor for the delayed alarm circuit of Fig. 7-12.*

The main sensing device here is the photoresistor (R1). As you read in chapter 2, a photoresistor is a junctionless, nonpolarized semiconductor component that varies its resistance in response to the amount of light striking its sensing surface. This light sensor circuit will trigger the alarm if the photoresistor does not detect a sufficient amount of light.

The light sensor should be mounted some distance from a light source, as shown in Fig. 7-14. If an intruder (or any other nontransparent object) passes between the light source and the sensor, the alarm will be triggered.

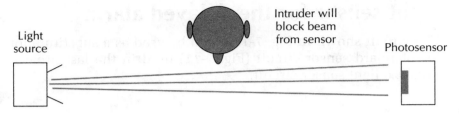

Fig. 7-14 *The light sensor should be mounted a short distance from the light source.*

Although this light sensor circuit was designed for use with the alarm circuit of Fig. 7-12, it can easily be adapted to work with many other alarm circuits, and even in other (nonalarm) applications, if you choose. A suitable parts list for this project is given in Table 7-5.

Table 7-5 Parts list for project 31.
Light sensor for the delayed alarm circuit (Fig. 7-13).

Q1	PNP transistor (Radio Shack RS1604, GE21, SK3025, ECG159, 2N3906, or similar)
Q2	NPN transistor (Radio Shack RS2009, GE20, SK3122, ECG128, 2N3904, or similar)
R1	Photoresistor
R2	100 kΩ ¼ W 5% resistor
R3	500 kΩ potentiometer
R4	10 kΩ ¼ W 5% resistor
R5	4.7 kΩ ¼ W 5% resistor

Potentiometer R3 is a sensitivity control for the light sensor. The setting of this control determines the light level that will trip the circuit and set off the alarm. In some applications, you might want to replace resistor R2 and potentiometer R3 with a single fixed resistor of a suitable value.

Normally, when the light source is shining on the photoresistor, the collector of Q2 is held near ground potential (zero volts). This biases transistor Q1 so that its collector carries the circuit supply voltage (V+), more or less.

If an object (such as an intruder's body) blocks the light from the photoresistor, that component's resistance will increase, dropping the signal fed to the base of transistor Q2. Notice that the photoresistor (R1) forms one half of a simple resistive voltage-divider string between V+ and ground. The other half of this voltage divider comprises of R2 and R3. Reducing the base voltage on transistor Q1 causes its collector voltage to rise, turning off transistor Q1, which sets off the alarm.

Alternate delayed alarm

Another delayed intruder alarm circuit is illustrated in Fig. 7-15. A suitable parts list for this project is given in Table 7-6. This project is built around the popular 555 timer IC, always a good choice whenever an electronic application calls for some sort of timing function.

Basically, the 555 timer (IC1) is wired as a simple monostable multivibrator circuit, or a timer. Normally, the output (pin 3) of this chip is held LOW. When the monostable multivibrator is triggered (by briefly opening sensor switch S1), the output of the 555 goes HIGH for a period equal to:

$$T = 1.1RC$$

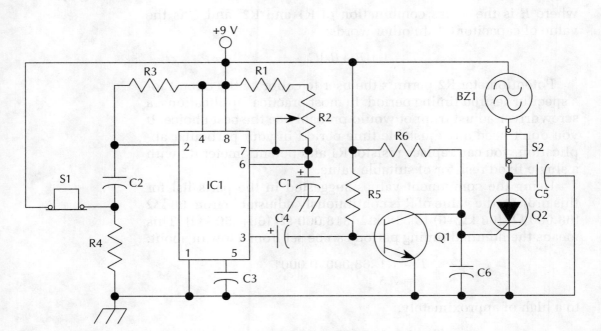

Fig. 7-15 *Project 32. Alternate delayed alarm.*

**Table 7-6   Parts list for project 32.
Alternate delayed alarm of Fig. 7-15.**

IC1	555 timer
Q1	NPN transistor (Radio Shack RS2009, GE20, SK3122, ECG128, 2N3904, or similar)
Q2	SCR 6 A, 200 V PIV
C1	100 µF 25 V electrolytic capacitor
C2, C5	0.1 µF capacitor
C3	0.01 µF capacitor
C4	47 µF 25 V electrolytic capacitor
C6	0.22 µF capacitor
R1	68 kΩ ¼ W 5% resistor
R2	250 kΩ potentiometer
R3	47 kΩ ¼ W 5% resistor
R4	2.2 kΩ ¼ W 5% resistor
R5	22 kΩ ¼ W 5% resistor
R6	1 kΩ ¼ W 5% resistor
BZ1	Buzzer—see text
S1	Normally closed SPST sensor switch
S2	Normally closed SPST push-button switch

where R is the series combination of R1 and R2, and C is the value of capacitor C1. In other words:

$$T = 1.1(R_1 + R_2)C_1$$

Potentiometer R2 permits the user to calibrate the circuit for a specific desired timing period. In most practical applications, a screwdriver-adjust trimpot would probably be the best choice. If you don't need an adjustable time period in your particular application, you can replace resistor R1 and potentiometer R2 with a single fixed resistor of suitable value.

Using the component values suggested in the parts list for this project, the value of R is continuously adjustable from 68 kΩ (68,000 Ω) (68 kΩ+0) to 318 kΩ (318,000 Ω) (68+250 kΩ). This means the nominal timing period can be set from a low of about:

$$T = 1.1 \times 68,000 \times 0.0001$$
$$= 7.5 \text{ s}$$

to a high of approximately:

$$T = 1.1 \times 318,000 \times 0.0001$$
$$= 35 \text{ s}$$

Normally the base of transistor Q1 is held near the circuit supply voltage (V+) through resistor R3, so its collector is held near ground potential (0 volts), keeping the gate of the SCR (Q2) turned off.

When the timer is triggered and its output goes HIGH, it charges capacitor C4 up to a value just a bit below the supply voltage (V+). When the 555 times out and its output goes LOW, the positive end of capacitor C4 is effectively shorted to ground, which turns transistor Q1 off. The collector of this transistor goes HIGH (near V+), and this signal is applied to the gate of the SCR (Q2), turning it on, and sounding the alarm (buzzer BZ1). Although a piezoelectric buzzer is shown here, you can use almost any sounding or indicator device. In some cases, you might have to use a heftier SCR to drive certain alarm sounding devices. The SCR suggested in the parts list is intentionally overrated for use with the buzzer.

To turn off the alarm once it has sounded, reset switch S2 must be briefly opened to turn off the SCR. Notice that the triggering sensor does not have to remain activated through the entire timing period. A very brief pulse (interruption of the circuit) will be sufficient to trigger the 555, and it doesn't much matter what happens to the sensor switches from that point on (until the circuit is manually reset). There will just be a delay between the time sensor switch S1 is opened and the alarm actually sounds.

Additional sensor switches can be placed in series with S1 shown here.

Alarm sounder with automated shutdown

In many practical situations, you want your alarm system to protect your property when you are not around. The siren, bell, or other alarm sounding device serves as a deterrent to scare off an attempted intruder. But if you're not there, you obviously can't reset the alarm circuit after the intruder has left.

In addition to needlessly consuming power, an alarm that continues to sound indefinitely is bound to annoy your neighbors quite a bit, and rightfully so. A possible solution to this type of problem is the circuit shown in Fig. 7-16. A suitable parts list for this project is given in Table 7-7.

This circuit can be used in between the alarm control circuitry and any standard alarm-sounding device. The alarm

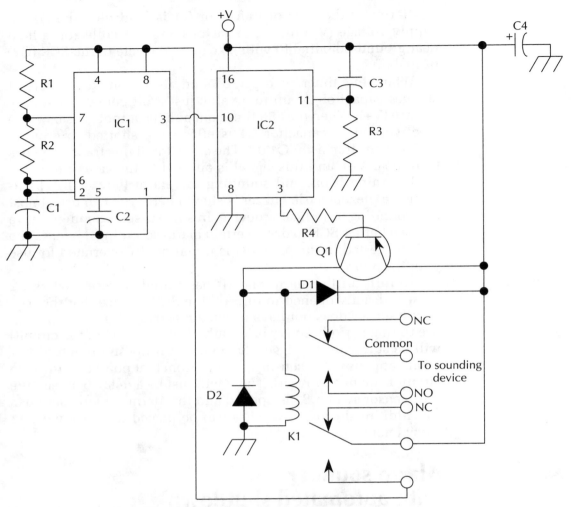

Fig. 7-16 *Project 33. Alarm sounder with automated shutdown.*

sounds when it receives a suitable V+ voltage from the control circuit. Anything from about +9 to +15 V should work just fine. When the supply voltage is applied to this circuit, the alarm will sound for a period of about 6.5 minutes (using the component values suggested in the parts list). The alarm will then automatically shut itself down. If an intruder has not been frightened off within five or six minutes, it is doubtful that continuing to sound the alarm will have much impact.

IC1 is a 7555 timer chip. This is a CMOS equivalent to the popular 555 timer IC. The 7555 and the 555 are 100% pin-for-pin

Table 7-7 Parts list for project 33.
Alarm sounder (Fig. 7-16) with automated shutdown.

IC1	7555 timer (see text)
IC2	CD4020 14-stage binary counter
Q1	PNP transistor (Radio Shack RS1604, GE21, SK3025, ECG159, 2N3906, or similar)
D1, D2	Diode (1N4001 or similar)
K1	DPDT relay to suit load and supply voltage
C1, C3	0.1 μF capacitor
C2	0.01 μF capacitor
C4	470 μF 25 V electrolytic capacitor
R1	33 kΩ ¼ W 5% resistor
R2	330 kΩ ¼ W 5% resistor
R3	1 MΩ ¼ W 5% resistor
R4	6.8 kΩ ¼ W 5% resistor

compatible, so you can substitute a standard 555 chip if you prefer. The 7555 suggested in the parts list will consume a bit less power, but other than that, the circuit operation will be unchanged by the substitution.

The 7555 timer is wired here as an astable multivibrator or a rectangular-wave generator. It puts out and continuous stream of regular pulses as long as power is applied to the circuit. The frequency (F) of these pulses can be found with this formula:

$$F = \frac{1}{(0.693(R_1+2R_2)C_1)}$$

Using the component values suggested in the parts list, the timer will be putting out pulses with a nominal frequency (ignoring any inaccuracies due to component tolerances) of approximately:

$$F = \frac{1}{(0.693\times(33,000+2\times330,000)\times0.0000001}$$

$$= \frac{1}{(0.693\times(33,000+660,000)\times0.0000001)}$$

$$= \frac{1}{(0.693\times693,000\times0.0000001)}$$

$$= \frac{1}{0.048}$$

$$= 20.8 \text{ Hz}$$

The time period of the pulses is equal to the reciprocal of the frequency, or in this case:

$$T = \frac{1}{F}$$

$$= \frac{1}{20.8}$$

$$= 0.048 \text{ s}$$

Rounding off a little, there is one pulse about every 0.05 second.

These pulses are then fed to IC2, which is a 14-stage counter. When power is first applied to this circuit, the output of IC2 is LOW. This LOW signal is fed to the base of PNP transistor Q1 which switches on and activates the relay (K1). Notice that this is a DPDT relay, with two independent sets of switch contacts. One set is connected to the actual alarm sounding device in the usual way (probably using the normally open contacts). The other set of relay switch contacts (normally open also) control the power fed to the timer stage (IC1). As long as the relay is activated, the astable multivibrator gets power and puts out pulses, and power will be applied to the alarm sounding device.

The counter (IC2) counts the pulses from the timer (IC1). Nothing much happens until a count of 8192 is reached. At this point, the output (pin 3) of IC2 will go HIGH. This will turn off the transistor (Q1), and deactivate the relay. The normally open switch contacts of the relay will be released and open up. The power connection to the timer (IC1) will be disconnected, so no further pulses will be sent to the counter (IC2). Similarly, power will no longer be fed to the alarm sounding device, so it will stop sounding.

To reach a count of 8192 with pulses lasting approximately 0.05 second each will take a time period of about 409 seconds, or a little more than 6.5 minutes.

To change the timer period, you can alter the values of resistors R1 or R2 or capacitor C1. Increasing any or all of these component values will increase the timing period. If it is appropriate to your particular application, you might want to use a trimpot for resistor R2 to permit manual control over the timing period. You can calibrate it to the exact timing period you want. It is very, very strongly recommended that you put a 10 to 100 kΩ fixed resistor in series with the calibration potentiometer to prevent the possibility of setting this resistance to 0, which could damage the timer chip. At the very least, the circuit would not work properly.

A nice feature of this circuit is that it does not require any bulky, expensive electrolytic capacitors to achieve the rather long timing period. This gives you a more accurately predictable timing period because electrolytic capacitors have notoriously wide tolerances, and can be off from their nominal value by as much as 50 to 80%.

Suppose you want to know if the alarm was set off while you were gone? Any easy way to do this would be to add an LED and a current-limiting resistor (330 to 470 Ω) from the V+ to ground points of this circuit, as shown in Fig. 7-17. The LED will go on as soon as the alarm is triggered and will remain lit, even after the circuit times out and the audible alarm stops sounding. The LED will not be extinguished until the alarm control circuit is reset (or power to the circuit is otherwise interrupted).

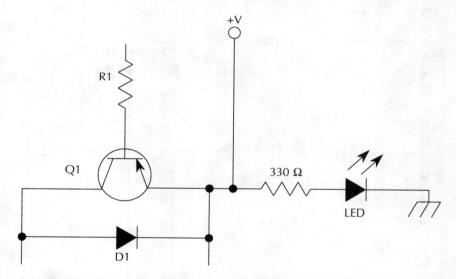

Fig. 7-17 *Adding an LED to the circuit of Fig. 7-16 will give an indication that the alarm had been set off.*

Multifunction intrusion-detector system

In a complete burglar alarm system, you might want to use both normally open and normally closed sensors, because each is more suitable for different purposes. Similarly, you want a time

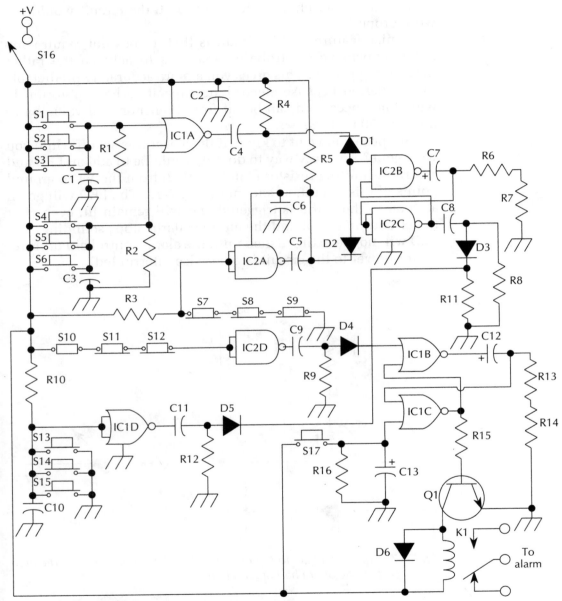

Fig. 7-18 *Project 34. Multifunction intrusion-detector system.*

delay for the main entrance(s) to the protected area (doors), but you might want other sensors to set off the alarm immediately, with no time delay.

The multifunction intrusion detector circuit shown in Fig.

**Table 7-8   Parts list for project 34.
Multifunction intrusion-detector system of Fig. 7-18.**

IC1	CD4001 quad NOR gate
IC2	CD4011 Quad NAND gate
Q1	NPN transistor (2N3904, GE20, SK3122, ECG128, Radio Shack RS2009, or similar)
D1–D5	Diode (1N4148, 1N914, or similar)
D6	Diode (1N4001 or similar)
C1–C6, C8–C11	0.01 µF capacitor
C7	10 µF 25 V electrolytic capacitor
C12	47 µF 25 V electrolytic capacitor
C13	33 µF 25 V electrolytic capacitor*
R1, R2, R3, R10	1 MΩ ¼ W 5% resistor
R4, R5, R8, R9, R11, R12	100 kΩ ¼ W 5% resistor
R6, R14	2.2 MΩ ¼ W 5% resistor
R7, R14	820 kΩ ¼ W 5% resistor
R15	10 kΩ ¼ W 5% resistor
R16	1 MΩ ¼ W 5% resistor*
S1–S6, S13, S14, S15	Normally open sensor switch
S7–S12	Normally closed sensor switch
S16	SPST key switch
S17	Normally open SPST push button
K1	Relay to suit load

*Timing component—see text.

7-18 will permit you to simultaneously utilize all of these various options for different sensors at different locations throughout the system. A suitable parts list for this project appears as Table 7-8.

S1 through S6, and S13 through S15 are normally open sensor switches. Normally closed sensor switches are used for S7 through S12. The schematic arbitrarily shows three sensor switches in each section of the circuit. In many practical applications, you won't really need this many sensors. If so, you can simply eliminate the unneeded sensor switches from the circuit without affecting the operation of the circuit, except there must be at least one switch in each section, or the alarm will be set off as soon as it is activated (by closing switch S16).

Sensor switches S1 through S9 activate a timer circuit, so there will be approximately a 30 second delay before the alarm sounds. You can change the time delay by altering the value of either or both of the timing components—resistor R16 and capacitor C13.

Sensor switches S10 through S15, on the other hand, trip the alarm immediately. There is no time delay before these sensors sound the alarm.

Push-button switch S17 is a manual reset button for the alarm system. It should be placed somewhere that is not directly accessible or obvious to an intruder, but the location should not be too inconvenient for any legitimately turning off the alarm.

Switch S16 arms or disarms the alarm system by applying or interrupting power to the circuit. A key switch is recommended for this switch. Again, even if a locking switch is used, try not to be too obvious about the positioning of this switch, because some experienced burglars might be able to pick the relatively simple mechanical lock used in such key switches. The supply voltage for this circuit can be anything from +9 to +15 Vdc.

❖ 8
Installing a home intrusion-detection system

SOME READERS MIGHT BE RATHER SURPRISED, AND PERHAPS EVEN A bit disappointed by the simplicity of the circuits presented thus far in this book. There is a tendency to believe that a security system must be complex, sophisticated, and expensive to be effective.

Such a belief just isn't true. In fact, the projects presented up to this point are sufficient to provide more than adaquate security for the average home, if the system is properly set up and built. Such a system might not be as exciting and impressive as a high-tech project, but it can do the job.

Some people seem to spend so much on a top-of-the-line burglar alarm system that you have to wonder if they could possibly have any property left worth protecting after they've paid for the burglar alarm.

A super-sophisticated motion detector with a crosshatch of laser beams might look very nifty, but it is almost certainly security overkill for most homes in the real world. Unless you are publicly known to have something of special value, most burglars would just as soon go next door than expend a lot of effort trying to defeat a well-designed but inexpensive burglar alarm system. The potential burglar usually doesn't know what you have until he or she gets in. The burglar just wants to steal whatever can be found and quickly sold. A burglar alarm system built around some of the projects described so far in this book will be plenty to discourage all but the most persistent burglars. It would be in the burglar's self interest to give up and try to find another home without any security system at all (or perhaps a poorly installed one that is easy to defeat).

As a matter of fact, an obviously very expensive super alarm system may actually work against your interests. Instead of discouraging the professional burglar, it might increase the motivation to find a way to get into your home. After all, a burglar might assume anyone who would spend that much on a burglar alarm must be protecting something really valuable. The unintended message sent is that there is a potential prize that is very much worth winning.

And remember, no burglar alarm system (or anything else in this world) is 100% perfect. There is no such thing as a truly unpickable lock or undefeatable burglar alarm system. What one person has designed, another person can figure out a way to get around. Some people even enjoy and actively seek out such impossible challenges. Look at the malicious ingenuity of computer hackers who try to get into restricted data systems or send out virus programs. As soon as a new form of protection is put into use, some hacker figures out a way to do the dirty work anyway.

No burglar alarm system will keep out a truly determined intruder. The point is to discourage potential intruders who are not quite so highly motivated, which accounts for the vast majority of home burglars.

An industrial complex or high-level office building might require the most sophisticated and up-to-date alarm system available, regardless of the price. But such a system is probably inappropriate and unnecessary in your home, and it is very unlikely to provide more real security than the projects presented here. This is assuming, of course, that your home-made security system is well laid out and properly installed.

This chapter discusses the factors you should consider in setting up and installing a practical security system. Some of information might seem almost insultingly obvious. No insult is intended. Consider such obvious statements as checklist reminders. There are so many things to think of in laying out and installing an alarm system that it is all too easy to overlook something very simple and terribly obvious, once you remember it. Most hobbyists make their share of such silly and careless mistakes, but they avoid making the same mistakes twice. The obvious points made in this chapter are included just to make things a little easier for you.

One the other hand, this chapter cannot possibly include everything that you need to consider when installing your security system. Every system is different, and it is impossible to predict, much less cover, all of the possibilities. In addition, your individual application may have unusual or even unique factors to take into account.

Although the focus here is on protecting a home, much of the same information can be applied to a small office or store.

Entrances

The most important job of any burglar alarm system is to discourage a potential intruder from getting into the protected area in the first place. Specialized monitoring within the protected area (such as motion detectors or cameras) can be important, but it should be considered secondary. If the intruder is within the protected area before the alarm is set off, he or she might be able to grab something and run. How much better it would be to get the burglar to run away empty handed instead of entering your property.

For this reason, the first step in laying out an intrusion-detection system is to make a list of all possible entrances to the protected area. For most home-security systems, the protected area would probably include the entire building. In some specialized cases, the protected area might be just a single room. For your purposes here, it doesn't matter. The same principles apply. From here on, assume your system is intended to guard your entire home unless otherwise noted.

Consider all exterior doors, including any that are "never" used or "permanantly" locked. Even if a doorway is boarded up, a reasonably strong intruder can get in with a crowbar.

Next, consider all of the windows in your home, with two possible exceptions. A tiny window, such as those found in some bathrooms, that is clearly too small for anyone, even a small child, to pass through can probably be ignored. Similarly, a barred window, or one protected with a metal grate of some sort might be impassable, but such a window should be ignored by your security system only if the bars or gratings are permanently installed and nonmovable. A window with a fold-away grating held in place by a lock should still be considered a potential entrance. Remember, no practical lock is ever truly unpickable. Any padlock can be defeated by a heavy hacksaw and a little patience. In fact, a determined intruder might be able to use a hacksaw or similar metal-cutting tool to get past any bars or gratings.

Whenever there is the slightest room for doubt, count it as a potential entrance. Usually protecting the extra unlikely entrance won't cost you much more than a couple dollars for the additional switch sensors.

Don't neglect to include any upstairs windows on your list. Of course, it would be more difficult to get inside your home that way, it is far from impossible. A nearby tree or rainspout can make it very easy for an agile intruder to climb up. Even without such aids to access, an upstairs window can be reached with a ladder.

Some professional burglars seem to make it a habit to try upstairs windows first, because they are much more likely to be left unlocked and unprotected by a burglar alarm, because many people naively assume the height makes them safe.

If you live in a high-rise apartment building on an upper floor, the windows are less likely to be used for entrance by an intruder, but it is still far from impossible. If there is any kind of ledge, your window might be reached from a nearby apartment. Are you sure that all of your neighbors have adaquate security systems? Once an intruder gets into your neighbor's apartment, will that give relatively easy access to yours?

Burglars have also been known to get inside high-rise apartments with a window washer's scaffold.

Admittedly, such burglars are rather unlikely. Most burglars won't take such physical risks and go to such extra effort unless they think there is a very good reason to assume it will reward them with a good haul. Such tricks are much more likely to be resorted to in a ritzy high-rise apartment building, where it is obvious that all of the residents have plenty of money, and therefore, lots of profitable items to steal. You decide whether the risk of such determined and gutsy burglars will make it worth your while to fully cover your windows in an upper-floor apartment.

Now, for most modern homes, the doors and windows will account for all the entrances to the building, but just to be on the safe side, do not prematurely trust this generalized assumption. Take a few minutes to use your imagination. Pretend that you are outside the house and it is a matter of life and death for you to get inside without using any of the doors or windows.

Would it be possible to crawl in through an air conditioning vent or perhaps through some sort of plumbing fixture? Could someone get into the house by sliding down the chimney? Be as imaginative and creative as you possibly can. Try to cover all possibilities no matter how absurd. You can consider the odds and practicalities later. For now, just freely brainstorm, making a list of each idea as it occurs to you, whether it is good or bad, realistic or silly.

Later, when you have completed this fanciful list of ways to get into your house, you will get more critical with each item. Just how practical is each of your suggestions? What are the odds that a determined burglar might try to get inside your home that way? There is no way to set these odds definitively, of course. You will just have to guess.

Now, you have to decide whether the "guesstimate" odds make it worthwhile to protect that mode of entry with your security system. This whole exercise might seem silly and a waste of time. In most cases, you probably won't end up making any additions to your security system this way, but you might. It is a better-safe-than-sorry procedure. If there is an alternate way of entering your home, don't you want to know about it? This little exercise will only take a few minutes, and it can't hurt. It can even be fun, if you approach it with the right attitude.

At this point you should have a list of all possible and probable ways to get into your house. Can each entry be locked? This is the best form of security. In many cases, simply locking the doors and windows will be a sufficient security system in itself. Most burglaries seem to be done pretty much by chance, in a hit-or-miss fashion. The casual burglar keeps an eye open for a handy opportunity and quickly takes advantage of any opportunity that happens to come along. He or she might move quickly from house to house until an unlocked door or window appears. That home will be the one robbed.

Of course, many burglars are very good at picking locks, and most home door and window locks are not really very imposing, especially to an experienced or determined burglar.

A favored method of illegal entry is to break a window or use a glass cutter to noiselessly make a hole in it. The intruder then reaches in through the opening and releases the latch holding the window shut. The window can now be opened fully.

The susceptibility of locks is the reason intrusion-detector alarms are necessary. The locks are the first line of defense, and the alarm system is the second.

Consider what type of sensor switch would best protect each entry point on your list. Refer to chapter 2 for more information on the various types of sensor switches available for you to choose from. For standard doors and most windows, magnetic reed switches will probably be the best and most convenient choice.

Of course a magnetic reed switch should be mounted on the inside of the protected door or window. It wouldn't be a good idea for the potential intruder to have access to the sensor switch before setting off the alarm. After the fact, it won't do him any good.

The actual reed switch (the parts with wires leading to the alarm circuitry) should be mounted on the fixed door frame or window frame. The magnet section should be mounted on the movable door or window. Be careful to align the two halves of the magnetic reed switch properly with one another. They should be physically as close together as possible when the door or window is fully shut, but as far apart as possible when the door or window is opened. This arrangement suggests that the switch unit should be mounted away from the hinged side of the door. Figure 8-1 shows an improper and ineffectual mounting of a magnetic reed switch. Figure 8-2 shows a correct setup.

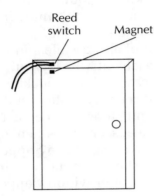

Fig. 8-1 *This is an improperly and ineffectually mounted magnetic reed switch.*

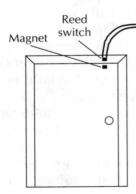

Fig. 8-2 *This is a correctly mounted magnetic reed switch.*

For doors, the magnetic reed switch is usually mounted along the top of the door, as illustrated in Figs. 8-1 and 8-2. But in some cases, it can be mounted on the nonhinged side. Usually it will be most convenient and secure if the switch unit is mounted as high on the door as practical. For a window, it will usually be best to mount the magnetic reed switch along the side.

For some applications, you might want your alarm system to know how wide the window is open. Mount several reed switches on the side of the window frame at different positions.

Mount a single magnet unit on the movable window itself. As the window is moved up (or down), the magnet activates each of the switches individually. The control circuitry can then determine which switch is activated, which indicates how far the window is opened.

It is usually difficult, if not impossible, to mount magnetic reed switches on windows with metallic frames. Some other sort of sensor switch might be required.

In addition to a sensor switch that indicates when the window is opened, it is a good idea to use foil tape, as described in chapter 2, as a guard against an intruder simply breaking the window or using a glass cutter. Position the tape so that no one can cut a hole in the window big enough to crawl through without setting off the alarm.

The use of foil tape is particularly important for nonopenable windows. Don't forget to protect any windows in your door. Many doors, especially in older houses, have a small decorative window (which also serves as an obvious peep hole) inserted in the wooden door. Don't make it too easy for a potential intruder to break this little window and reach in to unlock the door and possibly disable your magnetic reed switch using a small permanent magnet. Foil tape is very desirable here.

Housing the alarm circuitry

An important consideration in setting up and installing an intrusion-detection alarm system is how you will house the circuit. Of course, to some extent, this is a part of any electronic project. You usually don't want to just have the naked circuit boards out in the open. This is unattractive and can subject the circuitry to unnecessary potential damage from environmental conditions. But in most electronic projects, the decisions on housing the circuit boards are usually based on cosmetic considerations. After all, almost any case or enclosure will do the job—it's just something to hold the circuitry in. So, why not use the housing that looks the best?

But in an alarm system, other factors are far more important than how the project looks. You can use attractive cases if you want, but that should not be the primary consideration. Usually the alarm control circuit will not be displayed in open view anyway, so the appearance of its housing is almost irrelevant. What is important in this application is that the project's housing is secure.

You don't want to encourage an intruder to try to disable your alarm system by pulling wires. And if you get an intruder who has some knowledge of electronics, definitely do not allow access to your alarm system circuit boards.

The case for your alarm circuit should not be too easy to open. You especially want to avoid any type of quick-opening case here. Hold-down screws are a good idea. If possible, use screws with unusual, nonstandard heads. Many burglars carry a few common tools, such as screwdrivers, with them.

Another way to thwart an intruder with a screwdriver is to put a little nail polish or epoxy over the screw head once it is in place. It will then be very, very difficult to remove the screw and open the case. Of course, this means you should first thoroughly check out the circuit and make sure everything is working properly. It will be just as difficult for you to open the case for servicing as it is for the intruder. Also, you should not use this sort of trick on a case that must periodically be opened to replace batteries or for any other reason.

Normally, you will use only enough screws to do the job of holding the project case together securely. A lot of electronics hobbyists (and a surprising number of commercial manufacturers) tend to use a lot of excess screws that don't really accomplish much but add to the frustration factor if you ever have to open the case. But for an alarm circuit, it might be a good idea to add to the frustration factor.

In fact, you might even add some dummy screws, which aren't really holding the case shut or doing anything at all. An intruder won't know which screw is which. The intruder probably won't bother with trying. Even if he or she does, it will take a long time to get the case open.

Use a moderately heavy metal case for alarm circuits. A plastic case or a thin metal box could be broken. If possible, it is a good idea to mount and attach the alarm circuit case directly to a wall or a heavy piece of furniture. This will make it harder for an intruder to break it and get the alarm to shut up that way.

The actual alarm-sounding circuit or other sounding device should be similarly protected, especially the wires connecting it to the alarm controller circuit. Don't let an intruder simply cut a connecting wire to silence your alarm.

In a permanent installation, it is probably worthwhile to run the connecting wires inside the walls, with the alarm circuits mounted directly to the wall and without direct external access to the connection points.

A siren or alarm bell can be protected by enclosing it in a metallic cage or box-type housing. A good sturdy lock would help slow down someone desperately trying to silence the alarm once it has been set off.

Position the alarm control circuitry and the primary alarm-sounding device well within the protected area, so that an intruder cannot get to them without first setting off the alarm. The worst the intruder can do then is shut off the alarm prematurely, and the above suggestions are designed to make that as difficult as possible to accomplish.

Some people mount the alarm-control circuit box on the exterior of their house, right by the front door. This allows them to conveniently use a key switch to enable and disable the alarm. But it also practically invites an intelligent intruder to break or otherwise destroy the control circuit before the alarm is triggered.

Use great care in the placement of any reset or disable switches. Disguise their function, if possible. Such switches must be placed where legitimate users have convenient and ready access to them when entering or leaving the protected area, but not where they are obvious to an intruder.

A key switch is fine, especially for discouraging casual intruders who aren't too highly motivated to get in. But the lock mechanism of most key switches is relatively simple and rather easy to pick. A key switch is often a good choice but don't rely on it totally, because it by itself can only offer limited security.

If the switch is concealed or not obviously visible, or if it looks like it is for some other purpose, an intruder might not find it until it is too late.

There is no reason the reset or disable switch must be mounted right on the case of the alarm controller circuit. It could be at a remote location. This is particularly advisable if the switch must be placed at the entrance to the protected area for some reason. You don't want the control circuit to be that accessible.

Protect the connecting wires as much as possible, especially if opening the switch disables the alarm. Cutting a connecting wires will effectively look like an open switch to the control circuit. If the reset or disable switch must be closed to turn off the alarm, cutting a connecting wire will not help the intruder. Unfortunately, this feature will usually require more complex circuitry to reset or disable the alarm system.

❖ 9
Automotive security

AMERICANS ARE SPENDING MORE AND MORE TIME IN THEIR CARS. For many, a car is far from a luxury but is an absolute necessity. If a car is stolen or damaged, it could qualify as a disaster.

In addition, many people have some fairly expensive equipment in their automobiles, including such things as car phones and stereo systems. Such items are obviously appealing to thieves. And of course, many thieves specialize in stealing and reselling cars, not to mention kids who steal cars for joy rides.

Clearly, an automotive security system is a valuable accessory for any car. In addition to automotive burglar alarms, this chapter considers some other aspects of automotive security that can help keep you and your property safe.

As far as basic principles go, an automotive security system is essentially the same as a home security system, except some different sensor switches are used. It makes good sense to power the automotive security system from the car battery. This means in almost all cases, the circuit must be designed to operate off of a 12 V supply. It also must draw little or no current while in the monitoring mode. This is important, because the ignition will probably be off at such times, and a significant drain on the battery could run it down so the car won't start the next time you use it. When the engine is running, the battery is automatically recharged, but this can't happen when the engine is off.

When the alarm is set off, the circuit will almost certainly draw more current, but the alarm should not be allowed to stay on long enough to run down the battery. Ideally, the noise of the alarm should summon you to manually reset the system. If this is not possible (and often is isn't), a time-delay circuit to shut down the alarm after a few minutes is highly desirable. Time-delay circuits are discussed in chapter 7. When the time-delay circuit turns off the alarm, it should also automatically reset the system, otherwise, the vehicle will be left unprotected.

In addition to preventing the possibility of a dead battery, a time-delay shutoff will also keep you from becoming a public nuisance. Your neighbors would not be happy to listen to your alarm continuing to sound off for hours, long after the potential thief has been frightened off. This is especially annoying at night, which is when the alarm is most likely to be set off because thieves like the cover of darkness.

False alarms can be a serious problem with car alarms. Part of the function of any alarm is to make noise to summon help. But after a few false alarms, neighbors tend to ignore any further alarms—except perhaps a to file a complaint in the morning. You even could be ticketed and fined for leaving an alarm sounding too long, and disturbing the public peace.

Excessive false alarms, especially in systems without an automatic shutdown timer will place undue drain on the car's battery. What security is there in getting into your car and discovering the battery is dead?

Vibration sensors are strongly subject to false alarms, especially if the sensitivity is set too high, or if they are not properly installed. (Ironically enough, a car parked near the author's window had an alarm go off falsely as he was writing this chapter.)

Automotive sensor devices

Special automotive door switches are the most commonly used types of sensors for car alarm systems. These door switches can be of either the normally open or the normally closed type. When the door is open, the switch is in its normal position. The switch is activated when the door is closed, as it usually should be. Do not be confused by what is normal as far as the switch is concerned.

In some cases, you might be able to use the existing door switches in your vehicle (used to activate the dome light when the door is open) in your alarm system. In most cases, however, it is necessary or desirable to install independent door switches.

Automotive door switches are fairly inexpensive and are widely available. You can usually purchase them from any store that sells alarm systems or automotive supplies.

Do not forget to use sensor switches to protect the trunk and hood. Valuable items stored in the trunk can be stolen. Trunk locks are notoriously easy to pick or force open. In many automobiles, a small, agile thief can get inside the vehicle through the trunk.

The hood of a car usually isn't locked, although a latch can be controlled by a dashboard control. Still, it is easy enough for a thief to force the hood open, despite the latch. Once the hood is open, the thief can hot wire your car or steal your battery or other valuable engine parts. This is not unusual.

It is a good idea to set up your alarm system so that the alarm will sound if the engine is started before the alarm system is disabled. Do not monitor the engine at the ignition switch, because hot wiring the vehicle will usually bypass the ignition switch.

Vibration switches or motion detectors are often used in automotive alarm systems. Such sensors are useful in protecting the vehicle from being towed away by car thieves, and it will usually be set off by attempts to pick the car locks or by other attempts to break in. Unfortunately, sensitivity can be a real problem with vibration sensors. You want it sensitive enough to set off the alarm when necessary, but false alarms can be a real problem. A passer-by might bump into a parked car, especially when squeezing between two parked cars. Someone might innocently lean against your car in a parking lot. A cat jumping onto the car can set off a vibration detector.

Foil tape to guard the windows against breakage might be a good idea, but the tape must be carefully placed to avoid obstructing the driver's view.

Most automotive alarm systems are armed and disarmed by an external key switch. Such locks are relatively easy to pick, especially when there is no vibration sensor in the system. If the alarm system has a time-delay circuit (see chapter 8), you can place the disarm switch inside the protected vehicle. If a key switch is used here, the potential thief won't be able to use it and won't have time to pick the lock before the alarm is set off.

Simple automobile alarm system

A simple, but reasonably effective automobile burglar alarm circuit is shown in Fig. 9-1. A suitable parts list for this project is given in Table 9-1.

A 556 dual timer IC is used in this project (IC1). You can replace this chip with two separate 555 or 7555 timers, without affecting the circuit operation in any way. The only modification you will have to make is correcting the pin numbers. Refer to chapter 7 for the necessary details.

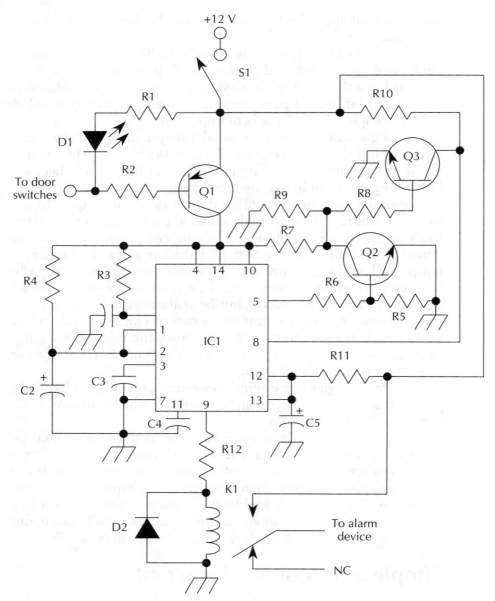

Fig. 9-1 *Project 35. Simple automobile alarm system.*

The input to this alarm circuit is labeled "To door switches" in the schematic. Multiple normally open switches can be connected in parallel or multiple normally closed switches in series.

These door switches can be specially installed automotive door switches, or, in some cases you can tap into the built-in

**Table 9-1 Parts list for project 35.
Simple automobile alarm system of Fig. 9-1.**

IC1	556 dual timer
Q1	PNP transistor (2N3906 or similar)
Q2, Q3	NPN transistor (2N3904 or similar)
D1	LED
D2	Diode (1N4148, 1N914, or similar)
C1	0.1 µF capacitor
C2	22 µF 25 V electrolytic capacitor
C3, C4	0.01 µF capacitor
C5	100 µF 25 V electrolytic capacitor
R1	680 Ω ¼ W 5% resistor
R2	18 kΩ ¼ W 5% resistor
R3, R8, R10, R12	10 kΩ ¼ W 5% resistor
R4	620 kΩ ¼ W 5% resistor
R5	5.6 kΩ ¼ W 5% resistor
R6	47 kΩ ¼ W 5% resistor
R7	39 kΩ ¼ W 5% resistor
R9	4.7 kΩ ¼ W 5% resistor
R11	820 kΩ ¼ W 5% resistor
K1	12 V relay to suit load
S1	SPST key switch (see text)

switches that turn on the dome light when one or more of the car doors is opened. It is assumed that an activated sensor switch will ground the base of transistor Q1 through resistor R2. This point is usually held HIGH through LED D1 and resistor R1. The LED indicates the circuit is armed.

In some cases, you might have to work with switches that will feed a high voltage (about +12 V) into the circuit. This should be easy enough to correct—just run D1 and R1 to ground instead of to V+. This connection is shown in the partial schematic of Fig. 9-2.

Other sensor devices can also be used with this alarm circuit, including vibration sensors and/or foil tape protecting the windows from breakage.

The system is armed by closing switch S1. A lock switch is recommended for this purpose. When this switch is opened, the circuit can't get any power, so it can do nothing at all.

When the alarm circuit is armed (on) the alarm will be sounded when any door is opened (or other sensor switch is activated). There is a built-in delay feature to give you time to disarm

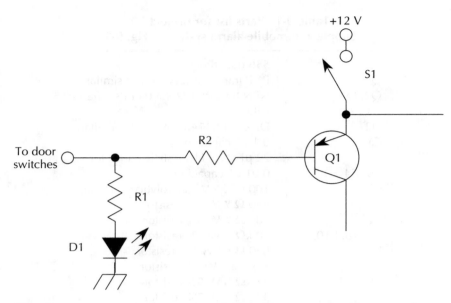

Fig. 9-2 *In some vehicles, you might need to rewire the door switches as shown here.*

the alarm when legitimately entering your own vehicle. The locking arm/disarm switch (S1) can be mounted on the outside body of the car, but greater security can be obtained by installing this switch inside the vehicle, perhaps under the dashboard. Position the switch where it is conveniently accessible to someone legitimately entering the vehicle, but try not to make it too obvious to an intruder. Physically protect the connecting wires to the switch as much as possible. The intruder should not be able to disable the alarm by yanking out or cutting wires. If possible, install the switch in a drilled hole, with its connecting wires inside the body of the car. Often the automobile's own horn can be used for this purpose, or you can use a separate, specialized siren circuit.

A relay (K1) controls an external alarm sounding device. Any of those discussed in chapter 3 will do. Your best choice would be an alarm-sounding device that works comfortably off the +12 V supplied by the automobile battery. If necessary, you can drop this voltage to a lower value with a simple resistive voltage-divider string.

When the alarm circuit is triggered, the relay (K1) is activated and feeds the 12 V from the battery to the external alarm-sounding device. The alarm will be automatically shut off after a preset period of time.

This alarm circuit features two timers (the two halves of IC1). One timer sets the delay between the time the sensor switch is activated and the alarm is sounded (permitting a legitimate user to first disarm the alarm system.) The second timer determines how long the alarm will sound once it is triggered.

The timing components for timer A (which controls the initial time delay) are resistor R4 and capacitor C2. Don't make this time delay too long, or you will make it too easy for a potential thief to find a way to get around the protection of your alarm system. On the other hand, make the time delay long enough to permit convenient legitimate disarming of the system. Using the component values suggested in the parts list, the time delay will be approximately 15 seconds. To increase the delay time, simply increase the value of either resistor R4 or capacitor C2 or both. Similarly, reducing the value of either or both of these components will reduce the delay time.

Timer B controls how long the alarm will continue to sound once it is triggered. The timing components here are resistor R11 and capacitor C5. With the values given in the parts list the alarm will sound for about 90 seconds, then it will shut itself off and automatically reset. If an intruder hasn't been scared off within 90 seconds or so, letting the alarm continue to sound probably won't be much additional deterrent.

If you want to increase the time the alarm sounds, it is again simply a matter of increasing the value of either resistor R4 or capacitor C2, or both. Reducing the value of either or both of these timing components will shorten the time the alarm sounds when the circuit is triggered.

Emergency flasher

There is a lot more to automotive security than just a burglar alarm. If you have ever had an accident, a flat tire, or some other problem at night or in stormy weather, you know that visibility can be a real problem. Oncoming vehicles might not be able to see the obstacle (stopped vehicle), which obviously would be a dangerous invitation to an additional accident. It is all too easy for another driver to collide with a stalled or otherwise stopped vehicle he or she cannot see in time.

Therefore, it is a very good idea to carry an emergency flasher of some sort in your car at all times. In the case of a problem, set out the flasher and turn it on. It produces a bright, flashing light that is almost impossible to miss. In addition to warning other drivers, an emergency flasher can aid in summoning help.

Figure 9-3 shows a simple but effective emergency flasher circuit. A suitable parts list for this project appears in Table 9-2.

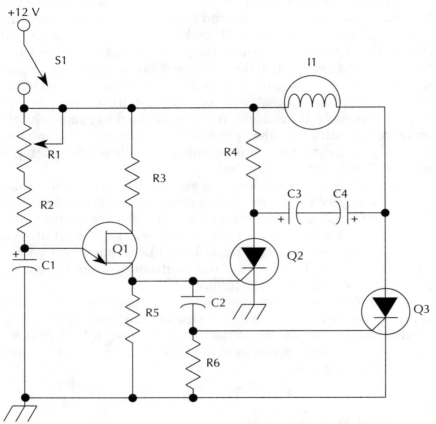

Fig. 9-3 *Project 36. Emergency flasher.*

Potentiometer R1 can be manually adjusted to determine the flash rate. Using the component values suggested in the parts list, the flash rate can be adjusted over a range of about 35 to over 150 flashes per minute. A moderately slow flash rate—say about 50 to 75 flashes per minute—would probably be the best choice.

You can operate this emergency flasher circuit directly from the vehicle battery. It is a good idea to carry a 12 V lantern battery along with the flasher, just in case the emergency involves a dead car battery.

Table 9-2   Parts list for project 36.
Emergency flasher of Fig. 9-3.

Q1	UJT (unijunction transistor) (2N2646, Radio Shack RS2009, or similar)
Q2, Q3	SCR (C1064 or similar)
I1	12 V lamp (GE #1073 or similar)
C1	4.7 µF 25 V electrolytic capacitor
C2	0.01 µF capacitor
C3	100 µF 25 V electrolytic capacitor
R1	250 kΩ potentiometer
R2	3.9 kΩ ¼ W 5% resistor
R3	220 kΩ ¼ W 5% resistor
R4	2.2 kΩ ¼ W 5% resistor
R5	10 Ω ½ W 5% resistor
R6	1 kΩ ½ W 5% resistor
S1	SPST switch

This project is fairly inexpensive and can be built quite compactly, so it can be stored in the car without taking up a lot of space. Keep it under one of the seats, or perhaps in the trunk.

Headlight delay timer

Have you ever parked your car in a dark garage and then had to fumble around to find the light switch? You could leave the headlights on until you've turned on the garage light, and then reach back in the car to turn the headlights off. But this is a very inelegant solution at best. Besides, it is all to easy to forget, especially if you are distracted in any way and leave the headlights on all night. This will give you an excellent chance of finding a dead battery in the morning.

The circuit shown in Fig. 9-4 is a handy, automated headlight control timer that will prevent such a problem. The parts list for this project appears in Table 9-3.

When activated via switch S1, this circuit turns the headlights on through the relay (K1) for a predetermined period. After the circuit times out, it automatically turns the headlights back off. You don't have to worry about it.

The length of time the headlights will stay lit is determined by the values of capacitor C1 and potentiometer R1. You can manually adjust R1 for the desired time period within a fairly wide range. In most applications, it would make sense to use a

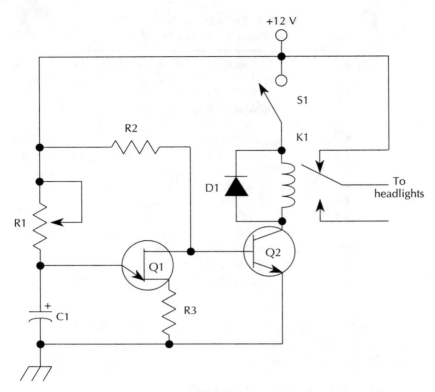

Fig. 9-4 *Project 37. Headlight delay timer.*

**Table 9-3 Parts list for project 37.
Headlight delay timer of Fig. 9-4.**

Q1	UJT (2N2646 or similar)
Q2	NPN transistor (HEP50, GE-20, or similar)
D1	Diode (1N4003 or similar)
C1	10 μF 25 V electrolytic capacitor
R1	10 kΩ potentiometer
R2	330 Ω ¼ W 5% resistor
R3	1 kΩ ¼ W 5% resistor
K1	Relay (coil—180 Ω)
S1	SPST switch

trimpot instead of a front-panel control for R1. Depending on the setting of R1, the lights will remain on for a period of a minute or two. To extend the timer range for a longer on time, you can use a larger value for capacitor C1.

Switch S1 is a normally open SPST push-button switch. Briefly closing this switch activates the timer circuit. This project does not interfere with the ordinary operation of the head-lights in any way. If the ordinary headlight switch is in the on position, this timer circuit will not turn the headlights off.

Low-battery warning

The dreaded dead battery has probably faced every driver at some time or another. If the headlights or some other accessories are left on for an extended period while the engine is off, the battery will discharge. A defective battery might not be able to hold an adequate charge. Heavy drain on the engine while multiple accessories are in use can also weaken the battery.

To help prevent dead battery problems, the circuit shown in Fig. 9-5 will let you know if the battery is getting weak. The parts list for this simple project is given in Table 9-4.

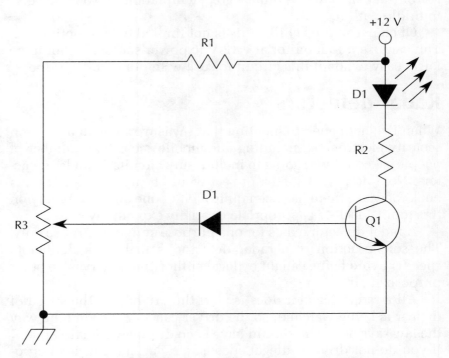

Fig. 9-5 *Project 38. Low-battery warning circuit.*

As you can see, this project is really quite simple. When the battery voltage drops below a preset value (set by trimpot R3), the LED lights up, letting you know there is some sort of prob-

Table 9-4 Parts list for project 38.
Low-battery warning circuit of Fig. 9-5.

Q1	NPN transistor (2N3904 or similar)
D1	6.2 V zener diode
D2	LED
R1	1.2 kΩ ¼ W 5% resistor
R2	680 Ω ¼ W 5% resistor
R3	10 kΩ trimpot

lem. This will give you a chance to try to correct the situation before the battery goes completely dead on you.

In most applications a screwdriver-adjusted trimpot should be used for R3, not a front-panel control. Once you've set the trigger voltage for the circuit, you probably won't want to change it. A front-panel control is often a great temptation for someone else to fiddle with it.

Of course, a project like this is not limited to automotive use. You can use it to monitor any 12 Vdc power source. It should be fairly easy to adapt this circuit for use with other voltages too.

Radar detectors

When I've happened to mention that I was working on a book on security electronics, including automobile security, a number of people asked if I was going to include any circuits for radar detectors. No, I don't feel such a project would be appropriate for this book. Because there has been quite a bit of one-sided publicity on this topic, I feel it is appropriate to briefly explain my reasons.

A radar detector exists for one purpose and one purpose only. The sole function of a radar detector is to help a deliberate speeder avoid being caught by legal authorities. It serves no other purpose at all.

All a radar detector does is alert the driver that the speed of the car is being watched, so the driver can start driving the way the law says he or she should have been driving in the first place. If you do not drive at illegal speeds, a radar detector is of absolutely no use to you whatsoever.

Much has been said about the supposed inaccuracy of radar. It is so "inaccurate" that it is used to protect thousands of lives at major airports and military installations all over the world. Police radar is just a stripped-down version of the same technology.

Admittedly, as with any high-technology equipment, police radar guns require some degree of training for proper use, and in some cases, adequate training may be lacking. There have been reports of trees radar clocked at speeds of 70 mph (miles per hour), and similar absurdities. But such an extreme, obvious error would certainly be easy to identify in a practical road situation. A misused radar gun will give outrageous readings, which are obviously meaningless. If the reading is 5 or 10 mph off, that is a problem, but such low-level errors are not likely to occur with radar, though they would be quite likely with most other methods of speed measurement.

Certainly a radar gun clocks speeds more accurately and is less prone to error than other standard methods of determining the speed of a passing vehicle. When a mistake is made, it will almost always be quite easy to spot.

And even if police radar were totally inaccurate, how on earth could a radar detector possibly help a law-abiding driver? If the radar detector goes off, you know you're being watched. What can you do about it, except drive at the posted speed limit—which you should be doing anyway. If the police clocked you inaccurately, knowing you are being watched would be of no practical value because there wouldn't be anything you could do about it.

So, the supposed inaccuracy of police radar is not a legitimate justification for radar detectors at all. It is just an excuse for radar detector manufacturers and habitual speeders to hide behind.

The same thoughts apply to so-called *speed traps*. If you are obeying the law, a radar detector is utterly unnecessary. In some cases, there might be a tricky and improper speed trap where the speed limit is not adequately posted. But how can a radar detector help here? It can't. If the radar detector tells you that you're being watched, and you don't know the speed limit, there isn't much you can do but guess and hope, which would be no different than passing through such a dishonest speed trap without a radar detector.

A few people offer the curious argument that at least chronic speeders will slow down when their radar detectors go off, which would at least be some benefit to public safety. Well, yes, but they'll also feel more secure to speed when they're not being watched. Drivers are not being watched the majority of the time they're on the road, so the radar detector directly encourages illegal speeding. Of course, that is the sole and only function of this device. That is the entire reason for its existence.

Radar detectors are currently permitted, only because of some legal loopholes, which could probably be closed if a little common sense were used.

Most of the legal loopholes are related to the Federal Communications Act. But radar detectors really aren't legitimately covered by this legislation at all. A radar detector has nothing to do with the Communications Act because it is not a communications device. Yes, a radar detector does receive a radio-wave signal, but it merely detects the absence or presence of the signal. Any transmitted intelligence or data (communications) cannot be received by any radar detector presently on the market. It is no more a communications receiver than a field-strength meter. Because the design of a radar detector precludes the possibility of the reception of a communications signal, it is not at all protected by the Federal Communications Act, any more than the car cigarette lighter or headlights.

At least one radar detector proponent insists that this same argument would apply to a radio when no station was broadcasting. Wrong. The radio circuitry doesn't change. It was designed specifically to receive communications signals. A radar detector, on the other hand, was specifically designed not to receive any communications signals, but merely to detect the presence or absence of a carrier. This is not communications. One toaster occassionally picked up a strong commercial radio station in the area. This guy's argument would make more sense for the toaster, which can receive communications signals under certain conditions, than for a radar detector, which cannot.

Even if radar detectors were communications receivers as defined by the Federal Communications Act, it is still quite legal for authorities to ban the use of specific types of receivers in moving vehicles if such use presents a threat to public safety. Because the only possible purpose of a radar detector is to encourage speeding, the case is pretty clear cut. If someone wants to operate a radar detector in his basement, there would be no complaint.

Many radar detector owners claim they are protesting what they consider unfair and unreasonable speed limits. The basic idea here is legitimate, but it doesn't really justify radar detectors. By all means, people who feel this way have the right to fight to change the laws. Agreement or disagreement with them is not the issue here. And there are times when civil disobedience is a legitimate and responsible choice for a citizen to make. But there is a difference between responsible civil disobedience and wreckless and selfish law breaking. True civil disobedience means willingness to accept responsibility for breaking the law—a willingness to go to court and fight it and to accept the legal consequences if necessary. The purpose of a radar detector is to aid and abet someone in breaking a law and avoid getting caught. That is, radar detector users, by definition, are unwilling to face the legal consequences of violating the speeding laws, so their claims of civil disobedience are weak, at best.

In light of all this, I hope you can see why I'd consider it highly irresponsible to publish plans for a radar detector project. I would then be guilty of aiding and abetting law breakers. I don't think that would be appropriate at any time, but especially not in a book on electronic security.

Overspeed alarm

Speeding is doubly dangerous. The higher the speed, the greater the required stopping distance. By the time a driver can react to a hazard, there might not be sufficient distance to stop the vehicle. The result is a collision. Speeding increases the risk of such accidents. Some radar detector advocates point to statistics that allegedly "prove" that speeders have fewer accidents. This is clearly ridiculous, and just plain false. Statistics can be manipulated to "prove" almost anything, which means that statistics alone make weak proof for anything.

The second risk of speeding is that the higher the vehicle speed, the greater the energy that must be suddenly dissipated in a collision. The higher the speed involved in a given collision, the greater the potential for harm.

Someone truly interested in automotive safety and security will not invest in a radar detector but perhaps in something like an overspeed alarm. A radar detector only lets you know when you are being watched. An overspeed alarm lets you know if you exceed a preset speed.

The circuit for a simple but practical overspeed alarm is shown in Fig. 9-6. A suitable parts list for this project is given in Table 9-5.

The input to this circuit is in the form of pulses taken from the engine distributor points. Transistor Q1, along with its associated components, converts these input pulses into a dc voltage that is proportional to the engine rpm, which is directly related to the automobile speed. (The reference to distributor points applies only to older vehicles.)

IC1A and IC1B basically act as a comparator and Schmitt trig-

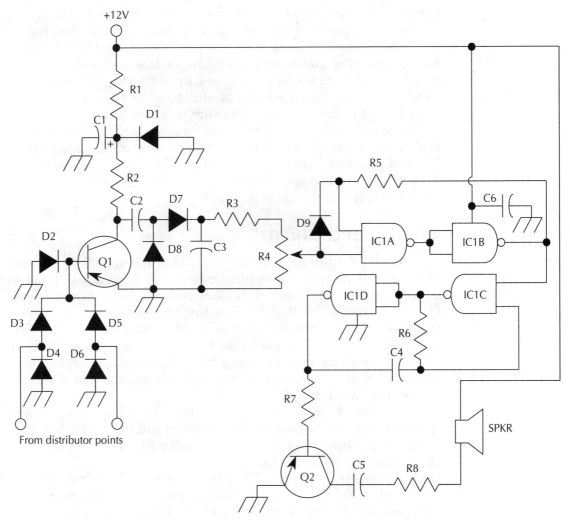

Fig. 9-6 *Project 39. Overspeed alarm.*

ger. When the dc voltage exceeds a specific preset value (set by potentiometer R4), these gates enable the gated oscillator made up of IC1C, IC1D, and their associated components. The signal from this oscillator is fed to the speaker, producing an attention-getting tone. This tone continues to sound as long as you exceed the preset speed. Reducing the speed causes the alarm to shut down and reset itself.

With this project installed in your car, you will never accidentally or unknowingly speed again. You can still speed if you

Table 9-5 Parts list for project 39.
Overspeed alarm of Fig. 9-6.

IC1	CD4011 quad NAND gate
Q1	PNP transistor (2N3904, Radio Shack RS2009, or similar)
Q2	PNP transistor (TIP3055, Radio Shack RS2020, or similar)
D1	9 V zener diode
D2	4.7 V zener diode
D3–D9	Diode (1N4148, 1N914, or similar)
C1	100 μF 25 V electrolytic capacitor
C2, C3, C6	0.1 μF capacitor
C4, C5	0.01 μF capacitor
R1	1 kΩ ¼ W 5% resistor
R2	4.7 kΩ ¼ W 5% resistor
R3	47 kΩ ¼ W 5% resistor
R4	250 kΩ potentiometer (see text)
R5	1 MΩ ¼ W 5% resistor
R6, R7	22 kΩ ¼ W 5% resistor
R8	270 kΩ ¼ W 5% resistor

really want to, of course. But this device will let you know you are doing so, even when you aren't paying attention to the speedometer. An overspeed alarm like this is best if it is set for the maximum legal highway speed in your area.

Calibration of this project should be done by two people. Do not attempt to do it by yourself, or you might wind up in an accident caused by your attempt to calibrate a safety device. In the calibration process, the driver carefully maintains a specific speed, and the second person adjust potentiometer R4 to the point where the alarm just goes off at that speed.

You could use a trimpot for R4 to set the overspeed alarm for one specific speed. In this case, the trimpot should then be replaced with a fixed resistor of suitable value, or held in position by a drop of glue or paint. Otherwise, the vibrations of the moving vehicle will eventually jiggle the trimpot shaft out of its calibrated position.

Alternately, and perhaps even better, you can make R4 a front-panel control with a calibrated dial, indicating the position for a number of common speed limits.

The best approach is to find the potentiometer settings for several common speed limits, then replace the potentiometer with a series of fixed resistors of suitable value that can be selected via some push-button switches. That way, the driver can easily and safely change the speed limit while driving.

To minimize the possibility of getting a ticket due to the margin of error in this project, set each alarm speed limit a little low. For example, in an error with a 65 mph speed limited posted, you might set the overspeed alarm to go off at 63 mph or so. This will not make any noticeable difference in how soon you reach your destination, but you will be less likely to receive an undeserved speeding ticket from a police officer whose speedometer or radar gun isn't perfectly calibrated. (Incidentally, a radar detector cannot protect you against such undeserved tickets.)

❖ 10
Advanced security systems

THE BURGLAR ALARM PROJECTS PRESENTED IN THIS BOOK ARE fairly simple and inexpensive, yet they can be quite effective. The projects shown here will be more than sufficient for most home and small business security needs.

Well, if that is the case, then why are so many expensive, deluxe alarms sold every year? Are all the customers of commercial alarm installers being ripped off? Not necessarily. These projects usually will be adequate, but in some cases, you may want more than merely adequate. The more deluxe instrusion-detector systems will be even more difficult for a determined burglar to defeat (though this will probably never be 100% impossible).

Most commercially installed home burglar alarms are pretty much similar to the projects offered in this book and typically cost just a few hundred dollars. Most of the expense is for the labor involved in building and installing the alarm equipment. When you use do-it-yourself projects like these, you are providing this labor yourself, so you don't have to pay someone else for it. Whether this is worthwhile for you depends on what your time is worth (to you) and how much you enjoy building electronic projects (and how good you are at it). Many avid electronics hobbyists would almost be willing to pay for the chance to do it themselves, so they get a real bargain out of the deal.

But can those expensive super-alarm systems ever be worth the (considerable) extra cost? That depends. It is largely a trade-off of cost against effectiveness. It doesn't make much sense to spend $5000 on an alarm system to protect $3000 worth of stealable property. For a large industrial complex, a $5000 alarm system would not be unreasonable, when someone could come in and steal $69,000 worth of equipment.

If you are wealthy enough to have that much stealable property, then a deluxe commercial alarm system might be worthwhile, but such a person is unlikely to be reading a do-it-yourself book like this anyway.

But what if you are installing an intrusion-detector alarm not so much to protect your property as to ensure the personal safety of yourself and your loved ones? How can you put a price tag on human lives?

This is a valid point, but you have to look at how much extra protection the added expense will truly offer. No burglar alarm will keep a very determined intruder out. When someone is home, the function of the alarm is to scare off the intruder and to warn you of the attempted intrusion. The projects presented in the previous chapters will do this quite well. The advantages of the super deluxe alarm systems with the high price tags are mainly for areas where no one should be present (while the alarm is armed). They are also useful for protecting a large area with just a handful of guards.

When no one is in the protected area, the alarm system should frighten off the intruder and/or summon help. Some systems might be designed to physically trap an intruder until help arrives. These functions aren't really applicable to protecting the occupants of a home.

In fact, many of the deluxe alarm systems really can't be used when someone is home, because they depend heavily on sensitive motion detectors and the like. The legitimate occupants would set off the alarm just as easily as an intruder would.

In this chapter, you briefly look at some examples of high-tech security that you might find interesting. If you actually have a need for such things, the information presented here will help point you in the right direction when you go shopping for your security equipment.

There aren't any actual projects in this chapter. One reason is that these devices are rather exotic, and aren't likely to be of much practical use for most readers of a book like this. Also, the technology involved with such equipment is necessarily complex, and such projects would be beyond the scope of this book. For one thing, they would take up too much space. One high-tech project of relatively limited application would take space from five or six (or more) general projects with much wider potential applications. The trade-off would probably not be worth it.

If you are really interested in building something along these lines, projects for most of the high-tech security devices discussed here have appeared from time to time in the electronics hobbyist magazines and some advanced project books.

Lasers for intrusion detection

You have probably heard of the use of laser beams in advanced intrusion-detector systems. You might have even seen such systems on TV or in movies, with the impressive cross-hatch of laser beams. (In many practical systems, the laser beams are likely to be in the infrared region and therefore invisible to the unaided human eye.)

Of course, these laser beams are not used as death rays or anything like that. The potential danger for accidents would be too great, and it would probably be illegal. It would certainly hold the owner of the lasers open to potential lawsuits.

Actually, these are very low-power laser beams. Anyone can walk right through them without suffering any harm. They might damage their eyes if they stare into the source of the laser beams for an extended period, but otherwise, there is no direct physical risk involved. The laser beams don't really do anything to keep anyone out of the protected area. Instead, they are sensors used to set off the alarm if someone enters the protected area while the system is armed.

Basically, the laser cross-hatch system is similar to the simple broken-beam photosensor systems discussed in chapter 2. Such a simple system is shown in Fig. 10-1. If someone (or some object) passes between the light source and the photosensor, the light beam will be broken. The difference in the light level detected by the photosensor can be used to set off the alarm. Of course, if the intruder knows that the photodetector is there (which can be very obvious when a visible light beam is used), he or she can probably avoid setting of the alarm with relative ease. All that is needed is to avoid breaking the light beam. The intruder can probably go over it or under it, or in some cases, go behind the light source or the photosensor. This means these items must be carefully placed and concealed as much as possible to maximize the security. Multiple light beams and photosensors offer greater protection, because they cover more area. Ideally, if the intruder avoids one light beam, that will force him or her to break another, setting off the alarm.

Multiple light beams is precisely the idea behind the cross-hatch laser systems. A complex, overlapping pattern of laser beams fill the protected area, making it very, very difficult, if not

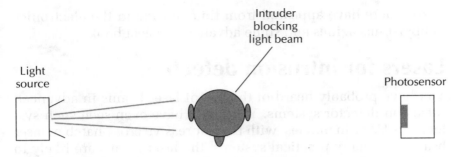

Fig. 10-1 *A broken light beam can indicate the presence of an intruder.*

impossible, for anyone to enter the area without breaking at least one of the laser beams.

Breaking one beam is all that is necessary to set off the alarm.

If invisible, infrared laser beams are used, it will be even be harder for an intruder to avoid breaking any of the beams. How can you avoid what you can't see?

Why are lasers used instead of ordinary light sources, which would surely be less expensive? It's not just because the laser beams look nifty. Actually, the use of lasers in this application is much more efficient and practical than ordinary light sources.

If you are using just a few beams, such as in the simple systems described in chapter 2, it makes sense to use a separate, independent light source for each beam. But this would quickly become impractical and unwieldy (not to mention expensive) for a complex cross-hatch pattern of beams. In such a system, one or just a few lasers provide all of the necessary beams. Reflectors are used to split the original beam into multiple paths throughout the protected area, as shown in the simple, partial system of Fig. 10-2. Each reflected beam is aimed at its own photosensor. If you tried to do this with ordinary light sources, you'd pretty much end up with just a well-lit room. Even if one of the light beams was broken, the photosensor is likely to be fooled by bleed-over light from other nearby beams.

The reason for this limitation is that ordinary light does not make a very good beam. It tends to spread out as it moves away from its source. A laser beam, on the other hand, is naturally very tightly focused, and will spread out very little with distance from its source. Even if you shot a laser beam to the moon, it would still hold its beamlike shape by the time it got there, although it is likely to be a somewhat wider beam after that much distance. With ordinary light, the beam would be almost completely dissi-

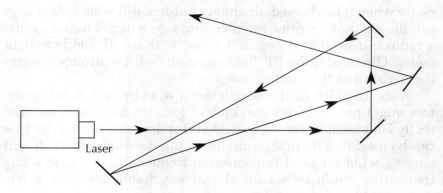

Fig. 10-2 *In a laser security system, a system of mirrors is used to split the beam into multiple paths.*

pated after just a mile or two at best, no matter how many focusing lenses are used.

The upshot of this is that the reflected laser beams in your cross-hatch system remain narrow, well-directed beams throughout the system, but ordinary light beams spread and dissipate. Ordinary beams blend into one another, rendering the system more or less useless.

A good laser cross-hatch system can make a very effective motion detector. In fact, such systems sometimes have problems with false alarms caused by breezes moving lightweight inanimate objects slightly.

Of course, in a home with a pet that might enter the protected area, such a system would be completely worthless. (Well, maybe a goldfish would be OK.)

Bugs

These days it isn't just necessary to protect physical, material property. Sometimes it is just as important, if not more so, to protect intellectual property—information. This is more likely to be a business concern, rather than something the average private home is liable to be faced with, but there are always exceptions.

Modern technology has advanced to the point where a tiny electronic bug can be planted almost anywhere. Most bugs are miniaturized radio transmitters. With modern integrated-circuit technology, they can be made very small indeed. Some types of modern bugs would fit comfortable on your thumbnail. Obviously, it would be difficult to find something that small, especially when it has been deliberately hidden. But what technology can do, technology can overcome. Because a bug is basically just a radio transmitter, it can be located with an RF field-strength meter. Obviously, the RF field strength will be stronger nearer the transmitter than farther away.

A standard RF field-strength meter used by ham radio operators might not do a very good job of locating bugs, because that really isn't what it was designed for. But the same basic principle can be used in a dedicated circuit. A bug-seeking circuit should cover a wide range of transmission frequencies, because a bug transmitter could be set for almost any frequency from a few dozen hertz up into the microwave range.

A bug-seeker circuit must also be very sensitive to small, low-level RF signals. Most bugs are very weak transmitters. The receiver and listening post are usually as close as possible to the bugged site. After all, the people who planted the bug obviously don't want to make it too easy on their victim by using a strong transmission signal—they use the weakest signal that will do the job.

But if you must protect sensitive information, you must be aware that not all modern bugging uses actual RF transmitters. The type of bug described so far is known as *active bugging*. But *passive bugging* is also possible. Passive bugging is usually more difficult and expensive for the person doing the bugging, but it is also a lot harder for the victim to detect passive bugging.

In passive bugging, no bugging signal is transmitted at all, so it can't be detected by watching for such a signal. Instead, existing phenomena is read by the person doing the bugging.

There are many types of passive bugging in use today. Just one is discussed here to give you an idea of the problems involved. A low-power, invisible (infrared) laser in another building is aimed at a window in the area to be bugged. The laser beam is reflected from the window back to a sensor. Any sound near the window (including speaking voices in the bugged room) will cause tiny vibrations in the glass. Sound, of course, is nothing but rhythmical variations in air pressure. The window glass acts like a pseudoeardrum. These vibrations will cause small but definite changes in the reflected laser beam. These changes are detected by the sensor, and special circuitry converts the pattern of the laser beam movement back into acoustic sound waves. The person bugging the area can hear what is being said in the room.

Now, theoretically, this type of bugging could be detected by placing infrared detectors all over every window and mirror or other potential reflecting surface in the area, but this would probably be wildly impractical.

This type of bugging also has the advantage (to the person doing the bugging) of not requiring entry to the bugged area to plant a physical bug. There is no chance of someone accidentally finding the bug, because there is no physical bug to find.

But even passive bugging can be defeated. Have you ever seen an old spy movie when someone goes into the bathroom to tell a secret with the water running? The white noise of the running water helps drown out the speaking voices, so a listener through a bug can't make out what is being said.

The same idea can be applied to high-tech passive bugging techniques such as the laser beam/window trick. Just set up mechanical vibrations that will drown out the relatively small fluctuations caused by speaking voices. This could be a loud noise source, but that would be annoying, especially if you can't predict just when you might be bugged. Some sort of mechanical vibrator that simply shakes the windows (and other reflecting devices) can often be left running continuously, making no more noise in the room than an air conditioner, but to the listener, these mechanical vibrations will be converted into a loud noise, drowning out your words.

Voice scramblers

The most common type of electronic bugging is tapping telephone calls. It isn't always necessary to plant a physical tap on the bugged phone, although that is (technologically) the easiest way to do it.

And, of course, if you use a cellular phone, you are actually transmitting a radio signal that can be picked up by anyone with a suitable receiver.

If you need to discuss sensitive, private matters by phone, and are afraid someone might be listening in, you can use a voice scrambler. This is an electronic circuit that converts the ordinary voice signal into gibberish. The effect usually calls to mind Donald Duck at his most incoherent. The person you are talking to must have an appropriate descrambler unit to reconstruct your voice.

Most practical voice scrambler/descrambler circuits permit the users to set up their own unique scrambling codes, so someone with a similar circuit cannot descramble the signal without the appropriate code.

There are a number of different types of voice scramblers

around today. One of the simplest uses the frequency-inversion method. Although relatively simple, this system is quite effective and provides very good security. The circuit generates a *carrier* signal of some specific fixed frequency. Both the scrambler and the descrambler must use the exact same carrier frequency. This carrier signal is mixed with the normal *audio signal* (your speaking voice) in a special way that the normal audio spectrum is translated into a different spectrum. Anyone listening in will hear an unintelligible "Donald Duck."

If someone tries to listen in with a frequency-inversion descrambling circuit, but uses the wrong carrier frequency, the signal will still be unintelligible. Police in many areas use frequency-inversion scrambling for sensitive radio transmissions.

Stunners

Many people today are understandably afraid of being mugged or attacked. They want to protect themselves in some way. A lot of people keep guns around for their protection, but often they get the opposite result. A gun can often increase rather than decrease the danger. It can protect you against an armed intruder if and only if you get to the weapon first, and if you're a better shot. Because an armed assailant will probably already have a gun drawn and at the ready, you're automatically at a disadvantage.

Every day the newspaper carries stories of accidental shootings or family arguments where someone impulsively reaches for a handy gun. There are strong feelings on both sides of the gun-control issue, and this is not the place for a debate on gun control. Just say a lot of people want to protect themselves, but don't want to carry a gun. They might want to only disable an attacker but not risk killing.

An electronic weapon for this purpose is the stunner or stun gun. This is a small, handheld device that generates a high-power electrical shock.

Discharging a high-voltage burst on the surface of the skin sends the current racing through the nervous system. The nervous system is largely electrical in nature. A small electrical signal at an synapse produces some action—for example, if the synapse is connected to a muscle, a signal can cause the muscle to move. When the rather large stun current reaches a synapse connected to a muscle, it will be a lot stronger than an ordinary synapse signal. The muscle will contract violently, and it might even go into spasms.

The longer the high-voltage burst is applied to the skin, the more muscles will be affected. Once muscle spasms have started, it may take ten or fifteen minutes for the brain to reestablish its control over the nervous and muscular systems.

The key problem with stunners is the question of just how much power is enough. If there is too little power, it will hurt, but not disable your attacker. It will probably just make the attacker angry, which really isn't a very good idea.

On the other hand, too high a voltage can do serious damage. It can even cause death. Remember, the heart is a muscle—imagine what would happen if it goes into violent spasms.

Different people have different susceptibility to electrical shock. For example, there is an age correlation. An epileptic is likely to have a severe over-reaction to a stun gun.

A stunner is not a toy. It might be preferable to a gun (at least for some people), but is still a potentially dangerous weapon.

11

Fire and temperature alarms

SMOKE ALARMS ARE CERTAINLY VALUABLE SECURITY DEVICES, and no home should be without one. But it can be dangerous to rely on a smoke alarm exclusively. Most fires, especially in a home, are likely to put out quite a bit of smoke before they get out of control, so a smoke alarm is normally adequate protection. But there are exceptions in the real world. Many fires might not set off a smoke alarm in time, because there might not be much smoke until it is too late.

For greater security against fires, you might need to add a thermal alarm, which responds to excessive heat instead of smoke. Please note that such a thermal alarm is recommended here as a supplement to a standard smoke alarm, not as a replacement for it. The two types of alarms are good for different purposes. If well-placed smoke alarms and thermal alarms are used, you should have reasonably adequate warning of almost any fire. (But please remember, no alarm system is ever perfect, or 100% foolproof. You must use some common sense too.) This chapter features several temperature sensitive alarm projects.

Simple nonlatching fire alarm

Figure 11-1 shows a very simple, but effective thermal alarm circuit. If the temperature in a monitored area exceeds a specific, preset level, the buzzer will sound. This circuit is not a latching type. That is, it will reset itself, and the buzzer will be silenced as soon as the over-heating problem is removed. In this particular application, there is really no point in latching the alarm on when it is triggered. If the temperature corrects itself on its own, it was presumedly a false alarm anyway. If an actual fire sets off

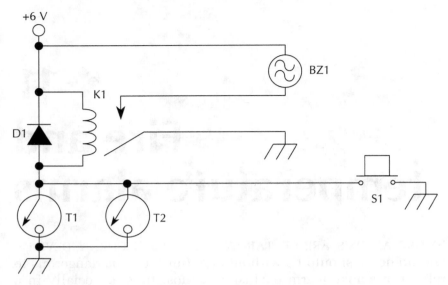

Fig. 11-1 *Project 40. Simple nonlatching fire alarm.*

the alarm, the only way it will go off before the fire is extinguished is if the fire burns up the alarm circuitry itself. A suitable parts list for this simple project appears as Table 11-1.

As you can see, there really isn't very much to this circuit. Electromechanical thermostats are used as the sensors. Although only two thermostat sensors are shown in the schematic diagram, you can add as many as you want to the circuit. All thermostat switches are simply wired in parallel, just as T1 and T2 are shown here. Each individual thermostat switch can protect a different area.

These thermostat switches are the same type used in portable heaters, water heaters, and furnaces. You should be able to find suitable devices of this type at a large hardware store. Or you could cannibalize the thermostat switch out of an old, discarded

**Table 11-1 Parts list for project 40.
Simple nonlatching fire alarm of Fig. 11-1.**

D1	Diode (1N4001 or similar)
K1	6 V relay
BZ1	6 V buzzer
T1, T2	Thermostat switch
S1	Normally open SPST push-button switch

unit. A third possibility is to check with a shop that services heat-related appliances.

You probably won't come across any thermostat switches with normally closed (NC) contacts, but if you do, such devices will not work in this circuit. The thermostat switches must have normally open (NO) contacts. As long as the monitored temperature is in the safe range, the buzzer will remain silent. As soon as one of the parallel thermostat switches in the circuit detects a too-high temperature, the alarm circuit is triggered and the buzzer starts to sound until the temperature drops back down to a safe level again.

Set each thermostat switch to a temperature a little above the highest expected normal temperature. Remember, a real fire will produce quite a bit of heat, so it might be a good idea to set the thermostat a little higher. A too-low setting can result in false triggering of the alarm, especially during the summer. For example, assume you don't expect the temperature in a protected area to ever exceed 90 degrees. Don't set the thermostat for 90 degrees or even 92 degrees. Set it at least for 100 degrees, and 120 degrees would be even better. The lower temperature setting won't make any real difference in warning you of a real fire, but it could be prone to annoying false triggering.

Push-button switch S1 is included to provide a manual test of the alarm circuit. This is especially important if you use batteries to power the project, which is strongly advised. This must be a normally open (NO) momentary-action switch. Briefly closing this switch should cause the buzzer to sound, just as if one of the thermostat switches was tripped. Releasing the test switch should turn off the buzzer. If the buzzer does not go off when this button is pressed, something is wrong in your circuit. The most likely culprit is a dead battery. If the battery is OK, the relay might be damaged. The coil could be burned out, or the switching contacts could be bent, dirty, or otherwise damaged. A defective buzzer is less likely, but possible.

Of course, when you first test the circuit after constructing the project, there might be an error in the wiring. Check that out first.

You could power this project with an ac-to-dc converter power supply, but this is not a very good idea for a fire alarm. One of the most common types of fires, particularly in homes, are electrical fires. The wiring to the socket you're using for the alarm could burn through within the walls before the thermostat sensors can detect the problem and set off the alarm. Of course, if this happens, the buzzer will never sound, because it can't get any power.

In most cases, it would be best to mount the thermostat switches at ceiling level or at least as high up as possible. Remember, heat rises, and cold air sinks. A thermostat on the floor might not detect a fire overhead until it has become very strong.

For maximum protection, use multiple thermostat switches at strategic locations throughout the room or area to be protected. This will help the circuit to spot localized fires while they are still fairly small.

Do not rely on this simple fire alarm project by itself. This project is designed as an addition to a smoke alarm, not as a replacement. The smoke alarm will detect many fires that can produce a lot of deadly smoke and damage before they start burning hot enough to trigger this simple thermal alarm circuit. By using both a thermal alarm and a smoke alarm, you can greatly increase your overall protection. Remember, each type of alarm is sensing different things, so what one misses, the other may detect.

Temperature range detector

For a fire alarm, you basically just need to know if the temperature is too hot. But there are many other potential applications for temperature alarms. In some cases, you might be concerned about temperatures that are too hot, but in other applications the problem might be a temperature that is too cold. Often, you want to be warned of either extreme. For example, most electronic equipment functions best within a specific temperature range.

The circuit shown in Fig. 11-2 gives an indication whenever the monitored temperature goes out of a preset range—either too hot or too cold. A suitable parts list for this project is given in Table 11-2.

This circuit is basically a window comparator, comparing voltages derived from two resistive voltage-divider strings. One of these voltage dividers is made up of R1 and R2, and the second voltage divider comprises R3, R4, and R5.

The key to this project is R1, which is not an ordinary resistor, but a thermistor. This is a component specially designed to vary its resistance in proportion to the ambient temperature it senses. A thermistor is a junctionless semiconductor device, and its response to changes in temperature is quite controlled and predictable. In action it is a little like a potentiometer, except the "shaft" is "controlled" by the sensed temperature. Potentiometer R2 is used to calibrate the sensitivity of the thermistor. In most practical applications, a trimpot should be used here.

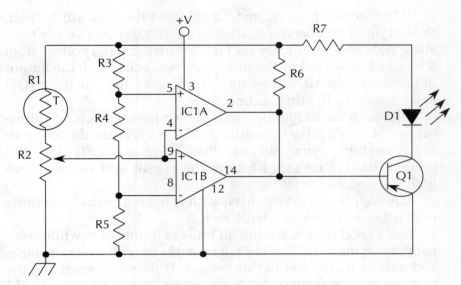

Fig. 11-2 *Project 41. Temperature range detector.*

Table 11-2 Parts list for project 41.
Temperature range detector of Fig. 11-2.

IC1	LM339 quad comparator
Q1	PNP transistor (Radio Shack RS1604, 2N3906, or similar)
D1	LED (Optional—see text)
R1	Thermistor
R2	500 kΩ trimpot
R3, R4	10 kΩ ¼ W 5% resistor (see text)
R5	33 kΩ ¼ W 5% resistor (see text)
R6	18 kΩ ¼ W 5% resistor
R7	330 Ω ¼ W 5% (optional—see text)

The critical too-high and too-low temperatures are determined by the values of the resistors in the reference voltage divider string—R3, R4, and R5. These three resistances interact, but roughly speaking, the size of R3 determines the highest maximum voltage before the comparator is triggered, and R5 determines the lowest minimum voltage before the comparator is triggered. The value of resistor R4 controls the width of the window, or the separation between the two critical voltages. Each voltage is compared to the voltage taken off the tap of trimpot R2. This voltage is determined by the setting of the trimpot and the ambient temperature sensed by the thermistor (R1).

If the voltage from R1 and R2 is higher than the upper limit, the output of comparator IC1A will go HIGH, turning on the transistor (Q1) and lighting up LED D1. Similarly, if the voltage from R1 and R2 drops below the minimum reference level, the output of comparator IC1B will go HIGH, turning on the transistor (Q1) and once again lighting up LED D1.

Although the output device is shown here, you could substitute an SCR or a relay to control an alarm sounding device or almost anything you choose. Just eliminate LED D1 and current-limiting resistor R7 from the circuit and replace them with the desired device.

The supply voltage for this circuit is not too critical, anything from +9 to +15 V should work well.

It is a good idea to ground all unused inputs of any idle comparators on the chip. The LM339 contains four comparator stages and only two are used in this project. Unless you are using the two spare comparators in some other circuitry, you should ground these inputs to avoid potential stability problems.

The critical switch points for the comparators can be determined by utilizing Ohm's law. Using the component values suggested in the parts list, the total series resistance in the reference voltage divider string is:

$$R_t = R_3 + R_4 + R_5$$
$$= 10,000 + 33,000 + 10,000$$
$$= 53,000 \ \Omega$$

Assuming the circuit supply voltage is +12 V, Ohm's law tells you that the current flowing through this string of series resistors is equal to:

$$I = \frac{E}{R}$$
$$= \frac{12}{53,000}$$
$$= 0.0002264 \ A$$
$$= 0.2264 \ mA$$
$$= 226.4 \ \mu A$$

The same amount of current will flow through each of the resistors in the series string. The voltage drop across each resistor is equal to that component resistance multiplied by the current:

$$E_a = IR_3$$
$$= 0.0002264 \times 10{,}000$$
$$= 2.264 \text{ V}$$

$$E_b = IR_4$$
$$= 0.0002264 \times 33{,}000$$
$$= 7.471 \text{ V}$$

$$E_c = IR_5$$
$$= 0.0002264 \times 10{,}000$$
$$= 2.264 \text{ V}$$

The sum of these voltage drops should be equal to the original supply voltage:

$$V+ = E_a + E_b + E_c$$
$$= 2.264 + 7.471 + 2.264$$
$$= 11.999 \text{ V}$$

You should have gotten 12.0 V, of course. The small error is simply due to rounding of values during the calculations. As you can see, the error of this rounding off is quite negligible.

The lower voltage limit for the comparators is simply equal to the voltage drop of the bottom resistor (E_c), or 2.264 V in this case. The upper voltage limit is equal to the original supply voltage ($V+$) minus the voltage drop across the upper-most resistor. That is:

$$E_u = V+ - E_a$$
$$= 12 - 2.264$$
$$= 9.736 \text{ V}$$

Using these component values, any sensed temperature producing a voltage higher than 9.736 V or lower than 2.264 V will trip the comparators, lighting the LED (D1) or activating the external alarm sounding (or other) device.

Pulse-output temperature sensor

There are many ways temperature can be monitored electronically. In the last project, you converted the temperature into a proportional voltage. In some applications, it might be more useful to express temperature as a proportional frequency. The pulse

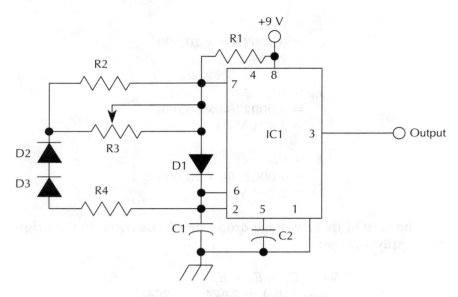

Fig. 11-3 *Project 42. Pulse-output temperature sensor.*

output temperature sensor circuit illustrated in Fig. 11-3 will accomplish this. A suitable parts list for this project is given in Table 11-3.

This circuit is essentially a variation of the basic 555 astable multivibrator, or rectangular-wave generator circuit. A 7555 CMOS timer chip is recommended for this project, but you can substitute a standard 555 timer IC if you prefer. The 555 and the 7555 are pin-for-pin compatible, so no changes need to be made in the circuitry to support such a substitution.

The actual temperature sensor in this circuit is made up of diodes D2 and D3. The voltage dropped across these diodes will

Table 11-3 Parts list for project 42.
Pulse-output temperature sensor of Fig. 11-3.

IC1	7555 timer (or 555)
D1, D2, D3	Diode (1N4148, 1N914, or similar)
C1	0.1 µF capacitor
C2	0.01 µF capacitor
R1	470 Ω ¼ W 5% resistor
R2	4.7 kΩ ¼ W 5% resistor
R3	1 kΩ potentiometer
R4	690 Ω ¼ W 5% resistor

vary with their temperature. In other words, the diodes act like a temperature-dependent variable resistance. This resistance is part of the 7555 timing network, so the output frequency will change in step with any changes in the sensed temperature.

You can experiment with alternate values for any of the resistors in this circuit and for capacitor C1. These component values affect the nominal output frequency and thus, the effective range of the project. The ideal frequency range will depend on just how you intend to use the output signal.

Potentiometer R3 is used to fine tune and calibrate the pulse output temperature sensor. You could replace this potentiometer with a fixed resistor of suitable value if your application is not too critical and you don't want to bother with periodic calibration.

Differential-temperature sensor

In some applications, you might be less concerned with the absolute temperature than the difference between two temperatures. If you have such a need, you can use the circuit shown in Fig. 11-4. A suitable parts list for this project is given in Table 11-4.

This project uses two LM3911 ICs. These chips are dedicated temperature-sensor circuits in IC form. The LM3911 is a somewhat unusual component, and it might be difficult to find a source for it (or an appropriate equivalent device). Of course, there is no way to guarantee that any particular device won't be discontinued without advance notice before you start to build a

**Table 11-4   Parts list for project 43.
Differential temperature sensor of Fig. 11-4.**

IC1, IC2	LM3911
C1	0.001 µF capacitor
R1, R5	3.9 kΩ ¼ W 5% resistor
R2	150 kΩ ¼ W 5% resistor
R3	6.8 kΩ ¼ W 5% resistor
R4	680 Ω ¼ W 5% resistor
R6	1.8 kΩ ¼ W 5% resistor
R7	1 kΩ ¼ W 5% resistor
R8	25 kΩ trimpot (gain)
R9	180 kΩ ¼ W 5% resistor
R10	100 kΩ trimpot (zero trim)

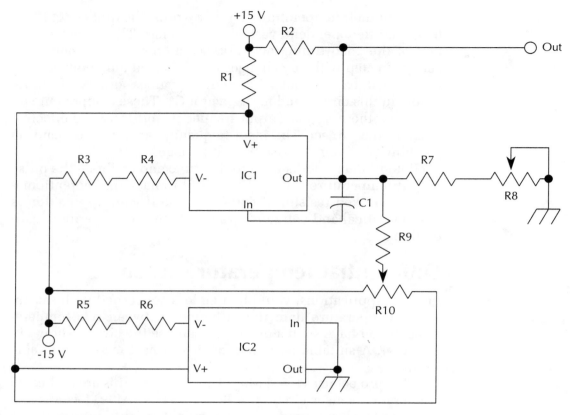

Fig. 11-4 *Project 43. Differential temperature sensor.*

project. By all means, first make sure you can get the LM3911s before investing any money in the other components for this project. Don't set yourself up for unnecessary disappointment and frustration. The LM3911 is now available from many electronics parts suppliers, but that might change at any time.

Two trimpots are used in this circuit for calibration purposes. Potentiometer R8 adjusts the circuit gain, and R10 helps set the zero output point.

The output voltage from this circuit will be proportional to the difference in the temperatures sensed by the two LM3911s, which are presumedly mounted at different locations. If the two sensed temperatures are equal, the output voltage should be zero. (Adjust trimpot R10 to ensure this.) The greater the difference between the two sensed temperatures, the greater the circuit output voltage will be.

Freezer melt alarm

This next project wouldn't be of much practical use as a fire alarm, but it can warn when it is getting too warm inside your freezer. This project has a very clever twist, although it is a mechanical trick, rather than an electronic gimmick.

The schematic diagram for the freezer melt alarm circuit is shown in Fig. 11-5. A suitable parts list for this project is given in Table 11-5.

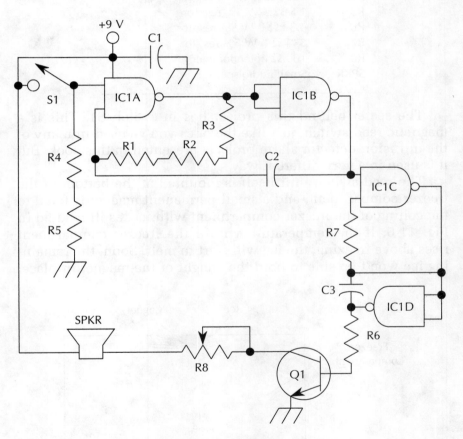

Fig. 11-5 *Project 44. Freezer melt alarm.*

This circuit is fairly straightforward. When switch S1 is closed, an alarm is sounded through the speaker. Potentiometer R8 controls the volume of the alarm tone. Nothing is too terribly critical in this circuit. Almost any low-power NPN transistor should work just fine for Q1.

Table 11-5 Parts list for project 44.
Freezer melt alarm of Fig. 11-5.

IC1	CD4011 quad NAND gate
Q1	NPN transistor (Radio Shack RS2009, GE20, 2N3904, or similar)
C1	0.01 µF capacitor
C2, C3	0.1 µF capacitor
R1, R4	2.2 MΩ ¼ W 5% resistor
R2	470 kΩ ¼ W 5% resistor
R3	820 kΩ ¼ W 5% resistor
R5	1 MΩ ¼ W 5% resistor
R6	3.3 kΩ ¼ W 5% resistor
R7	33 kΩ ¼ W 5% resistor
R8	100 Ω potentiometer
SPKR	Small audio speaker

The secret behind this project lies in switch S1. This is a magnetic reed switch, just like the ones you've used in many of the intrusion-detector alarm projects presented in this book. But it is used in a very different way.

The reed switch unit itself is mounted at the bottom of the freezer compartment, and a small permanent magnet is fixed to the ceiling of the freezer compartment with ice, as illustrated in Fig. 11-6. If the temperature within the freezer compartment rises above freezing, the ice will start to melt. Soon, the remaining ice won't be able to hold the weight of the magnet in place,

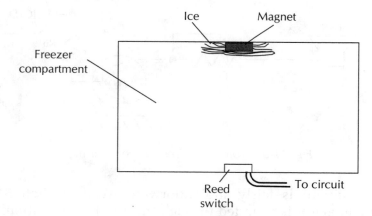

Fig. 11-6 *In Project 44, the reed switch is mounted at the bottom of the freezer compartment, and a small permanent magnet is affixed to the ceiling of the freezer compartment with ice.*

and it will fall to land on top of the magnetic reed switch, activating it. This closes the switch and sounds the alarm.

For maximum reliability, you must position the switch and the magnet so the magnet will be sure to fall where you want it to. If it misses the switch unit, the alarm won't sound, and the circuit won't do anything at all. You might try mounting the switch unit on a small raised shelf, so the magnet doesn't have so far to fall. You could also install a simple mechanical guide of some sort. For example, a cut-down cardboard toilet paper or paper towel tube will often work well. This arrangement is shown in Fig. 11-7.

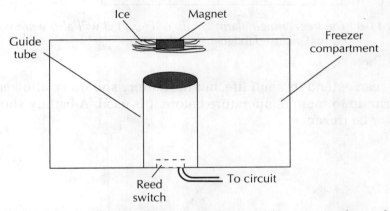

Fig. 11-7 *A small cardboard tube can help guide the magnet when it falls.*

An alternate approach would be to use a normally closed magnetic reed switch. In this case, the switch unit is mounted to the top of the freezer compartment with bolts, not ice. The magnet is held in position to keep the switch open with ice. This arrangement is shown in Fig. 11-8. Again, when the temperature exceeds freezing, the ice will begin to melt, and the magnet will drop. But the switch unit remains in place. The switch is deactivated, and so it closes (its normal state), setting off the alarm.

This project is a good demonstration of how a little bit of imagination can put a simple electronic circuit to work in unusual but practical ways. Be creative. You'll be able to adapt many of the projects presented in this book (and other sources) for some unusual applications.

If you use battery power for this project, install the battery outside the freezer compartment. Using a battery at such low temperatures will tend to change the internal chemical reactions and significantly shorten the life of a battery. Refrigerating a bat-

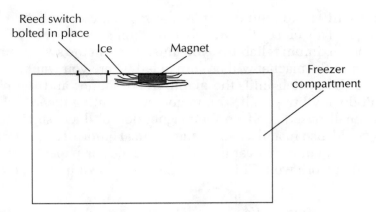

Fig. 11-8 *The freezer melt alarm circuit of Fig. 11-5 will also work with a normally closed magnetic reed switch.*

tery can extend its shelf life, but the battery should be allowed to warm up to room temperature before it is used. A battery should never be frozen.

12

Other environmental sensors and alarms

AN ELECTRONIC ALARM CIRCUIT CAN BE DESIGNED TO RESPOND TO almost any environmental condition. This chapter covers a few additional possibilities not covered elsewhere in this book.

Several of these projects are designed to respond to light (or the absence of light) because there are so many potential applications for such sensing circuits. Some of the most common of these applications was discussed in chapter 2. Others will occur to you as you read about these projects.

Other projects in this chapter respond to other environmental conditions. In some cases, the connection to security systems might seem rather strained, but remember the function of any electronic security system is to alert you (or perform some automated response) to some critical environmental condition. Will these projects be of any use in your security system? That depends entirely on your requirements. These miscellaneous sensor projects are presented to increase your options and aid your creativity in designing your own ideal security system, specifically developed to suit your applications.

Light-detector alarm

The circuit shown in Fig. 12-1 will sound an alarm whenever it senses the light level exceeds some specific preset level. If the light is below this level, the speaker will remain silent. A suitable parts list for this project appears as Table 12-1. You are encouraged to experiment with alternate component values.

Either a standard 555 timer chip or a 7555 CMOS timer IC can be used in this project. These two devices are pin-for-pin compatible and neither requires any modification of the circuitry.

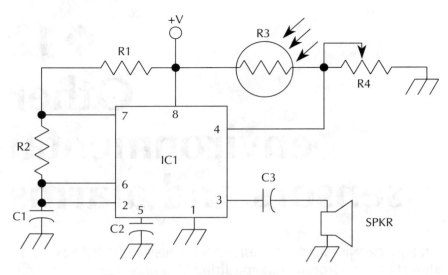

Fig. 12-1 *Project 45. Light-detector alarm.*

**Table 12-1 Parts list for project 45.
Light-detector alarm of Fig. 12-1.**

IC1	555 timer (or 7555)
C1, C2	0.01 µF capacitor
C3	0.1 µF capacitor
R1	100 kΩ ¼ W 5% resistor (see text)
R2	2.2 kΩ ¼ W 5% resistor (see text)
R3	Photoresistor
R4	25 kΩ potentiometer
SPKR	Small speaker

The frequency of the alarm tone is determined by the values of resistors R1 and R2 and capacitor C1, just as in a standard 555 astable multivibrator circuit. The frequency formula for this type of circuit is:

$$F = \frac{1}{(0.693C1 \ (R_1 + 2R_2))}$$

Using the component values suggested in the parts list for this project, we get a nominal alarm frequency of approximately:

$$F = \frac{1}{(0.693 \times 0.0000001 \times (100,000 + 2 \times 2200))}$$

$$= \frac{1}{(0.693 \times 0.0000001 \times (100{,}000 + 4400))}$$

$$= \frac{1}{(0.693 \times 0.0000001 \times 104{,}400))}$$

$$= \frac{1}{0.0007234}$$

$$= 1382 \text{ Hz}$$

This (1382 Hz) is a good frequency, clearly audible to most people. Some people will have more difficulty hearing very high-frequency sounds or very low-frequency sounds. If you would like a different alarm frequency for whatever reason, simply change the values of any or all of these three timing components—R1, R2, and C1. Increasing any of these component values decreases the tone frequency and vice versa.

You could use a potentiometer for R1 to provide a manual frequency control, if that suits your particular application. It would be a good idea to include a small resistor in series with the potentiometer to avoid the possibility of setting the resistance too close to zero, which would cause the circuit to misfunction and could possibly damage the IC.

The secret of this light-detector alarm circuit is in the way the timer reset pin (pin 4) is used. A simple resistive voltage divider is made up of potentiometer R3 and photoresistor R4. The relative resistances of these two components determine the voltage seen by the reset pin. If this voltage is too low, the astable multivibrator cannot operate, and the speaker will remain silent. Increasing the amount of light shining on the photoresistor will increase the pin 4 voltage. At some point, the timer will be enabled, and the alarm will sound.

Potentiometer R3 is manually adjusted to determine the sensitivity of the light detector alarm circuit. This resistance defines how much light will be required to set off the alarm.

The photoresistor (R4) used in this project can be any standard CdS cadmium sulfide photoresistor. In some cases you might have to use a larger or smaller potentiometer for R4 to achieve the desired sensitivity with a given photoresistor. For most practical applications, the values given here will be perfectly adequate.

Alternate light-activated alarm

An alternate circuit for setting off an alarm when the sensed level exceeds a specific preset level is shown in Fig. 12-2. A suitable parts list for this project is given in Table 12-2.

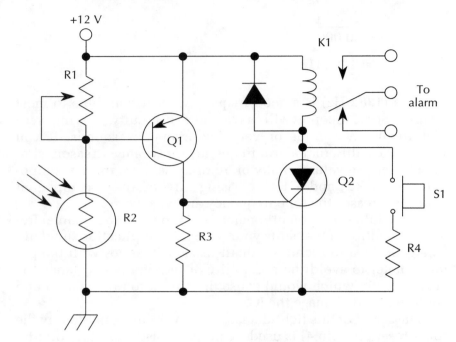

Fig. 12-2 *Project 46. Alternate light-activated alarm.*

**Table 12-2 Parts list for project 46.
Alternate light-activated alarm of Fig. 12-2.**

Q1	PNP transistor (Radio Shack RS1604, GE21, 2N3906, or similar)
Q2	Low-power SCR (to suit load—relay)
D1	Diode (1N4001 or similar)
K1	Relay—to suit load
S1	Normally open SPST push-button switch
R1	1 MΩ potentiometer
R2	Photoresistor
R3	10 kΩ ¼ W 5% resistor
R4	470 kΩ ¼ W 5% resistor

This project, unlike the last one, does not have a built-in alarm sounding device. Instead, the sensed light level controls the action of a relay (K1), which can drive almost any desired alarm sounding device or virtually any other electronic circuit or electrically powered device. To drive a large load with this circuit, you might need to add a larger intermediate relay in cascade with the one shown here.

Another difference between this circuit and the preceding project is that this one is latching. Once the alarm circuit has been triggered, it will remain on until it is manually reset via push-button switch S1, even if the light level is reduced below the critical turn-on point. In the last project, the alarm sounds only as long as the light level exceeds the trip point. When the light level is reduced, the alarm is silenced and automatically reset. This is a key difference, and it will be a major factor in determining which of these light-detector alarm circuits is the best choice for any given applications.

The basic operating principle of this circuit is similar to that of the preceding project. A voltage-divider network is made up of potentiometer R1 and photoresistor R2. The setting of the potentiometer determines the sensitivity of the circuit, or how much light will be required to trip it.

Once the potentiometer has been set, the resistance of photoresistor R2 determines the voltage seen by the base of transistor Q1. Of course, this resistance is, in turn, determined by the amount of light striking the sensing surface of the photoresistor. At some point, there will be sufficient voltage to turn on transistor Q1, which functions here as a simple electric switch. The collector voltage then triggers the SCR (Q2), turning it on and activating the relay. To turn the SCR back off and deactivate the relay, you must briefly close the manual reset switch (S1).

If the alarm sounding device (or other load) is connected to the relay normally open contacts, the circuit will act as a light-detector alarm. In some applications, you might want this circuit to turn off the load (probably not an alarm sounding device) when the detected light level exceeds the preset value. In this case, simply use the normally closed contacts of the relay.

To reverse the operation of the circuit—that is, to create a dark-detector alarm, simply reverse the positions of potentiometer R1 and photoresistor R4.

Dark-detector alarm

In some applications, you might need to be warned when the light level gets too low (dark), rather than too high. You can modify the light detector alarm circuit of Fig. 12-1 to create a dark-detector alarm circuit, as illustrated in Fig. 12-3. A suitable parts list for this project is given in Table 12-3.

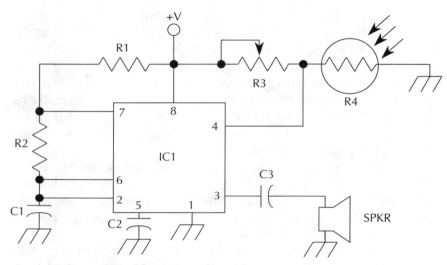

Fig. 12-3 *Project 47. Dark-detector alarm.*

**Table 12-3 Parts list for project 47.
Dark-detector alarm of Fig. 12-3.**

IC1	555 timer (or 7555)
C1, C2	0.01 μF capacitor
C3	0.1 μF capacitor
R1	100 kΩ ¼ W 5% resistor (see text)
R2	3.3 kΩ ¼ W 5% resistor (see text)
R3	25 kΩ potentiometer
R4	Photoresistor
SPKR	Small speaker

Basically, all you have done here is reverse the positions of the sensitivity control potentiometer and the photoresistor in the voltage divider string controlling the timer's reset input (pin 4).

As in the earlier project, the relative resistances of R3 and R4 determine the voltage seen by the reset pin. If this voltage is too low, the astable multivibrator cannot operate, and the speaker will remain silent. Decreasing the amount of light shining on the photoresistor will increase the pin 4 voltage. At some point, the timer will be enabled, and the alarm will sound.

Potentiometer R3 is manually adjusted to determine the sensitivity of the light detector alarm circuit. This resistance defines how much light will be required to turn off the alarm.

The photoresistor (R4) used in this project can be any standard CdS photoresistor. In some cases you might have to use a larger or smaller potentiometer for R4 to achieve the desired sensitivity with a given photoresistor. For more practical applications, the values given here will be perfectly adequate.

Once again, either a standard 555 timer chip or a 7555 CMOS timer IC can be used in this project. These two devices are pin-for-pin compatible and neither requires any modification of the circuitry.

The frequency of the alarm tone is determined by the values of resistors R1 and R2 and capacitor C1, just as in a standard 555 astable multivibrator circuit. The frequency formula for this type of circuit is:

$$F = \frac{1}{(0.693C1\ (R_1 + 2R_2))}$$

Using the component values suggested in the parts list for this project, you get a nominal alarm frequency of approximately:

$$F = \frac{1}{0.693 \times 0.0000001 \times (100{,}000 + 2 \times 3300))}$$

$$= \frac{1}{(0.693 \times 0.0000001 \times (100{,}000 + 6600))}$$

$$= \frac{1}{(0.693 \times 0.0000001 \times 106{,}600))}$$

$$= \frac{1}{0.0007387}$$

$$= 1354\ \text{Hz}$$

If you would like a different alarm frequency for whatever reason, simply change the values of any or all of these three timing components (R1, R2, and C1). Increasing any of these component values decreases the tone frequency and vice versa.

You could use a potentiometer for R1 to provide a manual-frequency control if that suits your applications. It would be a good idea to include a small resistor in series with the potentiometer to avoid the possibility of setting the resistance too close to zero, which would cause the circuit to misfunction and could possibly damage the IC.

Light-range detector

In some applications, you might need to know both when the lighting level gets too bright and when it gets too dark. In other words, you want to be alerted whenever the light level goes outside a preset range. This requirement is a natural application for a window-comparator circuit.

A simple but effective light range detector circuit is illustrated in Fig. 12-4. A suitable parts list for this project appears in Table 12-4.

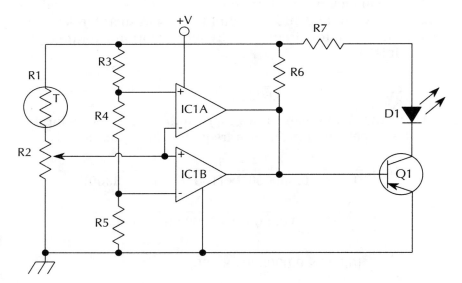

Fig. 12-4   *Project 48. Light-range detector.*

In this circuit, a pair of comparators (IC1A and IC1B) compare two dc voltages. The variable input voltage is taken from a voltage-divider network made up of photoresistor R1 (the sensor) and potentiometer R2, which serves as an overall sensitivity control for the circuit.

The second voltage being fed into the comparators is a fixed-

**Table 12-4 Parts list for project 48.
Light-range detector of Fig. 12-4.**

IC1	LM339 quad comparator (see text)
Q1	PNP transistor (Radio Shack RS1604, GE21, ECG159, or similar)
D1	LED (optional—see text)
R1	Photoresistor
R2	500 kΩ potentiometer
R3, R4, R5	10 kΩ ¼ W 5% resistor (see text)
R6	10 kΩ ¼ W 5% resistor
R7	330 Ω ¼ W 5% resistor (optional—see text)

reference voltage derived from a voltage-divider network made up resistors R3, R4, and R5. Notice that two different tap-off points are used from this reference voltage-divider string, one for each of the two comparator stages.

The input voltage divider produces a voltage that is directly proportionate to the amount of light striking the surface of the photoresistor (R1). This voltage is compared to each of the reference voltages set up by the second voltage-divider network. If the input voltage is higher than a specific maximum level (set by the relative value of resistor R3), then the output of the upper comparator (IC1A) will go HIGH, turning on a transistor switch (Q1), which lights up the LED (D1). Similarly, if input voltage is lower than a specific maximum level (set by the relative value of resistor R5), then the output of the bottom comparator (IC1B) will go HIGH, turning on the transistor switch and lighting up the LED. As long as the voltage is within the window range, the outputs of both comparator stages will be LOW, and the LED will remain dark.

The width of the window range is determined by the relative value of resistor R4. Notice that it is the relative resistance values that are important here, not so much the absolute values of the voltage-divider resistors. The resistor values interact with one another.

Setting the window limits is fairly easy to do using Ohm's Law. You are encouraged to experiment with alternate values for resistors R3, R4, and R5. These three resistors do not necessarily need to be equal in value, even though this is the case in the suggested parts list.

To determine the window limits, first find the total resistance of the voltage-divider string. This is simply the sum of the component resistances. Using the component values suggested in the parts list, total string resistance is:

$$R_t = R_3 + R_4 + R_5$$
$$= 10000 + 10000 + 10000$$
$$= 30000 \ \Omega$$
$$= 30 \ k\Omega$$

Next, use Ohm's Law to find the current flow through the voltage-divider string. Assume the circuit is running off of a +9 V power supply. In this case, the current flow works out to:

$$I = \frac{V+}{R_t}$$
$$= \frac{9}{30,000}$$
$$= 0.0003 \ A$$
$$= 0.3 \ mA$$
$$= 300 \ \mu A$$

The next step is to use Ohm's Law again, this time to find the voltage drop across each of the individual resistors in the voltage-divider string. In this particular case, all three resistors have identical values, so you only have to perform the equation once. In most such circuits, however, you will probably have to repeat this step three times—once for each individual resistor in the string.

The voltage drop across each resistor in the sample circuit is:

$$E = IR$$
$$= 0.0003 \times 10,000$$
$$= 3 \ V$$

The sum of these three voltage drops should equal the original supply voltage:

$$V+ = E_a + E_b + E_c$$
$$= 3 + 3 + 3$$
$$= 9 \ V$$

In this particular example, everything worked out very neatly. Often, however, you will find a slight error, due to rounding off of values during the equations. Don't worry about it. Remember, the component tolerances will also introduce some error in the calculated value. Adjusting the sensitivity control (R2) can help compensate for such small errors.

The upper limit of the window is equal to the circuit supply voltage minus the voltage drop across resistor R3 (E_a) or in the example:

$$V_u = V+ - E_a$$
$$= 9 - 3$$
$$= 6 \text{ V}$$

The lower limit of the window is very simply equal to the voltage drop across the resistor R5 (E_c), or 3 V in the example. The acceptable window runs from 3 to 6 V. Values in this range will not light up the LED.

The width of the window range is equal to the voltage drop across the middle resistor R4 (E_b), or 3 V in the example.

Try another example, this time with unequal resistor values. This time, use the following component values:

$$
\begin{array}{lll}
\text{R3} & 22 \text{ k}\Omega & (22,000 \ \Omega) \\
\text{R4} & 47 \text{ k}\Omega & (47,000 \ \Omega) \\
\text{R5} & 10 \text{ k}\Omega & (10,000 \ \Omega)
\end{array}
$$

In this case, the total voltage-divider string resistance is:

$$R_t = R_3 = R_4 + R_5$$
$$= 22,000 + 47,000 + 10,000$$
$$= 79,000 \ \Omega$$
$$= 79 \text{ k}\Omega$$

Once again, assume a +9 V power supply for the circuit. This means the current flowing through the voltage-divider string works out to approximately:

$$I = \frac{V+}{R_t}$$

$$= \frac{9}{79,000}$$

$$= 0.000114 \text{ A}$$
$$= 0.114 \text{ mA}$$
$$= 114 \ \mu\text{A}$$

Next, find the voltage drop across each individual resistor in the voltage-divider network:

$$Ea = IR_3$$
$$= 0.000114 \times 22{,}000$$
$$= 2.5 \text{ V}$$

$$Eb = IR_4$$
$$= 0.000114 \times 47{,}000$$
$$= 5.35 \text{ V}$$

$$Ec = IR_5$$
$$= 0.000114 \times 10{,}000$$
$$= 1.14 \text{ V}$$

Double checking the total of these individual voltage drops:

$$V+ = E_a + E_b + E_c$$
$$= 2.5 + 5.35 + 1.14$$
$$= 8.99 \text{ V}$$

The original supply voltage is +9 V. This small (0.01 V) error is simply due to rounding off during the equations. Nothing is wrong.

In this example, the upper window limit is:

$$V_u = V+ - E_a$$
$$= 9 - 2.5$$
$$= 6.5 \text{ V}$$

The lower window voltage limit is simply equal to the voltage drop across R5 (E_c), or about 1.14 V. The LED will remain dark as long as the input voltage is between 1.14 and 6.5 V. This is a window range of about 5.35 V (E_b).

As you can see, this circuit is quite versatile and can be set for many different window parameters to suit your own individual application.

This circuit is built around the popular LM339 quad comparator IC. Only two of the four available comparator sections on this chip are used in this project. To avoid possible stability problems, the inputs of any unused comparator stages should be grounded. Of course, you could also use the extra comparator stages in some other circuitry, as part of a larger system.

Standard op amps can be used in place of the dedicated comparators in this circuit. Almost any low-power PNP transistor will work well for transistor Q1.

As shown here, the output of this light range detector circuit is a simple LED that lights up when the monitored light level goes outside the acceptable window range (either too low or too high). You can easily modify this circuit to drive some other load. Just replace LED D1 and its current-limiting resistor (R7) with an appropriate relay coil or SCR.

Automatic night light

Have you ever come home late at night when you've forgotten to turn on the porch light? Isn't it frustrating trying to get the key into the lock in the dark?

Or have you ever gotten up in the middle of the night and tripped over a toy or the family cat? (That last one has happened to me a lot, because I happen to have a black cat, who is very difficult to see in the dark.) Then you have to fumble around to find the light switch.

Such situations are always potentially dangerous. An unlit area is also more likely to provide a hiding place for a prowler or other intruder. Most burglars will think twice before going to work in a well lit area.

A small night light can make life easier and more secure by preventing such problems. However, in these times of conservation awareness, it seems wasteful to keep a night light burning during daylight hours when it does no one any good at all. But who can remember to turn the light on every evening and then turn it back off again in the morning? It's too easy to forget. This is an ideal application for electronic automation.

So how can you best automate a night light? You could rig up a timer of some sort, so the light automatically switches on and off at specific, preset times. But is that really appropriate to this type of application? The exact time the light turns on or off is pretty much irrelevant. You just want the night light to come on when it is dark. When there is sufficient light in the area (from whatever source), the night light should turn itself off.

Timer systems can also be ineffective in discouraging burglars. Often people will use a timer to control lights while they are away to create the illusion that someone is home. The trouble is, smart burglars will "case" a house they plan to rob a few nights in advance. If the lights always turn on and off at the same time every night, it's a dead giveaway that an automatic timer is being used.

All of this suggests that a better approach for automating your night light is to use a photosensor of some sort to determine the night light is actually needed. We will be using a pair of photoresistors—one to turn the night light on, and the other to turn it back off.

The schematic diagram for our automatic night light circuit is shown in Fig. 12-5. A suitable parts list for this project is given in Table 12-5.

Photoresistor R8 senses when the ambient light in the protected area drops below a specific level, producing a signal that is used to turn on the night light. Potentiometer R2 acts as a sen-

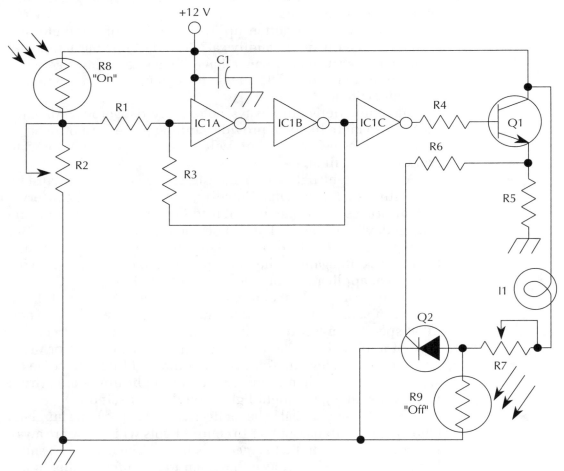

Fig. 12-5 Project 49. Automatic night light.

Table 12-5   Parts list for project 49.
Automatic night light of Fig. 12-5.

IC1	CD4049 hex inverter
Q1	NPN transistor (Radio Shack RS2009, GE20, ECG128, or similar)
Q2	SCR to suit load
C1	0.01 µF capacitor
R1	10 kΩ ¼ W 5% resistor
R2, R7	100 kΩ potentiometer (trimpot)
R3	10 kΩ ¼ W 5% resistor
R4, R5	1 kΩ ¼ W 5% resistor
R6	120 Ω ¼ W 5% resistor
R8, R9	Photoresistor
I1	dc lamp—see text

sitivity/calibration control for this photosensor. Notice that photoresistor R8 and potentiometer R2 form a simple voltage-divider network. The voltage applied to the input of IC1A through resistor R1 is determined by the setting of potentiometer R2, and the amount of light striking the sensing surface of photoresistors R8. When this voltage is high enough, the digital inverter (IC1A) will see a logic HIGH signal. Otherwise, IC1A has a LOW input.

When the sensed light level exceeds the calibrated turn-on point, transistor Q1 will be switched on, providing a gate signal to turn on SCR Q2, which causes the lamp (I1) to light up. In some applications, you might want to replace this lamp with a relay or a larger SCR to drive a heftier electrical load. As the circuit is shown here, the lamp (I1) should be only a small dc light bulb, such as those used in flashlights. This is useful for a bathroom or keyhole night light, but it won't discourage intruders. By using this circuit to control an appropriate relay, several larger lights can be controlled. The SCR must be able to safely handle sufficient current to power the lamp used, or to drive the relay coil. In most applications, an inexpensive, fairly low-power SCR will probably do the job just fine.

Once the SCR has been turned on, it will remain on, until the current flow from anode to cathode is interrupted. This is accomplished by the second photoresistor in the circuit—R9. This second sensor determines when the ambient light in the protected area is bright enough to make the night light unnecessary. The sensitivity of this sensor is calibrated via potentiometer R7.

Almost any handy low-power NPN transistor should work well for Q1 in this circuit.

The on sensor (R8) should be mounted where it will have a clear "view" of the ambient light level in the protected area and can't be too affected by stray shadows, which could cause the night light to flash on and off at inappropriate times. This probably wouldn't be a major problem in most applications, but it almost certainly would be annoying. You can avoid such problems by careful placement of the photoresistors.

Similarly, you must give careful thought to the physical placement of the off sensor (R9). It should be positioned so that the night light, when on, won't shine directly on it. This could confuse the circuitry and prevent the night light from being turned off when it should be, especially if calibration potentiometer R7 is set for fairly high sensitivity.

In calibrating this circuit, you should set the sensitivity potentiometers (R2 and R7) so that the on sensor (R8) responds to a lower light intensity than the off sensor (R9). This gives the circuit some hysteresis and prevents the lamp from blinking on and off too frequently when the ambient light level is close to the critical point.

Ultraviolet alarm

Many people enjoy getting a suntan, and feel it makes them look healthy. Paradoxically, there is growing concern that getting too much of the Sun's tanning rays could be decidedly unhealthy. The Sun's light includes light of many wavelengths, including some in the ultraviolet region, which can be harmful if absorbed in excess. If nothing else, absorbing too much ultraviolet radiation can cause sunburns, which certainly aren't any fun.

Just how much sun is too much? It is hard to say. Sometimes when the sky is overcase or partly cloudy, you might assume you aren't getting very much sunlight, because the visible light is restricted. But ultraviolet light can go right through the cloud cover and reach your skin anyway.

The circuit shown in Fig. 12-6 is designed to warn you that you've stayed out in the Sun long enough. A suitable parts list for this project appears as Table 12-6.

This ultraviolet alarm monitors the Sun's intensity, and more important, it keeps track of the accumulated exposure. When a preset exposure limit has been reached, the alarm sounds warning you that it's time to come in out of the Sun. This circuit

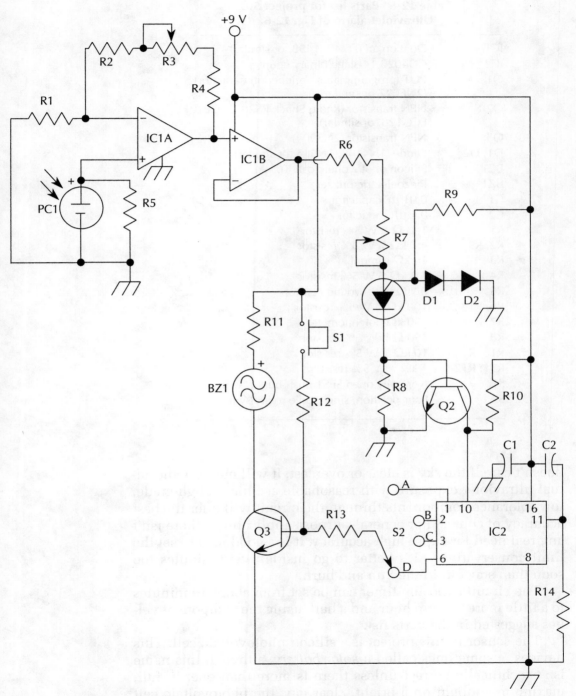

Fig. 12-6 *Project 50. Ultraviolet alarm.*

**Table 12-6 Parts list for project 50.
Ultraviolet alarm of Fig. 12-6.**

IC1	Dual op amp (747, 1458, or similar)
IC2	CD4020 14-stage binary counter
Q1	PUT (programmable unijunction transistor) (2N6027 or similar)
Q2	NPN transistor (Radio Shack RS2009, GE20, ECG128, or similar)
Q3	NPN transistor (2N3904)
D1, D2	Diode (1N4148, 1N914, or similar)
PC1	Silicon photovoltaic cell (0.3 A)
BZ1	Piezoelectric buzzer
C1	0.01 µF capacitor
C2	0.1 µF capacitor
R1	100 Ω ¼ W 5% resistor
R2, R9	4.7 kΩ ¼ W 5% resistor
R3	10 kΩ trimpot
R4	1.2 kΩ ¼ W 5% resistor
R5	0.2 Ω wire-wound resistor
R6, R14	100 kΩ ¼ W 5% resistor
R7	250 kΩ potentiometer
R8	150 Ω ¼ W 5% resistor
R10, R13	10 kΩ ¼ W 5% resistor
R11, R12	1 kΩ ¼ W 5% resistor
S1	Normally open SPST push-button switch
S2	Four-position, single-pole rotary switch

doesn't care if the sky is clear or overcast, it will measure the actual ultraviolet exposure with reasonable accuracy. High-grade, low-tolerance components through the circuit will offer the best accuracy of course. For general-purpose applications, there isn't any real need for super-high accuracy. It is a good idea to set the limit conservatively. It's better to go inside a few minutes too soon than stay out in the Sun and burn.

The circuit exposure timer can be set from about 10 minutes to a little more than an hour and a half, using the component values suggested in the parts list.

The sensor in this project is a silicon photovoltaic cell. This devices is sometimes called a *solar battery*, although this name isn't technically correct unless there is more than one. In full, maximum sunlight on a bright, clear day, the photovoltaic cell should put out about 03 A (300 mA). The current of a photovoltaic cell for a given amount of illumination is primarily determined by its surface area. A tiny photocell just won't cut it in this application. You will need a moderately large photovoltaic cell. If you have problems finding a large enough photovoltaic cell, you can use two 0.15 A (150 mA) photocells, wired in parallel (not in series to increase the voltage).

The output voltage from a photovoltaic cell is more or less constant with changes in the sensed illumination level. Only the current changes in proportion to the monitored light level.

Resistor R5 is placed in parallel with the photovoltaic cell to convert this current into a proportional voltage, in accordance with Ohm's Law. Because the current of the photovoltaic cell varies, while its voltage remains stable, it electrically looks like a variable resistance in series with a fixed voltage source. An equivalent shown circuit for this sensor portion of this project is shown in Fig. 12-7.

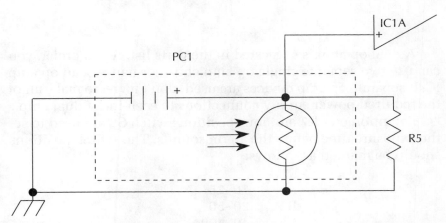

Fig. 12-7 *This is an equivalent circuit for the sensor portion of Fig. 12-6.*

The resistance of R5 must be very small to get a usable voltage. A 0.2 Ω wire-wound resistor was used in the prototype of this project. Such small wire-wound resistors are rather expensive and sometimes a little tricky to find. Some experimenters choose to make their own wire-wound resistor. It isn't hard to do. You just take a specific length of wire of a known resistance. Special ohmic wire is available for this purpose. Ohmic wire is just wire with a higher per-foot resistance than ordinary wire. You can use ordinary hook-up wire, but you will need a much, much longer length for a given resistance.

If you know how much resistance the wire has per foot, you

can readily calculate the required length for a specific resistance—0.2 Ω in this case.

For convenience, the resistance wire is usually wound around a nonconductive core of some sort, like a coil. You could use a pencil as an ordinary core. After the wire is wound into shape, remove the pencil, and you're left with an air core. The core material used isn't too important here, as long as it is a fairly good insulator.

The voltage proportional to the sensed light level is amplified by IC1A and then buffered by IC1B. Potentiometer R3 serves as a sensitivity (or calibration) control for the sensor.

For best accuracy, mount the following components physically as close to one another as possible:

> IC1A
> PC1   (the photovoltaic cell)
> R5
> R1

A dual op amp is suggested in the parts list. If you prefer, you can use two separate single op amp chips, or half a quad op amp IC. If separate op amp devices are used, don't forget to make all of the required power supply connections to each individual chip.

Potentiometer R7 and four-position switch S2 are used to set the exposure time before the alarm sounds. The switch positions should be marked as follows:

> A   10–25
> B   20–50
> C   40–100
> D   CALIBRATE

Notice that the three active ranges (A, B, and C) overlap.

To calibrate the project, you should pick out the brightest, sunniest days you can. If possible, try to perform the calibration on the summer solstice (June 21), which is when the sun is the closest to the earth (in the Northern Hemisphere). This means the Sun's rays will be strongest at this time. Connect a dc voltmeter between the output of IC1B (positive lead) and the circuit ground (negative lead). Adjust potentiometer R3 for a reading of about 5.5 V, give or take a tenth of a volt. A trimpot should be used for this calibration control. Do not use a full, front-panel control. Once this calibration potentiometer has been adjusted, you might want to use a drop of glue or paint to hold its shaft in place.

It is very, very, very important to perform this calibration procedure in the maximum sunlight to be encountered when using this device. The 5.5 V should be the maximum voltage ever seen at this point in the circuit.

In some cases, you might have to increase or decrease the value of wire-wound resistor R5 slightly to make the correct calibration possible. Using a homemade wire-wound resistor, as discussed above, would be an advantage here.

Potentiometer R7 should be a front-panel control for most applications. This control fine tunes the exposure time limit within the range set by switch S2. You can calibrate this control by setting switch S2 to position D. Ideally, you should break the connection from the output of IC1B and feed in a known 5.5 Vdc signal. Otherwise, calibrate the timer-limit control on a bright, sunny day as in the previous calibration procedure. At each reference point on a dial scale, measure how long (in seconds) it takes before the alarm buzzer sounds, after power is applied to the circuit. At least three index points are recommended on your dial scale:

	Calibration time	Scale Marking
a	20	10/20/40
b	30	15/30/60
c	50	25/50/100

Point a should be at or near the minimum setting of the potentiometer, and c should be near the maximum setting. Point b should be more or less in the middle. If you find your circuit is way off in the timing, you might try substituting a different value for resistor R6.

The suggested scale markings each have three values—one each for each active position of range switch S2. These markings refer to the time in minutes. For example, if switch S2 is set to position B, and R7 is set at position c, the exposure time limit will be about 50 minutes. Changing the setting of switch S2 to position C, without readjusting the potentiometer will extend the exposure time limit to about 100 minutes.

Notice that these are not absolute times. You could use an alarm clock or kitchen timer for that. In operation, this circuit takes into account the sensed-light intensity in its timing equation. So if you set the ultraviolet alarm for an exposure time limit of 25 minutes, for example, you might actually lie out in the Sun for 48 minutes before the alarm sounds, but the ultraviolet radiation you will absorb in this period will be the equivalent of 25 minutes in maximum sunlight.

When you start tanning, it is a good idea to start out with relatively short exposure times—10 to 20 minutes, and work your way up slowly. This gives your skin a better chance of getting accustomed to the Sun's rays and minimizes the risk of painful sunburns.

You could replace the piezoelectric buzzer in this project with some other alarm sounding device, if you prefer, but in this particular application, there is not much point in it, unless you find the buzzer a little too raucuous and annoying. A low-power and not-too-loud alarm sounding device would be appropriate in this case.

Electrical storm alarm

An electrical storm can do quite a bit of damage, especially if it catches you off guard. People who work outside and campers often need advanced warning of such storms. It can also be important for almost anyone with any electrically powered equipment.

Thunder and lightning are the results of large electrical discharges in the atmosphere. If such a discharge takes place near an ac power line, a large voltage source will be induced into the power cables. This works by the principles of induction, pretty much similar to the principles of a power transformer. The atmospheric electrical discharge will generate a strong magnetic field, which moves across the power line. Any conductor moving through a magnetic field (or vice versa) will have a proportional voltage induced into the conductor. The result in this case is a large power surge through the ac lines.

It is commonly said that such surges occur when lightning hits the power lines. This isn't quite true. If a power line actually took a direct lightning strike, it would probably snap and break, cutting off the power flow altogether. The surge occurs when the lightning strikes near enough to induce a voltage spike into the power lines.

Incidentally, most storm-related power outages also aren't the result of direct lightning strikes either. The power line systems include many distribution amplifiers and switching transformers. Although these items are well water proofed, they can leak, and in a heavy rain, enough water can get in to cause a short circuit. Also, a lightning strike near an amplifier or transformer can induce enough of a power surge to damage it, cutting off the power flow.

The power surges from a strong electrical storm can overload the power supply of ac-powered equipment. Because the power surge is so large, it can do quite a bit of damage to the circuitry before a fuse or circuit breaker has a chance to react and open up. Any equipment that is plugged in during an electrical storm is at risk. The equipment doesn't have to be on at the time. A few years ago, I was called in to repair some relative's TV set that had been damaged in exactly this way. They were amazed that a fuse blew, and it kept blowing until the television was unplugged. "But it wasn't even on during the storm!" they kept saying in confused amazement.

When you turn off a TV set, or any other piece of electrical equipment, the break in the circuit is only as large as the physical dimensions of the switch contacts. Have you ever walked across a rug in low humidity, then had a spark jump from your fingertip to a doorknob, or some other metallic object? The spark can jump several inches under some circumstances. Considering the size of a lightning-induced power surge, it shouldn't be surprising that a quarter inch or half inch gap between a set of switch contacts is going to stop it.

If you know an electrical storm is coming, you can unplug any sensitive equipment, which is the only sure way to stop such disasters. Surge protectors will usually help, if the equipment must keep running during the storm, but no surge protector is ever perfect or truly infallable. If possible, unplug your electrical equipment during a severe thunderstorm, rather than relying on a surge protector. This is not to say surge protectors are worthless—far from it. They have saved millions of dollars in repairs and equipment replacement. But lightning spikes are a severe test for them. (There are many potential causes of ac power surges, and dozens occur every day.).

Now, you don't need to get ridiculously paranoid about unplugging things. Unplugging things like lamps is just making unnecessary busy work. For a lamp, the worst that is likely to happen is that the bulb will burn out, which is going to happen sooner or later anyway. Even a bulb burning out is rather unlikely. But for electronic equipment, especially if it is expensive, even a relatively small power surge can damage sensitive (and usually expensive) semiconductor components.

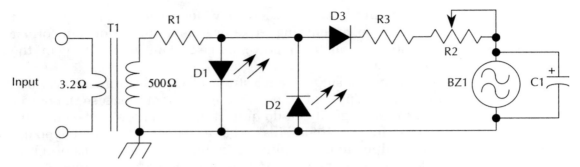

Fig. 12-8 *Project 51. Electrical storm alarm.*

Obviously it is important to know when an electrical storm is on the way so you can take the necessary precautions. The circuit shown in Fig. 12-8 will help you here. A suitable parts list for this project appears as Table 12-7.

Table 12-7 Parts list for project 51.
Electrical storm alarm of Fig. 12-8.

D1, D2	LED
D3	Diode (1N4002 or similar)
T1	Audio transformer 3.2 to 500 Ω (see text)
BZ1	Piezoelectric buzzer
C1	47 µF 50 V electrolytic capacitor
R1	390 Ω ½ W 10% resistor
R2	50 kΩ trimpot
R3	1 kΩ ½ W 10% resistor

To use this project, you need a small standard AM (amplitude modulation) radio with an earphone jack. Tune the radio between broadcast stations, near the upper end of the broadcast band (about 1600 kHz), and connect the input of the electrical storm alarm circuit to the radio earphone jack. Leave the radio playing continuously. When there are atmospheric electrical discharges in the area, the LEDs (D1 and D2) will flash, and the alarm (a piezoelectric buzzer) will sound. You could substitute some other alarm sounding device for this buzzer if you prefer.

If you only want a visual indication, you can eliminate the following components from the circuit:

R2
R3
C1
BZ1
D3

If for some reason, you want only an audible indication of an approaching storm and don't want the visual indication, you can eliminate the LEDs from the circuit, but frankly, there is not much point in that. You might as well include the LEDs. They certainly aren't going to hurt anything, and they probably won't add significantly to the cost of the project.

Potentiometer R2 serves as a simple volume control for the audible alarm. In some applications, you might want to eliminate this control from the circuit. You might want to increase the value of resistor R3 slightly in this case.

The input impedance of transformer T1 should more or less match the output of the radio being used as the signal source. The transformer suggested in the parts list is typical.

The alarm does not sound continuously, but it makes a brief "ping" type sound each time the circuit detects an atmospheric electrical discharge. Don't worry too much if you occasionally hear one or two stray pings, especially during clear weather. Other phenomena can cause interference bursts on the AM radio and. But frequent alarm pings (and flashes from the LEDs) are a good indication that there is an electrical storm in the area, and it would be a good idea for you to take any necessary precautions.

Flooding alarm

You know water is necessary, but if too much water (or other liquid) gets in the wrong place, it can do a lot of damage. It can create short circuits in electrical equipment. It can cause rust, mildew, and corrosion in many cases. A flooded basement can be very destructive to any property stored there.

A very simple but effective flooding alarm circuit is shown in Fig. 12-9. A suitable parts list for this project is shown in Table 12-8. As you can see, this project doesn't require very many components.

The circuit should be enclosed in a watertight housing of some sort. A plastic case or even a plastic bag will do. Only the

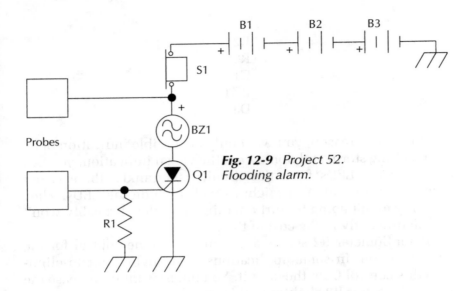

Fig. 12-9 *Project 52.*
Flooding alarm.

Table 12-8 Parts list for project 52.
Flooding alarm of Fig. 12-9.

Q1	SCR (Radio Shack RS1067 or similar)
BZ1	Piezoelectric buzzer
R1	1 MΩ ½ W 10% resistor
B1, B2, B3	9 V transistor-radio battery (27 V total)
S1	Normally closed SPST push-button switch

two probes should emerge from the water-tight housing. Use tight grommets, or duct tape to seal the exit points for the wires leading out to these probes.

The probes themselves are nothing special. They are just exposed electrical conductors. Small pieces of unetched, copper-clad board (about 1.5 inch square) will do well.

Ordinarily, the SCR (Q1) in this circuit is off. No current flows through the buzzer (BZ1), so it remains silent. The gate of the SCR is held near ground potential through resistor R1.

When flooding occurs, and water (or some other liquid) touches both probes, an electrical circuit from V+ to the SCR gate is completed. The SCR will be turned on, drawing current through the piezoelectric buzzer, which sounds the alarm. This alarm will continue to sound, even if the liquid dries up. To turn off the alarm, you must use manual-reset switch S1. Briefly opening this switch breaks the current path from the SCR anode to cathode, so the SCR turns off, and the buzzer is silenced until the circuit is triggered again.

Almost any low-power SCR will probably work just as well in this circuit. The device suggested in the parts list is simply what was used in the prototype of this project. Feel free to substitute other SCRs. It is a good idea to breadboard the circuit first, just to make sure the substitution SCR works properly.

This flooding-alarm circuit is powered from three standard 9 V transistor-radio batteries, connected in series to produce a supply voltage of 27 V. As long as no flooding is detected, virtually no current is drawn from the batteries, so they will have almost their full shelf life. Good quality batteries should last almost two years. Of course, whenever the alarm is sounded, it will draw current from the batteries, shortening their life. If the alarm is permitted to sound for an extended period of time, you will need to replace the batteries a lot sooner. It is always a good idea to test batteries in this type of circuit every few months, just to be sure.

It would not be a good idea to replace the batteries with an ac-to-dc power supply. There is always some finite chance of an electrical short, and if flooding has occurred, this could be a very serious fire or dangerous shock hazard. Ordinary batteries should last so long in this application, that there is no good reason to take any chances with ac power.

Liquid detector

A somewhat different flooding alarm, or liquid detector circuit is illustrated in Fig. 12-10. A suitable parts list for this project is given in Table 12-9.

This liquid-detector project is somewhat more versatile than the preceding one, because it controls a relay, which can be used to drive almost any electrical load your individual application might require.

Nothing is particularly critical in this circuit. Almost any low-power NPN transistor should work just fine for Q1 and Q2. Try to use the same type number for both transistors, however.

As with the previous flooding-alarm project, this circuit should be enclosed in a watertight housing of some sort. A plastic case or even a plastic bag will do. Only the two probes should emerge from the water-tight housing. Use tight grommets, or duct tape to seal the exit points for the wires leading out to these probes.

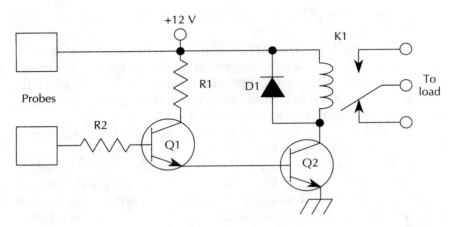

Fig. 12-10 *Project 53. Liquid detector.*

**Table 12-9 Parts list for project 53.
Liquid detector of Fig. 12-10.**

Q1, Q2	NPN transistor (Radio Shack RS2009, GE20, ECG128, or similar)
D1	Diode (IN4001 or similar)
R1, R2	3.3 kΩ ¼ W 5% resistor
K1	12 V relay with contacts to suit load

The probes themselves are nothing special. They are just exposed electrical conductors. Small pieces of unetched, copper-clad board (about 1.5 inch square) will do well.

When flooding occurs, an electrical current path forms between the two probes, turning on transistor Q1, which turns on transistor Q2, which in turn activates the relay. When the liquid short between the probes is removed, the circuit will automatically reset itself, deactivating the relay. In some applications, this can represent a major savings in power consumption. If no one is home when minor temporary flooding occurs, an alarm won't sound off for hours at a time after the trouble has corrected itself, draining the batteries needlessly.

In some applications, the relay can be used to control a pump to remove the flooded water. When the water is gone, the pump automatically is shut down until it is needed again.

It would not be a good idea to replace the batteries with an ac-to-dc power supply. There is always some finite chance of an electrical short, and if flooding has occurred, this could be a very serious fire or dangerous shock hazard. Ordinary batteries should last so long in this application, there is no good reason to take any chances with ac power.

Microwave detector

Microwave ovens are very popular appliances today, and they are becoming increasingly common. But many people are concerned about the potential health hazards of a possible leak in the microwave seal.

A simple, two-component circuit can help alleviate such fears. The schematic diagram, what there is of it, appears in Fig. 12-11, with the short parts list appearing in Table 12-10. Diode D2 must be a special microwave diode. Virtually any microwave diode will work, but an ordinary diode (such as a 1N4001 or a 1N914) will not work.

No circuit board is used for this project. The LED (D1) is mounted directly on the microwave diode (D2), and their leads are soldered together as close to the body of the diode as possible. Notice that the LED and the microwave diode must be wired with opposing polarity.

Do not cut off all the excess lead extending from the double-diode assembly. Leave 3.2 centimeters of lead on either side and trim off any excess beyond this. Make this measurement as exactly and precisely as you possibly can. These leads serve as an-

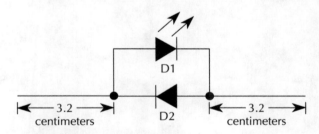

Fig. 12-11 *Project 54. Microwave detector.*

**Table 12-10 Parts list for the microwave
detector project of Fig. 12-11.**

D1	LED
D2	Microwave diode
	(Radio Shack RS1124, or similar)

tennae, and their length determines their sensitivity to the required microwave wavelength. With 3.2-centimeter leads, the circuit will be tuned for 2400 MHz, which is the microwave frequency used in most microwave ovens.

While the microwave oven is in operation, hold the microwave detector assembly horizontal to the oven. (Something must be in the microwave oven whenever it is operated. If nothing else, put a cup of water in the microwave oven to be heated up for the testing procedure.)

Move the detector up and down, while carefully keeping it in horizontal alignment. If there is a significant microwave leak, the LED will light up at that point. Many microwave ovens leak slightly near the door handle. If the leak seems very localized— that is, if moving the detector a fraction of an inch causes the LED to go out, the leak is probably not worth worrying about. On the other hand, if the LED remains lit over a relatively large area, something is seriously wrong. Turn off the microwave oven immediately, and unplug it. Call a qualified technician before using that oven again.

You should be aware that this is a very, very crude test. It obviously doesn't measure the intensity of a leak. It just lets you know if there is any measurable microwave radiation outside your microwave oven.

Index